The Color of Crime

CRITICAL AMERICA
General Editors: Richard Delgado and Jean Stefancic

White by Law:
The Legal Constructions of Race
IAN F. HANEY LÓPEZ

Cultivating Intelligence:
Power, Law, and the Politics of Teaching
A CONVERSATION BETWEEN LOUISE HARMON AND DEBORAH W. POST

Privilege Revealed:
How Invisible Preference Undermines America
STEPHANIE M. WILDMAN
WITH CONTRIBUTIONS BY MARGALYNNE ARMSTRONG,
ADRIENNE D. DAVIS, AND TRINA GRILLO

Does the Law Morally Bind the Poor?
or What Good's the Constitution When You Can't Afford a Loaf of Bread?
R. GEORGE WRIGHT

Hybrid:
Bisexuals, Multiracials, and Other Misfits under American Law
RUTH COLKER

Critical Race Feminism: A Reader
EDITED BY ADRIEN KATHERINE WING

Immigrants Out!
The New Nativism and the Anti-Immigrant Impulse in the United States
EDITED BY JUAN F. PEREA

Taxing America
EDITED BY KAREN B. BROWN AND MARY LOUISE FELLOWS

Notes of a Racial Caste Baby:
Color Blindness and the End of Affirmative Action
BRYAN K. FAIR

Please Don't Wish Me a Merry Christmas:
A Critical History of the Separation of Church and State
STEPHEN M. FELDMAN

To Be an American:
Cultural Pluralism and the Rhetoric of Assimilation
BILL ONG HING

Negrophobia and Reasonable Racism:
The Hidden Costs of Being Black in America
JODY DAVID ARMOUR

Black and Brown in America:
The Case for Cooperation
BILL PIATT

Black Rage Confronts the Law
PAUL HARRIS

Selling Words:
Free Speech in a Commercial Culture
R. GEORGE WRIGHT

The Color of Crime:
Racial Hoaxes, White Fear, Black Protectionism, Police
Harassment, and Other Macroaggressions
KATHERYN K. RUSSELL

The Color of Crime

Racial Hoaxes, White Fear,
Black Protectionism, Police Harassment,
and Other Macroaggressions

Katheryn K. Russell

NEW YORK UNIVERSITY PRESS

New York and London

NEW YORK UNIVERSITY PRESS
New York and London

Copyright © 1998 by New York Univeristy
All rights reserved

An abbreviated version of chapter 4, "Are We *Still* Talking about O.J."
appears in *Representing O.J.: Murder, Criminal Justice and Mass Culture,*
Greg Barak, ed. Harrow & Heston (1996).

Library of Congress Cataloging-in-Publication Data
Russell, Katheryn K., 1961–
The color of crime : racial hoaxes, white fear, black
protectionism, police harassment, and other macroaggressions /
Katheryn K. Russell.
p.   cm. — (Critical America)
Includes bibliographical references and index.
ISBN 0-8147-7471-7 (cloth : alk. paper)   ISBN 0-8147-7532-2 (pbk. : alk. paper)
1. Discrimination in criminal justice administration—United
States.   2. Crime and race—United States.   3. Afro-American
criminals.   4. Racism—United States.   I. Title.   II. Series.
HV9950.R87   1998 305.8—dc21   97-33806
                                                    CIP

New York University Press books are printed on acid-free paper,
and their binding materials are chosen for strength and durability.

Manufactured in the United States of America

10 9 8 7 6 5 4 3 2

To my parents,
Tanya Henrietta Johnson Russell
and Charlie Louis Russell, Jr.

Contents

Acknowledgments

A heartfelt thank you to Richard Delgado and Jean Stefancic for their invitation to participate in the Critical America series. Much gratitude to my editor, Niko Pfund, for his insights, suggestions, accessibility, encouragement, and most of all commitment to this project.

The University of Maryland's Department of Criminology and Criminal Justice provided release time to complete this project, which was greatly beneficial. Several people in the department were particularly supportive and helpful, including Charles Wellford, Lawrence Sherman, Gayle Fisher-Stewart, Denise Gottfredson, Sally Simpson, Brian Wiersema, Angela Gover, Barbara Churchill, and Christina Ruiz. Two criminology Ph.D. students, Melissa I. Bamba and Katharine Browning, were instrumental in gathering data for this project. Their painstaking research and insightful comments on early drafts were most helpful.

Ollie Johnson III, a University of Maryland colleague, was kind enough to lend his expertise to the focus groups with young Black men (discussed in chapter 1). I received support from a number of other university colleagues as well, including Sharon Harley, Robert Steele, David Wasserman, Linda Williams, and Rhonda Williams.

During my visit at the American University School of Law (spring 1997), I was provided with superb research assistance by two law students, Kharlton Moore and Sean O'Brien. My dear colleague Angela Jordan Davis, a continuing source of support and inspiration, provided incisive commentary on early drafts. Deans Claudio Grossman and Jamin Raskin were also helpful. Sherry Weaver was also a great resource. I greatly appreciate the technical support I received from Rosemarie Pal and Melissa Adler.

An extra-special thank you to other colleagues and friends who took time to offer substantive critiques of the manuscript, information, or a listening ear over the past few years: Garland Allen, Jody Armour, Gregg Barak, Rosemary Barbaret, Thomas Bernard, Deborah Blum, Delores Jones Brown, Rhonda Brownstein, Sue Bryant, J. Richard Cohen, Bernadette Hartfield,

Chinita Heard, Deborah Jeon, Kim Lersch, Colin Loftin, Coramae Richey Mann, Reginald L. Robinson, William Sabol, Becky Tatum, C. Keith Wingate, and Vernetta Young.

Throughout my ten years of teaching, my students have been a source of inspiration. A special nod to three former students, Jonathan Newton, Domiento Hill, and Brian Woolfolk, who have helped me realize that I picked the right profession.

To my friends, Taran Buckley Swan, Virginia Towler, and Krystal Wilson, for being there.

Most important, a heartfelt thanks to my family. In addition to my parents, I appreciate the support I received from Charlie Russell, Sr., Mildred Russell, Adam Jones, Jr., FranCione, Adam Jones III, Leah Wise, Tasha Wild, Ahlerman Lewis I, Ahlerman Lewis II, Fredric Lewis, Cleodel Russelle, Jessalyn Saffold, Madeline Williams, Millie Cleveland, Brenda Johnson, and Lakisha Lightner. Last, to the memory of my grandmother Paulene Loyola Speese Jones, who would have been most proud.

Introduction

In 1994, while living in New York City, I attended a film festival titled Young Black Film II. It was held at the Joe Papp theater in the Village. Lewis Payton, Jr.'s, film, *The Slowest Car in Town,* centered on a young Black man's elevator ride. In the short film, a Black man dressed in a business suit and carrying a briefcase enters an elevator on the eighteenth floor of an office building. The elevator makes four stops before reaching the lobby. With each stop someone White enters the elevator. Each White passenger sees something different. At the first stop, a White woman gets on the elevator and upon discovering the race and sex of her fellow passenger, she makes a quick exit. Two White people get on at the next stop. They look at the Black man and "see" an African bushman holding a spear and "hear" roaring African drum beats. The next Whites who board the elevator envision the Black man as a shackled convict, wearing prison stripes. Other passengers visualize him as a drooling crack addict, who looks like a homeless beggar. By the time the elevator reaches the lobby, the Black businessman no longer exists—he has been reduced to the image projected onto him by the White passengers.

Payton's short film captures much of what Black men and women face today—entrapment by media imagery. As a student of race and crime, I have studied the various criminal roles assigned to Blacks, Asians, Latinos, Native Americans, and Whites. I have taken particular note of the wide-ranging criminal personas attributed to Black people. Blacks are the repository for the American fear of crime. Ask anyone, of any race, to picture a criminal, and the image will have a Black face. The link between Blackness and criminality is routinized by terms such as "Black-on-Black crime" and "Black crime."

The images that are associated with other racial groups tend to be crime-specific. For instance, the image of Asian criminality is relegated to Asian gangs. Their crimes are viewed primarily as a reflection of internal group conflict. The public picture of Latinos and crime most closely resembles that of Blacks. Latinos too, are viewed as stealthy and criminal. They, however, are not perceived as posing the same kind of criminal threat as Blacks. Latinos, like Asians, tend to be viewed as involved in intraracial crimes. Native Americans are stereotypically portrayed as committing vice-related crimes, such as alcohol-related crime and gambling. Native American crimes are also typically portrayed as intragroup offenses.

Interestingly, as a group, Whites have managed to escape being associated with crime. This would not be so odd if Whites were not responsible, in raw numbers, for most of the crime that is committed. Each year, Whites account for almost 70 percent of the total arrests, and today they comprise about 40 percent of the prison population. When the media does connect someone White with a crime, for example, serial-murderer Jeffrey Dahmer, it does not implicate the entire White race. It is notable that phrases such as "White crime" and "White-on-White" crime are not part of our public lexicon on crime.

This book is an exploration of the images and realities of crime and race. It offers a detailed look at various phases of the American system of criminal justice and its dynamic relationship between Blacks and Whites. Chapter 1 critiques the media's racialized treatment of crime. The media tends to portray the extremes of Black life—the criminal versus the superstar entertainer. This has caused much confusion in the public mind. The public's perception of crime provides a backdrop for discussing the viewpoints that young Black men have about crime, justice, and race. This chapter concludes with the findings of interviews with young Black men about crime, race, and justice, how they view other young Black men, the O. J. Simpson criminal case, and the Million Man March.

Chapter 2 traces the historical role of race in the development and operation of the U.S. criminal justice system—from the slave codes to the Black codes to Jim Crow legislation. This history is used to determine what operating principles are necessary for a racially fair criminal justice system. These "fairness principles" lay the ground work for the book's assessment of whether the criminal justice system is racially biased.

Chapter 3 analyzes how racial discrimination in the criminal justice system is measured and assesses whether traditional measures have become obsolete and should be replaced. This chapter also takes a close look at the relationship between Black men and the police and why this relationship continues to be problematic.

Chapter 4 raises some new questions about the Simpson criminal case, including a look behind the poll numbers. This chapter analyzes why

Blacks were so steadfast in their support of Simpson, a "colorless" Black man. "Black protectionism" is offered as one explanation. Also, there is a discussion of how the public image of the case was represented in Black and White—excluding input from Asians, Latinos, and Native Americans, who together comprise close to 15 percent of the U.S. population.

The Susan Smith and Charles Stuart cases received widespread media attention. Both Smith and Stuart claimed they had been attacked by a lone Black man. After massive police investigations and international exposure, it was learned that Smith and Stuart were the actual murderers—Smith had killed her two young sons and Stuart had killed his pregnant wife. False criminal accusations against Black men are not as rare as we might hope. Chapter 5 looks at the phenomenon of racial hoaxes. This chapter details more than sixty racial hoax cases and concludes that they should be subject to greater criminal penalty.

Chapter 6 makes the case that researchers should have an ethical duty to respond to misrepresentations of research on race and crime. This "duty to rebut" places the burden on researchers to correct the public record when inaccurate statements about race are paraded as fact. An example of this includes research that purports to prove a genes-race-crime link, such as *The Bell Curve*. Chapter 7 examines how crime by Blacks is labeled as "Black crime," yet crime by Whites is not accorded a similar race label. Public language on crime does not include "White crime" or "White-on-White crime." This chapter examines whether racial labels should be attached to crime, and if so, which crimes it should encompass. The chapter closes with a critique of political scientist James Q. Wilson's argument that White racism is caused by the high rate of Black crime.

The final chapter assesses whether the U.S. justice system has adequate checks and balances against unexplained racial disparities. After reviewing three factors—existing laws (e.g., federal crack law and capital punishment), areas where more law is needed (e.g., Black reparations), and the current racial climate—it is concluded that the U.S. justice system falls short. The chapter details the harms associated with the law's failure to provide racial redress—including alienation, violence, and paranoia. The chapter concludes that more affirmative race law—law which acknowledges American racial history and operates to protect against racial discrimination—is needed. The afterword draws on the broad themes discussed and concludes that while the law cannot solve all problems of racial discrimination in criminal justice, the law can be made to operate much more effectively.

In 1997 President Bill Clinton called for a national discussion on race. While the call is a necessary one, it is important to bear in mind that there is already a national conversation about race—it's just that people are having the conversation with people like themselves. Blacks are talking to Blacks and Whites are talking to Whites. Asians are talking to Asians and Latinos are talking to Latinos. Even worse, most people talk about crime and race with few facts. This leads us to continue to exhort the opinions and ideas we already believe to be true. We rarely allow ourselves to entertain new perspectives. This book offers a different perspective in the ongoing debate about race and crime—new issues, more facts, some theories, and some tough but necessary solutions.

1

The Color of Crime
External and Internal Images

The media image of Blackness is primarily depicted through images of Black men. As detailed below, though the images are mostly ones of deviance, there are also enough images of Black success to create public confusion as to how Blacks fare in American society. The contradictory media portrayals of Blackness are analyzed and followed up with a look at how some young Black men interpret their public image and how they view the criminal justice system. At a time when young Black men are the focus of so much criminal justice attention, it is important to discuss their assessment of their image and their reality. The chapter concludes with a unique look at Blackness through White eyes: the story of a young White male college student who "became" Black.

The Media's Fictionalized Reality

It is both the best and worst of times for representations of Blackness in the media. On television, Blacks are regularly portrayed as lawyers, doctors, nurses, police officers, and best friends.[1] More Blacks appear in print, radio, and television journalism than ever before. At the same time, however, television programs continue to feature updated versions of centuries-old stereotypes.

In the 1990s, several trends caused television to revert to crude one-dimensional images of Blackness. The most remarkable trend has been the proliferation of daytime talk shows. These shows often feature Black guests who talk in loud, profane language (what some would label "Ebonics"), use animated gestures, and freely discuss their criminal involvement or sexual liaisons, sometimes both. Most talk shows, current and canceled—hosted by Ricki Lake, Montel Williams, Tempestt Bledsoe, Richard Bey, Sally Jessy Raphael, Mark Walberg, Rolonda Watts, Charles Perez, Jenny Jones, Maury

Povich, Gordon Elliot, and Geraldo Rivera—portray Blacks as amoral buffoons, sassy single mothers, arrogant absent fathers, and unfaithful friends. A common feature of these shows is a disproportionately high number of Black and Hispanic guests.

Another recycled image of Blackness is what some have labeled the 1990s version of Stepin' Fetchit.[2] The "comic relief" caricature of Black manhood is exemplified by the television characters Erkel (*Family Matters*), Martin (*Martin*), Mark (*Hangin' with Mr. Cooper*), and Will (*Fresh Prince of Bel Air*). Each offers a portrayal of Black manhood as bumbling, silly, neutered and nonthreatening. Although these representations are not completely negative, it cannot be said that they are completely positive either.

"Reality" police television programs, which showcase Black criminals front and center, are another throwback. For instance, on the shows *Cops, Final Justice,* and *Highway Patrol,* Black suspects are commonly videotaped cursing at law-enforcement officials and otherwise disrespecting the law. The poor, homeless, drug-addicted, mentally unstable, and hardened criminals are lumped together as Black crime threats. Shows such as these make it hard to believe that Black criminals represent a tiny fraction of the overall Black population.

Rap music videos provide yet another representation of Black men as social deviants. Black men are regularly filmed soliciting women, drinking beer, smoking marijuana, driving luxury automobiles, counting money, using cell phones, displaying pager devices, bragging about their gun collections, and wearing designer clothes—images widely associated with inner-city drug dealers. Further, the men in these videos are highly sought after by women—sending a clear message of sexual desirability. Black women do not fare much better. They are displayed in strictly sexual terms, as either subjects or objects—seeking, getting, or demanding sex.

Television news, with its focus on violent street crime, also fuels the stereotype of Black criminality. Many local news programs lead off with a crime story—e.g., often one showing a Willie Horton[3] prodigy, hunching over, shielding himself from the camera, being escorted away in handcuffs by the police. Though Black women are not usually the focus of crime news, they too have a recurring role. They are frequently shown as battle-weary, grieving mothers, photographed crying over the death or arrest of their sons and daughters.

For most of us, television's overpowering images of Black deviance—its regularity and frequency—are impossible to ignore. These negative images have been seared into our collective consciousness. It is no surprise that most Americans wrongly believe that Blacks are responsible for committing the majority of crime. No doubt, many of the suspects paraded across the nightly news are guilty criminals. The onslaught of criminal images of Black men, however, causes many of us to incorrectly conclude that most Black men are criminals. This is the myth of the *criminalblackman*. On balance, the picture that comes to mind when most of us think about crime is the picture of a young Black man.

Images of everyday Black life are overridden by images of Black deviance. This point was made dramatically by a *Washington Post* survey. In October 1995, in the midst of three powerful news stories—the O. J. Simpson acquittal, a Sentencing Project report (finding that one in three twentysomething Black men is part of the U.S. criminal justice system), and the Million Man March—the *Washington Post* published a fascinating series on racial perceptions.[4] The study reported the results of interviews with two thousand adults. Hispanics, Asians, Blacks, and Whites were polled to examine how information and misinformation shape public thinking about race.

Survey participants were asked to estimate the percentage of Blacks in the United States, the correct answer being 12 percent. Each racial group, including Blacks, overestimated the percentage of Blacks in the United States. On average, survey participants guessed that Black people comprise 20 percent of the population. Whites estimated that the United States is almost 25 percent Black. This is particularly surprising because Whites, who account for approximately 75 percent of the population, are the largest racial group. One White woman guessed that Blacks comprise 50 percent of the U.S. population. Upon being told that the actual figure was closer to 12 percent, she stated, "The Census must not have been done correctly. . . . It's only common sense. They [Blacks] have very, very large families."[5] The survey also found that at least 20 percent of all Blacks, Whites, Hispanics, and Asians responded that Blacks fare as well, if not better, than Whites. These respondents incorrectly believed that Blacks are on par with Whites in employment, education, housing, and income.

How is it that Blacks are widely seen as symbols of success and symbols of deviance? What accounts for these conflicting perceptions of Blacks and Blackness? At core, the presentation of Blackness is one of contradiction.

Images of Black deviance are promoted alongside images of Black achievement—sometimes they overlap.

The picture of Black success is partly presented in the form of fictional media portrayals of Black and White friendships. On the movie screen for instance, Blacks and Whites are paired as partners-in-crime, blood brothers, coworkers, and friends.[6] These images, however, do not effectively counter negative Black images. This is because sometimes underlying these Black and White pairings and images of Black success are subtle messages of Black deviance. Television and the movies frequently portray Black achievement as a "reform" case. On the television show *Designing Women*, the Black character, played by Meshack Taylor, was an ex-convict, hired as the gofer for four affluent Southern White women. On *Doogie Howser, M.D.*, the Black character was a rehabilitated stick-up kid. In the movie *The Shawshank Redemption,* two convicts, one Black, one White, become fast friends. Notably, the Black character, Red, was guilty of murder, while the White character, Andy, had been *wrongly* convicted of murder.

Another explanation for why Black success stories do not counterbalance images of Black deviance is that Black success is given a unique interpretation. In the minds of many, particularly Whites, Blacks have "made it." In many instances, Black superstars are not perceived in terms of their Blackness. A scene from Spike Lee's movie *Do the Right Thing* illustrates this point. Two young men, Mookie, who is Black, and Pino, who is Italian, have a discussion about racism. Pino hates Black people and refers to them as "niggers." In an attempt to point out his racial double standard, Mookie reminds Pino that all of his favorite celebrities are Black (Magic Johnson, Eddie Murphy, and Prince). Pino responds, "They're not really niggers. . . . They're not really Black, they're more than Black."[7] To some Whites those Blacks who achieve large-scale success—e.g., Michael Jordan, Oprah Winfrey, Michael Jackson—become colorless, while those Blacks who conform to the criminal stereotype remain "Black."

Given this complex imagery, it is predictable that Blacks are viewed as emblematic of both success and deviance. The contradictory media representations of Blacks reflects a double-edged resentment: the threat of both Black crime and Black success. The result is cross-wired thinking about Blacks and Blackness. As is true for most Whites, most Blacks are neither super-successful nor super-deviant. While the media portrays neutral and in some cases positive images of Blacks, these images cannot compete with the overwhelmingly negative characterizations.

Personal and Up Close—Shades of Crime, Shades of Difference

Fiction Meets Reality: Young Black Men Speak on Crime and Race

Volumes of press ink, forests of paper, and millions of research dollars have been devoted to the plight of the young Black male. He has been scrutinized, objectified, quantified, and memorialized—so much so that for most of us "young Black male" is synonymous with deviance. The negative criminal label is applied as though one characterization could accurately define such a vast group. Although some people have suggested that a generation of Black men has been lost, in reality, the criminal stereotype describes only a fraction of the entire group. A commonly quoted statistic is that one in three young Black men is under the jurisdiction of the criminal justice system.[8] What often goes unacknowledged is that if 33.3 percent are in the justice system, then 66.7 percent are not. Specifically, very little media attention is focused on the more than 400,000 Black men who are in college.

Law-abiding young Black men are frequently overlooked as a resource for analyzing crime and justice issues. To tap this source, focus groups were conducted with young Black male college students at the University of Maryland.[9] While an increasing number of books explore the breadth of the Black male experience,[10] very little research presents their specific viewpoints on crime, race, and society.

FOCUS GROUPS

Participants were first asked to share their reactions to receiving an invitation to participate in a focus group about young Black men. Several young men commented that they were "excited" about the invitation to participate in research. One student said it is "rare" for the perspectives of young Black men to be solicited. Each participant interpreted "race and crime" in the question "What does 'race and crime' mean?" as synonymous with "Blacks and crime." Malcolm, a 21-year-old from Columbia, Maryland, who has several family members in law enforcement, said the term is used as a way to "reinforce stereotypes . . . that certain crimes are committed by Blacks." For Jeff, a 21-year-old, who lived in France until age 12, it means "all Black males commit crime." David, a 23-year-old Washington, D.C., native said, "When I hear that phrase . . . I automatically think they're associating Blacks [with] illegal activities." Christopher, age 24, born in Jamaica, commented, "It makes me think of something my mother always says, 'They got another Black child on television.' With crime, the media emphasis is always on Blacks." Samuel, 22, from Takoma Park, Maryland, echoed Christopher's sentiments and said, "Many people don't realize that the media is the only way most Whites [see Blacks]."

Reflecting on crime and justice. More than any other race and gender group, Black men have the greatest probability of contact with the criminal justice system, as both victims and offenders. The young men responded passionately when asked to comment on the criminal justice system. "Racist" and "biased" were the terms invoked most frequently. Keith, 26, from Temple Hills, Maryland, said, "It [the criminal justice system] is just a microcosm of what the larger American society is. . . . [It] has been more or less an instrument to maintain the racism within the country."

Kwame, a 20-year-old Miami native, said, "My mother always told me that the criminal justice system is like slavery. When slavery was abolished, White people tried to find new ways to bring Black people down." Eric, 24, from Washington, D.C., who referred to the criminal justice system as "a sinking ship," said, "We know certain [policies and strategies] do not work, yet we continue to use them." According to David, the fact that the rights of Blacks are violated without recourse is evidence of racism in the criminal justice system. He analogized the constitutional rights of young Black men to an obstacle course, "[It is] almost like being on one side of a [seventy-five-foot] wall and you need to get to the other side without being seventy-five feet high. What can you do? You try to find a way around it but there doesn't seem to be one."

Hearing stories, creating boundaries. Given that young Black men have the greatest probability of falling victim to the violence of other young Black men, it would be reasonable to expect that they would be fearful of one another. The focus group participants said that whether they would be fearful of other young Black men would depend upon the situation. Kwame stated:

> I'm not fearful if I see a Black brother on the street. Really, I'd be more afraid of a White guy than I would a Black guy, simply because I [have] some relationship to the Black guy. I have no problem with one Black guy. But if I see a large group of them with joints [marijuana] in their mouths, wearing gold, I'd be afraid.

Kwame's sentiments were echoed by several young men. Some noted that if they were traveling alone, the presence of a group of young men, of any race, might be cause for concern. Factors including the behavior of the individual or group, time of day, physical size and conduct of the approaching person, and how the person is dressed would be evaluated. Overall, the young men appear to be fairly discriminating in assessing what constitutes a threat. It may be that because these young men are frequently targets of unfair negative stereotypes, they try not to unfairly stereotype other young Black men.

The participants were asked how old they were when they became aware of the negative public perception of young Black men. While the average age was 9, some said as early as *age 4*. Gregg, 21, from Lanham, Maryland, was one of the men who said he was aware of the stereotype by age 4. Raised in a small, mostly White town in Virginia, he recounted a frequent childhood occurrence, "[At the playground] everything is cool [until] an argument comes up, then, all of the sudden you're the 'nigger.'" Several others said that it was comments made by Whites that first made them aware of the negative image associated with Black men.

In response to the question, "How does the stereotype affect you?" several men commented that they have grown weary of the negative labels. Others expressed anger. Christopher said, "It becomes annoying. . . . I don't want to hear about another young Black male [and crime]." Derrick, a 23-year-old from Baltimore, said he is angry at Whites and Blacks:

> I'm upset about the negative portrayal of Black men on TV. I'm upset at Whites and Blacks. I'm upset at the media because they [say that] Blacks commit most of the crime. That's not true. . . . But I am also upset with Blacks because we perpetuate a lot of the stereotypes ourselves. Look at all the foolish movies we've made, like *Boyz N the Hood* and *Menace II Society*.

The participants also discussed their early perceptions of law enforcement. Most of the men had heard negative stories about the police. Many had concluded that the police were hired to enforce the law against Blacks. David said that as a little boy, when he acted up, his grandmother warned, "If I can't control you, the White man will." Gregg commented, "I was always told that the police are only as good as the people [who wear the uniform]. It is made up of people who lie, people who cheat, people from all walks of life. It is made up of guys off the street." In school Derrick learned about "Officer Friendly" and was taught that the police are the good guys. The picture of the helpful, pleasant, resourceful police officer, however, contradicted his direct experience:

It did not take long to realize that the police were not our friends. When I was a child they would come onto our block and tell us not to play ball in the street. "Go to a park." Well, we didn't have a park to go to, so that was harassment to us.

Fear, respect, and loathing. None of the young men directly acknowledged being fearful of the police. However, fear is the word that best describes their motivation for avoiding law enforcement officers. The incongruous result is that the young Black men interviewed are more fearful of the police than of other young Black men. The result is incongruous because the race and gender group with the highest rate of criminal offending and victimization, Black men aged 16 to 24, is the one most likely to need police assistance. Whether most Black men are fearful of the police is an important research question. Black fear of police, and the informal code of silence that it may erect, has implications for police relations with Black communities.

Another aspect of the fear dynamic is how Black men are perceived by others. The participants were asked, "How do Whites respond to you in public?" Most said that Whites are afraid of them. Several cited the never-ending slights that go along with being perceived as dangerous: difficulty getting directions from a stranger, hearing the click of automatic car locks as you walk or drive by, being stopped by police: being followed in a store, and being asked about crime ("Have you ever seen a drive-by?"). Actions taken by Whites to protect themselves or their property from Blacks are either aggressive moves towards Blacks (e.g., watchful eye of a shopkeeper) or aggressive moves away from Blacks (e.g., locking car doors, moving away from them on the street).

Oddly, the young Black men described White fear in ways that could be easily confused with White respect. Christopher, who is 5'11" and stocky, shared this:

Out in public I will see a White guy coming towards me. He may be 6'5" and 250 pounds and all of the sudden he will step aside and let me pass by. I may be six inches shorter, and less stocky, but [the White guy] just steps aside and [lets] me pass, no matter what I'm wearing.

This kind of reaction from Whites could be interpreted as either respect or fear. Other participants recounted similar experiences of deference from White men and women. At the same time that Black men are cast off as being criminals, they are also celebrated as being hypermasculine. They are idolized as cool, hip, and sexually gifted. These conflicting reactions may encourage some young Black men to capitalize on their macho image. Several of the young men said they believe that some Black men turn to crime and deviance as a "society"-fulfilling prophecy. That is, many engage in crime because people expect them to. Some of the participants expressed concern that crime by Black men is glorified and idolized by Blacks and Whites alike.

In his essay, "How Does It Feel to Be a Problem?" Black author Trey Ellis describes his response to the overlapping messages of fear and respect:

> My friends and I sometimes take perverse pride in the fear the combination of our own sex and skin instills in everyone else. . . . Imagine the weird power you'd feel if [your very presence made] a cop quake with fear and call for backup.[11]

Several focus-group participants expressed concern that the ability to frighten Whites is seen by some Black men as a way to gain respect. The fear-respect duality appears to be multi-layered. Not only is it an issue between Black men and White men, it also exists between Black men. This problem is highlighted in the 1991 movie *Grand Canyon*. In one scene, a young Black man, conversing with an older Black man, wryly comments on why he carries a gun, "No gun. No respect. That's why I always got the gun."[12] Some Black men, in an attempt to draw something affirming from the negative criminal stereotype, settle for the ability to instill fear in anyone.

O. J. AND THE MILLION MAN MARCH: REFLECTIONS ON TWO
ONCE-IN-A-LIFETIME EVENTS

Three months after the focus groups were held, O. J. Simpson was acquitted of murder and the Million Man March took place. Because the issues raised by both events bore directly on the issues addressed in the focus groups, follow-up interviews were conducted.[13]

The O. J. Simpson case. Most of the young men had predicted that Simpson would be acquitted. Though most agreed with the verdict, most said they believe Simpson committed the murders. There were a variety of responses to the question "What was your reaction to *the reaction* to the verdict?" Most said they did not anticipate the post-verdict fallout. Gregg commented:

> I thought it was shameful. The fact that it was so cut and dried shows the closed-mindedness of Blacks and Whites. It is nice to have unity and support within the race, but [people] should not be blinded by race membership.

Karl, a 24-year-old from Silver Spring, Maryland, said he was upset by the White response to the verdict: "[T]hey did not have the same reaction when Powell and Koon [two of the Los Angeles Police Department officers charged with beating Rodney King] were acquitted." All of the young men agreed that the outcome of the Simpson case and the reaction to it had deepened the U.S. racial divide. Most noted that the Simpson case underscored their belief that money plays a central role in securing justice.

The young men were asked whether they thought the verdict would have been different if the jury had been predominantly White (e.g., nine Whites, two Blacks, and one Hispanic). Most felt there would have been a hung jury if the majority of the jurors had been White. Christopher observed that if a mostly White jury had voted for acquittal there would have been a different White response: "It would have changed [White] perceptions about the legitimacy of the verdict."

Karl, like most of the men, predicted that in the long run the fallout from the Simpson case will prove to be a setback:

> There will be more racial polarity. There has not been enough of an examination [of the racial issues]. Whites are now going to internalize the verdict [as anti-White] and they will chalk it up to reverse-racism, discounting this country's history.

Though most of the men agreed with the jury's verdict, their opinions about the case were more complex than media reports and surveys indicated.

The Million Man March. Eight of the men had attended the March. Three did not go because they disagreed with the views of Nation of Islam leader Minister Louis Farrakhan. Some of the young men who went said that although they did not agree with all of Farrakhan's message, they concluded that "the March was bigger than Farrakhan."

"Peaceful," "bonding," "about love," "awestruck," "spiritual," "overwhelming," and "nonviolent" were among the adjectives used to describe the March. Many had difficulty expressing the impact of the March. Keith said, "The feeling cannot be explained. It's like you were a child again and [still] have the possibility of hope." The adjectives used to describe the Million Man March contrast with the negative adjectives that are typically used to describe Black men. This contrast makes the descriptions used by the young men particularly striking, considering that the terms are being used by Black men to describe a gathering of Black men.

Although only a few of the men believed that the March would yield any tangible, long-term benefits, most felt the March was beneficial. Several noted that the March would forever alter the public image of Black men. Others were bothered by the media debate over whether there were one million people at the March. One young man said that the argument about attendance figures distracted from the true focus of the March: a peaceful display of Black male unity. For this reason, most of the men said they felt the media did a poor job of covering the event.

Most of the young men said they respect and admire Farrakhan for his convictions and ability to amass such a sizeable crowd. However, several expressed reservations about his methods and his message. David's comments are representative:

> I have mixed reactions to him. I don't agree with his religious philosophy. Politically he scares me because he has a way with words. I don't agree with his belief in separatism because Blacks are not going anywhere and neither are Whites.

What lessons should we take from the comments of these young Black men? While they have high expectations for themselves individually, they feel encumbered by the negative labels attached to being young, Black, and male. A few wondered aloud how high they would be "permitted" to climb on the economic ladder. Their reflections and experiences with race, from their feelings of invisibility and fear to their feelings of frustration and anger, painfully illustrate the costs of negative stereotyping. The interviews provide a glimpse of what it is like to be an involuntary, lifelong, walking representation of deviance. The media's focus on the small percentage of young Black men who are criminals has exacted a burdensome toll on the majority who are law abiding. The noncriminal majority is an untapped resource. It may be that the young Black men who do not fit the criminal image can help us understand those who do.

With almost mirror-opposite intensity, the degree to which many young Black men experience the pain of being negatively stereotyped is the same degree to which Whites believe that Blacks overdramatize the existence of racism and negative stereotyping. The focus-group interviews present one viewpoint of life as a young Black man. The story of Joshua Solomon offers another.

Fade to White

At the age of 20, Joshua Solomon, a White college student, decided to do the unthinkable: he would become Black. Inspired by J. H. Griffin's book,

Black Like Me, he arranged to conduct his own short-term race experiment. Joshua is a native of Silver Spring, Maryland, a racially mixed suburb outside of Washington, D.C. He had observed that his Black friends in high school blamed racism for most social ills: "I'd sympathize with my friends and I wanted to support them, but secretly, inside, I'd always felt that many black people used racism as a crutch, an excuse."[14] He decided to test his friends' assertions, hoping to prove that race does not matter.

During his sophomore year, Joshua began taking psorlen, a skin darkening drug, under a physician's care. He took a one-semester leave of absence, planning to live as a Black man. As the psorlen began to take effect, Joshua shaved his head and began his sojourn as a young Black man. After using the drug for two months, he traveled south, as J. H. Griffin had done forty years earlier.

It is a gross understatement to say that Joshua had an eye-opening experience. As a young Black man in Atlanta, he found that he had to fight to get a fraction of the respect he had been accorded as a White person. In his new, darker skin, Joshua found he was "desperate for a little respect." He was now the target of offhanded, disrespectful comments by Whites (e.g., a homeless White man who referred to Blacks as "lazy niggers"). He also noticed that few Whites would look him in the eye and that shopkeepers followed him around in stores and police stopped him for no reason.

After being Black for two weeks—and after just two days of being Black in Georgia—Joshua had had enough. His experiment was over: "Maybe I was weak, maybe I couldn't hack it. I didn't care. This anger was making me sick and the only antidote I knew was a dose of white skin."[15] He returned to Silver Spring.

In an interview a year later, Joshua said that as a result of his experiment his views on race have changed drastically.[16] Joshua, who voted for George Bush in 1992, now supports affirmative action. Since his sojourn, he talks a lot more about race, is acutely aware of race and racial issues, and is frequently asked questions about race. Joshua commented that Whites rarely talk about race, except when talking about members of minority groups. The "racial" conversations that Whites have are usually about Blacks who are viewed as racist (e.g., Louis Farrakhan, Al Sharpton). Joshua has concluded that Whites are in denial about race. He commented that many Whites wrongly believe that they cannot be racist because they have Black friends. He says that Whites typically only see Whites as racist if they belong to groups like the Ku Klux Klan.

According to Joshua, Whites use the criminal stereotype of Blacks as an excuse for their racism: "Fear is used to rationalize racism."[17] He described the long-term effects of racism as a "drip-drop." This metaphor, in which racial slights accumulate, like water leaking from a faucet, symbolizes the repeated and cumulative impact of racism. Joshua indicated that he is not particularly optimistic about the future of race relations. He cynically concluded, "this is as good as it gets."

Joshua's sobering conclusion, the focus-group commentaries, and the widespread negative images of Blackness and crime raise several questions: What is the role of history in understanding today's criminal justice system? Does the criminal justice system discriminate against Blacks? Is there any way to improve the relationship between Blacks and the police? What role does the media play in fostering tension between racial groups? And finally, how can the law be used more effectively to address racial harms against Blacks? These questions are tackled in the pages that follow.

2

Measuring Racial Equity in Criminal Justice
The Historical Record

Central to the debate about the workings of the U.S. criminal justice system has been whether the system of police, courts, and corrections operates in a racially discriminatory manner. Those who conclude that the system is race-driven often point to the historical record of American criminal law and justice. Further, they observe that although blatant double standards are no longer a part of the law, subtle forms of race discrimination persist. On the other side, those who believe that today's criminal justice system is race-neutral argue that the racism of the past has been removed from the law and that any remaining discrimination is minimal. Part of the reason that little common ground emerges between the "discrimination" and "no discrimination" positions is that there is little agreement about *what* constitutes a racially fair criminal justice system. This chapter explores the history of race in American criminal law, including the slave codes, Black codes, and Jim Crow legislation. This history is used to distill the core principles of a racially equitable criminal justice system.

Slave Codes, Black Codes, and Jim Crow

Slave Codes

From 1619 to 1865, slave codes embodied the criminal law and procedure applied against enslaved Africans.[1] The codes, which regulated slave life from cradle to grave, were virtually uniform across states—each with the overriding goal of upholding chattel slavery. The codes not only enumerated the applicable law but also prescribed the social boundaries for slaves—where they could go, what types of activity they could engage in, and what type of contracts they could enter into. Under the codes, the harshest criminal penalties were reserved for those acts that threatened the institution of slavery (e.g., the murder of someone White or a slave insurrection). The slave codes also penalized Whites who actively opposed slavery.

The codes created a caste system under which Whites, Blacks, and mulattoes were accorded separate legal statuses and sanctions. This meant that in addition to the blatant double standards of the slave codes, Blacks were further marginalized by laws that assessed punishment by "degree of Blackness."

For example, some code provisions would except a mulatto from punishment if he had a White mother. Laws like this are direct descendants of the "one-drop rule." This rule defined a Black person as "any person with *any* known African black ancestry."[2] Accordingly, Blackness was treated as a default racial category. A person who was biologically more White than Black (e.g., a quadroon or octoroon) was classified as Black. This rule worked to the benefit of White slaveowners. Anyone with any remote African ancestry was presumed to be Black, thus presumed to be a slave.

Race was the most important variable in determining punishment under the slave codes. In addition to race, gender and class status of the offenders and victims played a role. These factors also determined whether justice would be meted out in White courts or slave courts.

Table 2.1 lists select provisions of the Virginia slave code. As indicated, slaves faced death for numerous criminal offenses. Harsh sanctions, such as brutal public executions, were imposed to keep slaves in their place. Under Maryland law, for example, a slave convicted of murder was to be hanged, beheaded, then drawn and quartered. Following this, the head and body parts were to be publicly displayed.

Enslaved Africans faced other barbaric sanctions, including iron brands. Typically, the brand letter was placed on the forehead with a hot iron. The letter was determined by the type of crime the slave was charged with, e.g., a "T" for theft. Whipping was the most commonplace punishment. Lashes were administered to the bare back with a leather strap. Thirty-nine lashes was a standard punishment. Slave owners believed that administering more than thirty-nine lashes in a single interval violated Christian tenets. Despite this, a sizeable number of slaves were subjected to whippings of one hundred or more lashes.[3] Another form of punishment consisted of placing slaves in the galleys or requiring them to wear a five-pound collar around the neck. Jail was reserved for slaves labeled incorrigible.

Slaves lived with the constant fear that at any moment they might be charged and convicted of crimes they did not commit. They also lived with

TABLE 2.1

Criminal Penalties by Race in Virginia

Crime	White Offender	Black Slave Offender
Murder (White victim) petit treason[a]	Maximum penalty, death	Death
Murder (Black victim)	Rarely prosecuted	If prosecuted, whipping, hard labor, or death
Rape (White victim)	10–20 years, whipping, or death if minor victim	Death or castration[b],
Rape (Black victim)	No crime	No crime, exile, or death[c]
Assault (White victim)	1–10 years (if done with intent to kill)	Whipping, exile, mutilation, or death

[a] Murder of a slaveowner.
[b] Same penalty for attempted rape.
[c] If rape of *free* Black women, penalty could be death.
SOURCE: A. Leon Higginbotham and Anne Jacobs (1992).

the knowledge that if they were the victims of crime, there was no avenue for redress. The slave codes of most states allowed Whites to beat, slap, and whip slaves with impunity. An 1834 Virginia case held that it was not a crime for a White person to assault a slave.[4] In some instances, however, Whites did face punishment for extreme acts of brutality against slaves. They were punished not because they violated a slave's rights, but because they had violated the rights of a slave owner. For example, under nineteenth-century South Carolina law, a White man found guilty of killing a slave could be fined seven hundred pounds. The fine was paid to the slave owner, not the family of the murdered slave.[5]

SEX CRIMES

Interracial sex crimes offer the best example of how racial double standards worked under the slave codes. A Black man who had sex with a White woman faced the most severe penalty, while a White man who had sex with a Black slave woman faced the least severe penalty. As Table 2.1 indicates, a Black man could be hanged for having sex with a White woman. There were more Black men executed for rape than there were

Black men executed for killing a White person.[6] White fear of Black male sexuality is the only possible explanation for why the rape of a White woman by a Black man was the only crime for which castration could be imposed under Virginia law.

The prohibition against interracial liaisons reflected the prevailing view that Whiteness and manhood were inextricably linked. A Black slave could never attain manhood; therefore, he could not marry a White woman. Under the codes the first line of defense against race-mixing were laws prohibiting interracial intimacy. A second line of defense were laws outlawing miscegenation.

Raping a Black woman was not a crime under most slave codes.[7] This reflected the reality that slave women were sexual as well as economic property. If a slave master wanted to force sex on his human chattel, this was perfectly legal. The number of mulatto children born to slave women was tangible evidence of this practice. Some codes, though, did punish White men for having sex with Black slaves. *In Re Sweatt,* a 1640 Virginia case, the court determined that a White man had impregnated a Black slave who was owned by another White man. For this race-mixing crime, the White man was sentenced to do "public penance" at a church. This was a slap on the wrist compared with the punishment the slave woman received. She was tied to a whipping post and beaten.[8]

In addition to the ever present threat of being raped by White men, Black women slaves had an additional burden to bear. It was also not a crime for a Black slave to rape another slave. The formal legal system might be invoked, however, if a rape caused an injury to the slave that affected her ability to work—since this amounted to economic interference. Eighteenth-century Virginia law reports few cases involving a Black male slave charged with raping a Black female slave. In the one case that did result in a criminal conviction, the male slave was removed from the county.[9]

Several rationales have been offered to explain why most slave codes neither acknowledged nor sanctioned the rape of Black women. One reason is that slaves were viewed as naturally promiscuous, making forced sex a legal impossibility.[10] Another reason is that the rape of a slave woman did not typically threaten the maintenance of slavery. In fact, if the rape resulted in offspring, this meant one more child was available for slave labor. Finally, there was little awareness or concern about the physical and emotional trauma caused by rape.

In addition to the heavy emphasis on prohibitions against interracial sex, the slave codes were replete with laws that punished Blackness. These laws made certain activities criminal only when committed by someone Black. For instance, a slave who "lifted his hand against" a White Christian or used "provoking or menacing language" against a White person faced a punishment of thirty-nine lashes. It was also an offense for seven or more Black men to congregate, unless accompanied by a White person. Under many slave codes, a free Black person who married a slave *became* a slave. Some states made an exception if the free person was a mulatto who had a White mother.[11]

Enslaved Africans were not the only group that faced punishment under the codes. There were also criminal laws that targeted Whites who opposed slavery. For example, in Mississippi, a White person who taught a slave to read or helped a slave obtain freedom risked being fined, imprisoned, or possibly executed.[12] Some states barred White abolitionists from jury service, some sentenced White women to prison for marrying Black men, others fined White women who had children by Black men. Notably, a White man who fathered a child by a Black woman was not guilty of any crime.

Slave patrols or "patterollers" operated to keep a tight rein on slave activity. Whites greatly feared slave insurrection and the slave patrols were established to monitor and quell suspicious slave conduct. These patrols, enumerated by the slave codes, were the first uniquely American form of policing. Slave patrollers, who worked in conjunction with the militia, were permitted to stop, search, and beat slaves who did not have proper permission to be away from their plantation. Whites in every community were enlisted to participate in the patrols. In Alabama, for example, all slave owners under age 60 and all other Whites under age 45 were legally required to perform slave patrol duties. By the mid-1850s, slave patrols existed in every Southern colony.[13]

At their core, the slave codes denied slaves political, social, and economic equality. Slaves, themselves property, were barred from owning property—including dogs. Further, they could be mortgaged. They were also prohibited from entering into contracts, including marriage. Not surprisingly, slaves were barred from holding elected office. This is yet another example of how the law was used to criminalize Blackness. Only *convicted* White criminals were barred from holding elective office. Blacks who had never been convicted of a crime were treated like Whites who had been.

Not only did the codes create separate crimes and punishments for Blacks, "justice" was administered in separate, special tribunals. These tribunals, ostensibly designed to protect slave rights, worked to uphold the rights of White slave holders. These separate forums had different procedural practices. In these courts, slave defendants did not have the right to a jury trial, could be convicted with a less than unanimous verdict, were presumed guilty, and did not have the right to appeal a conviction. Slaves could not serve as jurors or witnesses against Whites.

Racism in the administration of justice was not confined to the court system. In some cases, Blacks charged with a crime were subjected to "plantation justice." The codes gave slave owners private enforcement authority. This allowed them to act as judge and jury. Plantation justice was consistent with the classification of slaves as property. It permitted a slave owner to impose sanctions, including hanging, lashes, castration, and dismemberment (e.g., cutting off both ears). Slave laws sanctioned other forms of extra-judicial justice, such as slave owners hiring bounty hunters to capture runaway slaves. While most slave masters wanted their human chattel returned alive, some were satisfied with evidence that the slave was dead (e.g., return of a slave's body).

The above discussion barely conveys the harsh reality created and enforced by the slave codes. To say that slaves were viewed as less than human is a gross understatement. Slaves ranked below dogs, cats, and other breathing, feeling animals. Even horses and cows were legally protected against senseless cruelty. In their totality, the slave codes reveal the vast difference in how Whites and Blacks fared under the law. Under Virginia law, slaves could receive the death penalty for numerous offenses. First-degree murder, however, was the only offense for which Whites could be sentenced to death. What was considered a crime, which court justice would be administered in, what was meted out as punishment, and the applicable constitutional protections, were all determined by race.

Black Codes

The first Black codes were adopted in 1865. Newly freed Black women and men were given the right to marry and enter into contracts.[14] In some ways the Black codes operated as both shield and sword. At the same time that new rights were granted, laws were enacted that undercut these protections. For example, vagrancy laws allowed Blacks to be arrested for the "crime" of being unemployed. Mississippi's statute was representative:

[A]ll freedmen, free negroes and mulattoes . . . over the age of eighteen years, found on the second Monday in January, 1866, or thereafter with no lawful employment or business, or found unlawfully assembling themselves

together . . . shall be deemed vagrants, and on conviction thereof, shall be
fined . . . not exceeding fifty dollars . . . and imprisoned . . . not exceeding ten
days.[15]

In an attempt to protect White employment, licensing requirements were
imposed to bar Blacks from all but the most menial jobs. In South Carolina, for instance, Blacks were required to have a license for most jobs.[16]
Court approval and a fee were necessary to obtain a license to become a
mechanic, artisan, or shopkeeper. Blacks who were lucky enough to obtain
a license faced yet another barrier. A license could be revoked at any time, if
complaints were made. Laws criminalizing gun possession, voting, deser-
tion from work, and assembly after sunset were also used to limit Black
mobility and employment.

In their totality, the Black codes created a new system of involuntary
servitude, expressly prohibited by the newly adopted Thirteenth Amendment. The law was frequently applied in a discriminatory manner. Discrimination worked in two ways. First, Blacks faced harsher criminal
penalties than Whites. For instance, thousands of Blacks were executed for
offenses that Whites were given prison time for committing. Second, White
crimes committed against Blacks were largely ignored. For instance, the
Texas codes made it a crime for a White person to murder a Black person.
Yet, in Texas, between 1865 and 1866, there were acquittals in five hundred
cases where someone White was charged with killing someone Black.[17]

The enforcement arm of the law was not limited to the courts or legal
officials. In fact, newly granted Black rights served to mobilize White vigi-
lantes, including the Ku Klux Klan. The KKK and its sympathizers were
responsible for murdering thousands of Blacks. The *Cruikshank* case illustrates this point. In this 1874 Louisiana case, two Black men were ambushed
and killed by more than three hundred Klansmen. After the attack, ninety-
seven Whites were indicted on murder and conspiracy charges and only
nine went to trial. In all nine cases, the White defendants were acquitted of
murder. Only three were found guilty of conspiracy to murder.[18]

Lynching, the hallmark of the Klan, posed a new, oppressive threat to
Black freedom. This unique form of extra-legal Southern justice resulted in
death for thousands of Black children, women, and men.

The Lynching Ritual. Carried out as an extreme form of vigilante justice,
the lynching ritual rose to prominence after the Civil War. Those people
who were selected to conduct the lynching selected a site based upon the

location. This included finding a venue that would accommodate the expected onlookers and locating an appropriate tree. Following this, ritual instruments were gathered including rope, wood, guns, kerosene, tar, and feathers. Lynchings had many characteristics of a sporting event.[19] Entire families, including children, participated. Families packed food, drink, and spirits for the event.

White mobs, which sometimes included police officers, gathered to take part in the hanging, burning, or shooting.[20] After the tools were selected, the Black victim was required to strip naked. Black men were usually castrated and sometimes their bodies were used as target practice. The murderous assault ceremoniously concluded with Whites parceling out the remains of the Black victim. Teeth and other body parts were collected as souvenirs. In notorious cases, newspaper advertisements announced upcoming lynchings. Referring to a particularly violent 1917 lynching, W. E. B. Du Bois wrote:

> A Negro was publicly burned alive in Tennessee under circumstances unusually atrocious. The mobbing and burning were publicly advertised in the press beforehand. Three thousand automobiles brought the audience, including mothers carrying children. Ten gallons of gasoline were poured over the wretch and he was burned alive, while hundreds fought for bits of his body, clothing, and the rope.[21]

What could trigger so vile a reaction by Whites? Allegations that a Black person had killed someone White, assaulted someone White, or raped someone White could be the impetus for a lynching.[22] Blacks were also lynched for "stepping out of place" with a White person, insulting a White person, using offensive language, and engaging in boastful talk or behavior.[23] Lynch laws were so broadly interpreted that the act of a Black person buying a new car could be construed as an "insult to a White person" and result in a lynching.[24] The stated rationale for lynching was to protect the sanctity of the White female from the Black man. However, official records show it operated differently in practice. Allegations of sexual assault against White women accounted for *fewer than one-third* of all lynchings. Though the lynching ritual was designed to protect the White woman and thus the White family, it was primarily used as an extra-legal tool to punish Blackness.

U.S. records show that more than three thousand Blacks were lynched between 1882 and 1964.[25] Some historians, including Ida B. Wells-Barnett, place the figure at closer to ten thousand. Wells-Barnett estimated that between 1882 and 1899 alone, there were 2,553 Black people lynched.[26] Although Blacks were not the only people lynched, they did comprise the majority (75 percent). In 1892, 161 Blacks were lynched, the highest official figure recorded for a single year.

Table 2.2 lists some of the 1930 Black lynching cases. As indicated, in several cases White mobs forcibly removed Blacks from legal custody so they could be lynched. In many instances Blacks were murdered before they had been formally charged with any crime.

At the turn of the century, Blacks comprised about 10 percent of the U.S. population.[27] The continuation of "Black only" offenses, lynching, and discriminatory application of the law meant that Blacks were disproportionately targeted, arrested, convicted, and sanctioned. In 1910, for instance, 31 percent of the prisoners were Black—a haunting harbinger of today's incarceration figures.

Jim Crow Segregation Statutes

The slave codes and the Black codes represent two mutations of state-sanctioned double standards. "Jim Crow," which came into common usage in the early 1900s, refers to laws that mandated separate public facilities for Blacks and Whites. Segregationist practices, however, came before the term "Jim Crow"—as *Plessy v. Ferguson** illustrates. One constant remained as the slave codes became the Black codes and the Black codes became segregation statutes: Blackness itself was a crime. The codes permitted Blacks to be punished for a wide range of social actions. They could be punished for walking down the street if they did not move out of the way quickly enough to accommodate White passersby, for talking to friends on a street corner, for speaking to someone White, or for making eye contact with someone White.

Rules of racial etiquette were an integral part of Jim Crow. These unwritten rules required that Black men refer to White men as "Mister" or "Sir." At the same time, however, Whites would commonly refer to a Black man as "boy." The rules governing racial manners also required Blacks to step aside and bow their heads in the presence of Whites. This system of verbal and physical deference reflected the White belief that no matter how much racial equality the Constitution promised, Whites would never view Blacks as their social equals.

White fear of race-mixing remained steadfast. The notorious case of Emmett Till illustrates this fear. Till was a Black Chicago teenager who

* 163 U.S. 537 (1896)

TABLE 2.2

Selected Black Lynchings, 1930

Alleged Crime	Method of Lynching	Circumstances
1. Rape/Murder	Burned to death	No formal arrest
2. Murder	Shot to death	No formal arrest
3. Rape	Shot to death	Removed from jail
4. Rape	Burned to death	Jail where Black man was held was burned down. His burned body was removed and left in Negro section of town.
5. Murder	Shot to death	Body was tied to a car and dragged through town. Later, body was burned in front of a Negro church.
6. Rape	Shot and stabbed to death	Lynch mob broke into jail and removed victim.
7. Rape	Shot to death	No formal arrest
8. Rape	Shot to death	No formal arrest
9. Murder	Shot to death	Victim had been arrested but was left unguarded
10. No crime	Beaten to death	———
11. Rape/Assault	Hanged	Removed from jail
12. Resisting arrest	Shot to death	———
13. Rape	Shot to death	Removed from jail
14. Murder	Shot to death	Killed in jail
15. Robbery	Hanged	Taken from police officers
16. Attempted rape	Shot to death	Taken from police officers
17. No crime	Shot to death	Victim (Black man) had been the star witness in a case against two White men charged with raping a Negro woman. He was shot to death in his home.
18. Murder	Hanged	Removed from jail
19. Rape	Shot to death	No formal arrest

SOURCE: Arthur Raper, *The Tragedy of Lynching* (1933), 469–471. Raper notes that there were twenty-one lynchings in 1930, yet only lists twenty. The nineteen with Black victims are listed above.

visited Mississippi in 1955. While there, he told people that he had a White girlfriend back home. He made the fatal mistake of saying "Hello baby" to a White woman—thus violating the prohibition against interracial contact and the rules of racial etiquette. He was killed by several White men, including the woman's husband. Emmett Till's bloated body was found days later floating in a Mississippi river. An all-White jury acquitted the White men responsible for the lynch-murder.

Ostensibly limited to controlling racial interaction in public facilities, the long arm of Jim Crow reached private areas as well. Jim Crow regulations extended to the following:

prostitution

cemeteries

hospital wards

water fountains

public restrooms

church bibles

swimming pools

hotels

movie theaters

trains

phone booths

lunch counters

prisons

courthouses

buses

orphanages

school textbooks

parks[28]

The reach of these laws was so expansive that they effectively regulated the private lives of Blacks as well. Not only did Jim Crow laws determine which public facilities Blacks could use, they also determined who could serve Blacks in those facilities. For instance, there were laws prohibiting White female nurses from treating Black male patients—a clear indication of the taboo against interracial sex. Jim Crow laws made no pretense of being "separate but equal." Southern rail signs, designating separate areas for "White," "Colored," and "Negroes and Freight," captured the legal sentiment of the era. Although *Brown v. Board of Education* was decided in 1954, it had little practical effect. The goal of dismantling the formal barriers to racial equality was given new legs with the passage of the Civil Rights Act of 1964 and the Voting Rights Act of 1965.

"Fairness Principles." Can anything be learned from the slave codes, Black codes, and Jim Crow? These systems of punishment are object-lessons in how not to structure a racially fair criminal justice system. Antebellum and postbellum criminal law stood as the antithesis to a racially just system. Based on this 350-year history, several basic principles appear to be minimally required for a fair criminal justice system:

1. Criminal penalties apply to everyone equally, regardless of the race of the *offender.*
2. Criminal penalties apply to everyone equally, regardless of the race of the *victim.*
3. The race of the offender is not relevant in determining whether his actions constitute a crime. The offender's actions would have been considered criminal, even if he were another race.
4. The race of the victim is not relevant in determining whether the offender's action constitutes a crime.
5. The offender's racial pedigree (e.g., "degree of Blackness") is not used to determine punishment.
6. There are checks and balances that mitigate against racial bias within the legal system.

These fairness principles, while not exhaustive, provide a useful test for measuring the racial equity of a criminal justice system. The principles can be thought of as minimum requirements, since it is hard to imagine a nondiscriminatory legal system that does not adhere to each one. The following chapters analyze various aspects of race and criminal justice, including the criminal law, how it is applied, and how race and crime are framed in public discourse. The fairness principles provide a reference point for evaluating whether today's U.S. criminal justice system operates in a racially fair manner.

3

Racial Discrimination or Disproportionate Offending?

Study after study shows that Blacks and Whites hold contrary viewpoints about the fairness of the criminal justice system. Blacks are more likely to believe that the justice system works against them and Whites are more likely to believe that it works for them. Two common expressions capture these opposing viewpoints: "The system works" (Whites) and "Justice means 'just us'" (Blacks). Research on race discrimination tends to support the viewpoint that justice is blind. Because this research fails to include an analysis of the informal stages of the criminal justice system, it is not definitive.

This chapter examines the issue of whether racial bias affects the informal stages of the criminal justice system and thereby infects the formal stages. Detailing the social and economic costs of racial discrimination in the justice system, this chapter provides an overview of current research on racial discrimination, outlines the criticisms of this research, and considers whether the most important informal stage—pre-arrest contacts with police—should be subject to official measurement.

The Invisibility of Racial Discrimination

Mainstream criminology research leads one to conclude that racial discrimination in the criminal justice system is a historical concept: some discrimination exists, but with the exception of drug offenses, it is neither intentional nor widespread. Consider the following statements made by several well-known and widely quoted criminal justice system researchers:

MICHAEL TONRY: [F]or nearly a decade there has been a near consensus among scholars and policy analysts that most of the black punishment disproportions result not from racial bias or discrimination within the system but from patterns of black offending and of blacks' criminal records.[1]

ALFRED BLUMSTEIN: [T]he U.S. displays distressingly high rates of [Black incarceration]. . . . This is not so much due to racial discrimination, but to other factors outside the criminal justice system.[2]

JOHN DIIULIO: The bottom line of most of the best research is that America's justice system is *not* racist, not anymore, not as it undoubtedly was only a generation ago.[3]

WILLIAM WILBANKS: [T]here is racial prejudice and discrimination *within* the criminal justice system . . . there are individuals, both black and white, who make decisions . . . on the basis of race. I do not believe that *the system* is characterized by racial prejudice or discrimination against blacks.[4]

These conclusions are drawn primarily from 1970s and 1980s research on racial disparity. This research can be divided into two categories, "single" and "multiple" stage studies. Single-stage research examines criminal cases at one phase of the justice system. The research on racial discrimination has focused mostly on sentencing. At best, the findings are equivocal. Many studies conclude that there is very little overt discrimination. No longer do laws prescribe justice by race of the offender or victim. Researchers find, however, that race has an indirect effect upon criminal justice processing, primarily through its interaction with other variables (e.g., class status, prior criminal record). Arrest, bail, prosecutorial discretion, and incarceration have also been analyzed. The research on prosecutorial charging indicates there is evidence of racial discrimination, particularly in cases with a White victim. Studies measuring discrimination at bail and at sentencing show the existence of subtle, indirect racial bias.[5]

To assess whether the race of the offender affects criminal justice processing, multistage research examines cases at different points. The findings are split. A 1988 report by RAND, however, is widely cited as proof that race is not a factor in sentencing.[6] The study, which looked at the sentencing decisions made under California's Determinate Sentencing Policy, found race had no effect.

Disparity research, single and multistage, establishes no clear proof of racial bias in the criminal justice system. This has led many criminologists to adopt a "no discrimination" thesis. Other researchers, however, have rejected this conclusion. They cite four central criticisms, discussed below.

A Critique of the Research

First, the disparity studies have been characterized as being marred by tunnel vision. Studies that analyze race discrimination at a single stage of the criminal justice system cannot detect racial discrimination that exists in other parts of the system. For example, a study of how race impacts upon sentencing in State A may find no racial disparity. This finding, however, does not mean that State A does not have a racially discriminatory criminal justice system. Racial discrimination may not exist at sentencing but may permeate other stages (e.g., prosecutorial charging, plea bargaining).

Further, a study of several criminal courts could mask the discrimination of a few. For instance, an aggregate analysis of the sentencing decisions of ten courts might indicate there is very little racial discrimination. A look at these ten courts individually, however, might reveal sizeable discrimination. Aggregate studies, therefore, may minimize the existence of race discrimination in sentencing. At best, single-stage studies provide important, though limited information about the role race plays in the criminal justice system—they cannot reliably answer the broad question of whether racial discrimination exists in the American criminal justice system.

Multistage research, which is less problematic than single-stage research, still poses the same basic problem. This research covers more ground than single-stage studies. However, the fact that discrimination is not evident at two or three stages (e.g., bail and sentencing), does not mean that it is absent from other stages. Additionally, single and multistage studies cannot be generalized across states. In other words, a finding that there is no racial discrimination at the prosecutorial charging and sentencing phases in five states does not prove that there is no racial discrimination in the court systems of the remaining forty-five states. State variations, including differences in criminal code statutes, prosecutorial charging practices, jury-pool eligibility, and judicial selection, mean that the empirical findings for one jurisdiction do not necessarily apply to another jurisdiction. Many researchers have failed to acknowledge the limitations of single and multistage research, and this has led to an unreliable assessment of the degree and amount of racial discrimination in the criminal justice system.[7]

A second criticism of the discrimination research is that in it "disproportionality" is improperly defined. The term has been used to refer to whether a group is involved in the criminal justice system at a rate that exceeds its rate in the general population.[8] Using this formula for disproportionality, Blacks, who comprise about 12 percent of the U.S. population, are grossly overrepresented in arrest and incarceration figures. Blacks account for more than 30 percent of all arrests and more than 50 percent of the incarcerated population. Conversely, Whites are said to be underrepresented in arrest and incarceration figures because their rates are below 73 percent.

Some researchers reject this conventional formula for disproportionality, preferring a more complex analysis. They ask the question, *why* should a group's percentage in the population determine disproportionality? Specifically, some criminal justice researchers state that we should expect arrest rates to more closely mirror indicators of social marginality. Accordingly, the conventional measure of disproportionality is only useful assuming all racial groups are on equal social footing.

Table 3.1 provides data on select social indicators for Blacks and Whites. When compared with Whites, Blacks have much higher percentages of out-of-wedlock births, infant mortality, illiteracy, unemployment, female-headed households, and poverty. For almost every measure of social dysfunction, the Black rate exceeds the White rate. Notably, Black rates for out-of-wedlock births, female-headed households, unemployment, and poverty are more than twice the White rates. Given these data, is it surprising that Black arrest and conviction rates follow a similar pattern? In 1964, criminologists Marvin Wolfgang and Bernard Cohen reached a similar conclusion:

> [I]f a careful detached scholar knew nothing about crime rates but was aware of the social, economic and political disparities between whites and Negroes in the United States . . . what would be the most plausible hypothesis our scholar could make about the crime rate of Negroes? Even this small amount of relevant knowledge would justify the expectation that Negroes would be found to have a higher crime rate than Whites.[9]

Indicators of social marginality, such as high rates of unemployment and crime, are interdependent and we would reasonably expect them to be positively correlated—as unemployment rates rise, so do crime rates.

The current definition of disproportionality is not so much misleading as it is incomplete. Perhaps it better serves as one of the many indices of social status, rather than as a definitive measure for crime rates. Understanding why Blacks offend at rates that exceed their percentage in the population requires a consideration of other factors that may have a direct or indirect effect on crime. The empirical reality is that race, poverty, employment, crime, and education are interacting variables. Whether a

TABLE 3.1

Indicators of Social Marginality, Proportional Representation by Race, 1995

	White	Black
Arrests	4%	11%
Incarceration	<1%	1%
Nonmarriage births	22%	68%
Female head of house	14%	47%
Unemployment	6%	13%
Below poverty line	12%	33%

SOURCES: National Urban League, *The State of Black America* (1995).

group offends at a high or low rate typically reflects how it fares on other social indicators.

A third criticism of the research centers on the way issues of racial discrimination and racial disparity are presented. They are typically discussed as if they are competing, antithetical phenomena. In fact, they coexist. Those who are left-of-center tend to focus on racial discrimination, while those who are right-of-center tend to focus on the disproportionately high rate of Black offending. For example, liberals often focus upon the law (e.g., selective enforcement, disparate impact), while conservatives often focus on the criminals (e.g., the rising number of repeat offenders—so-called superpredators).[10] Despite these political distinctions, research shows evidence of racial discrimination against Blacks in the criminal justice system *and* evidence that Blacks disproportionately offend. The precise relationship between disparity and discrimination is unclear—the two may be correlated, causally related, or operate independently of one another.

It may be that the high rate of Black offending has caused many researchers to de-emphasize, to the point of ignoring, racial discrimination in the criminal justice system. It is almost as if disproportionate Black offending is viewed as a justification for race discrimination. The problem of racism in the justice system is too important to play second fiddle to other criminal justice system realities, including disproportionate offending rates. Researchers on either side of the disparity-versus-discrimination debate have been hesitant to acknowledge that both racial discrimination and racial disproportion exist, *and* both are problems that must be addressed.

Even some researchers who embrace the "no discrimination" thesis concede that the high rate of Black incarceration is not completely explained by disproportionate rates of offending. For instance, professor Alfred

Blumstein readily acknowledges that 20 to 25 percent of the incarceration rate for Blacks is *not* explained by disproportionate offending. He surmises, however, that a 20 to 25 percent gap is no great cause for alarm, because eliminating this gap would not change the incarceration picture dramatically. By Blumstein's calculation, the 20 to 25 percent of unexplained disparity between arrest and incarceration figures represents about ten thousand Black prisoners.[11] Although ten thousand prisoners is a statistical drop in the bucket of the overall prison population (less than 1 percent), socially it is no small number. Ten thousand Blacks, who may have been treated more harshly by the criminal justice system *because* of their race, constitutes an enormous social problem. If ten thousand Blacks have been subjected to discrimination, this means that some were unjustly convicted and unjustly sentenced to lengthy prison terms.

Further, the impact of the race discrimination would extend beyond those Blacks who were direct victims of discrimination. There would be the economic and social impact on their families (e.g., children, spouses, and parents). By what logic could we excuse or, worse, ignore this unexplained 20 to 25 percent gap? Blumstein states that the high rate of Black incarceration is "not so much due to racial discrimination." How could he know this to be true? Can the issue of discrimination be dismissed so easily? It is likely that Blumstein did not intend to belittle the impact of racial discrimination. His analysis, however, serves to illustrate another problem of aggregate analysis.

Some researchers studying the disproportionately high rate of Black arrests have questioned whether it is caused by disproportionately high crime rates, or whether other factors are at work. A few have suggested that the legal system may operate to promote Black disproportionality. For instance, national studies show that about half of all crack-cocaine users are White, yet they account for only 4 percent of the defendants convicted under the federal crack law.[12] Blacks, who make up 38 percent of all crack users, account for more than 85 percent of the federal crack convictions. This racial disparity illustrates one of the problems with current measures of racial discrimination in the criminal justice system. (The issues of differential enforcement and differential penalties under the federal crack law are discussed in more detail in chapter 8.)

The U.S. Supreme Court's decision in *U.S. v. Armstrong*[13] highlights how certain kinds of race discrimination can elude traditional checks and balances. In the *Armstrong* case, the Los Angeles federal public defender's office argued that the U.S. Attorney's office was selectively prosecuting

Black defendants under the federal crack-cocaine statute. The public defender's office, noting that the penalty for a crack conviction is much harsher under federal law than under California law, argued that Black offenders were being slotted for federal court. In 1991, all twenty-four of the federal crack cases handled by the public defender's office involved Black defendants. The public defender's office requested records from the prosecutor's office reporting how many Whites and Blacks had been prosecuted in state court. The U.S. Attorney's office was also asked to state its criteria for deciding whether to prosecute a case in federal court. The public defender sought to establish that White crack offenders were being prosecuted in state court because the penalties were less harsh.

The Court held that the defense would have to offer some minimal proof of racial discrimination *before* the prosecution could be legally required to turn over its case records. Not surprisingly, without the records from the prosecutor's office, the public defender's office was unable to meet this legal burden. The *Armstrong* decision does not mean that the U.S. Attorney's office is not selectively prosecuting Blacks in federal court. Rather, it means that the prosecutor can withhold evidence of it.

The Court's decision is just one example of a legal roadblock that makes it difficult to measure race discrimination in the criminal justice system. Its reasoning indicates that forms of discrimination that are difficult to measure may escape penalty. While *Armstrong* symbolizes the legal barriers to identifying race discrimination in the criminal justice system, empirical barriers also exist. This brings us to the fourth criticism of the racial disparity research, that researchers have failed to expand their examination of racial discrimination to include nontraditional measures.[14] Researchers, in their attempt to measure race discrimination, usually confine their analyses to the formal stages of the criminal justice system. Formal stages are those that are subject to criminal justice record keeping, such as arrest, bail, sentencing, and parole.

Criminologist Daniel Georges-Abeyie, who favors analyzing the informal phases, asks, "Does the focus of criminal justice analysis on the formal, easily observed decision-making process obscure or even misdirect attention from the most significant contemporary form of racism within the criminal justice system?"[15] He states that an examination of the formal stages is insufficient to determine the prevalence of racial bias. Police stops of motorists, which constitute an informal stage, determine in large measure who will be arrested and thus who will enter the criminal justice system. Accordingly, these encounters, which are not subject to official measure, must be included in an assessment of whether the justice system operates in a racially biased manner. Georges-Abeyie hypothesizes that a study of the informal phases would reveal a system of *"petit* apartheid"—that Blacks consistently and unfairly receive harsher treatment from legal officials than Whites receive.

In an attempt to explore the issue of racial discrimination in the informal stages, the next section looks at how police treat Black men *prior* to arrest. The discussion centers on why this informal stage should be measured, how it might be measured, and the social, economic, and criminal justice consequences of failing to measure it.

Black Men and the Police

As a group, Black men have an endless supply of police harassment stories. These include being mistaken for a criminal, being treated like a criminal, being publicly humiliated, and in some instances, being called derogatory names. Often their encounters with the police arise from being stopped in their cars. They are subject to vehicle stops for a variety of reasons, some legal, some not, including:

- Driving a luxury automobile (e.g., Lexus, Mercedes, BMW)
- Driving an old car
- Driving in a car with other Black men
- Driving in a car with a White woman
- Driving early in the morning
- Driving late at night
- Driving a rented automobile
- Driving too fast
- Driving too slow
- Driving in a low-income neighborhood, known for its drug traffic
- Driving in a White neighborhood
- Driving in a neighborhood where there have been recent burglaries
- Fitting a drug courier profile
- Violating the vehicle code (e.g., excessive speed, exposed tail light)

It seems that no matter what Black men do in their cars, they are targets for criminal suspicion. It is so commonplace for Black men to be pulled over in their vehicles that this practice has acquired its own acronym: "DWB"

(Driving While Black).[16] In Selma, Alabama, police harassment of Black men became so acute that Black leaders installed a telephone hot-line for people to call and report police use of unnecessary force.[17]

Police harassment comes in many forms. It is also demonstrated by the number of times Black men are stopped, questioned, and assaulted by police as they go about their daily lives. There are clear distinctions between police harassment and police brutality. Police brutality typically refers to the unlawful use of excessive force. Harassment covers a range of police actions, some lawful, some unlawful (e.g., conducting a stop on less than legal cause). For many Black men, consistently negative encounters with the police have caused the line between harassment and brutality to become blurred. For Black men, who are more likely to be stopped by the police than anyone else, each stop has the potential for police brutality. The frequency of contact between Black men and the police has led a generation of Black men to teach their sons "The Lesson"—instructions on how to handle a police stop.[18]

The comments made by the young Black men who participated in focus groups, detailed in chapter 1, attest to the general fear and loathing that many Black men have of the police. Jerome McCristal Culp, Jr., a Black law professor, who has faced police harassment, refers to this as "the rules of engagement of black malehood." According to Culp, these rules, which are taught to Black males over 5 years old, instruct that "at all times we [Black men] make no quick moves, remove any possibility of danger and never give offense to official power."[19]

Many Black men have developed protective mechanisms to either avoid vehicle stops by police or to minimize the potential for harm during these stops. The primary shield they use is an altered public persona. This includes a range of adaptive behaviors, e.g., sitting erect while driving, traveling at the precise posted speed limit, avoiding certain neighborhoods, not wearing certain head gear (e.g., a baseball cap), and avoiding flashy cars. Another preemptive strike that is available to a select few is vanity license plates that indicate professional status (e.g., "M.D." or "ESQ"). Of course, vanity tags can work as both a magnet and a deterrent for a police stop. Black men are used to structuring their encounters with police during car stops: placing both hands on the steering wheel, responding to an officer's questions with "sir" or "ma'am," and quite creatively, keeping the car radio tuned to a classical music station.[20] Black men are wise to take measures like these because studies consistently show that a suspect's demeanor influences whether he will be arrested.[21]

The difference in experiences with law enforcement may explain why Blacks and Whites have contrasting impressions of the legitimacy and trustworthiness of police treatment of Blacks. In 1996, the Joint Center for Political and Economic Studies conducted a national survey on citizen attitudes toward crime and policing. In response to the question, "Do you believe that police brutality and harassment of African Americans is a serious problem where you live?" 43 percent of the Blacks polled answered "yes." Notably, 52 percent of Blacks with incomes between $75,000 and $90,000 answered "yes." Only 13 percent of the overall sample (Black and White) answered "yes." Another poll conducted in 1996 by the *New Yorker* magazine reported similar findings. Most Blacks said they "agree strongly" that the police and the legal system are biased against Blacks.[22] Further, Gallup poll research consistently reports that at least 50 percent of the Blacks polled believe the criminal justice system is racially biased against them. In a 1995 Gallup survey, less than 30 percent of Whites polled said the criminal justice system is biased against Blacks.[23]

In addition to the experiences of the larger Black citizenry, Black police officers present an interesting twist on the issue of police abuse. They too have stories of abuse and harassment at the hands of other police officers (of all races). Out of uniform they are Black, not blue. The long list of cases involving Black undercover officers who have been mistaken for criminals by White officers illustrates this point.[24]

Black distrust of the justice system is not new. It is historically rooted in the role police played in enforcing the slave codes, Black codes, Jim Crow segregation, and the ultimate form of vigilante justice, lynching. In his treatise on race in America, Gunnar Myrdal reported that between 1920 and 1932, White police officers were responsible for more than half of all the murders of Black citizens.[25] Historical accounts also show that White policemen were often present at lynchings. Today, police brutality barely resembles its past forms. Many Blacks alive today, however, still remember the widespread, persistent, and inhumane abuse Blacks suffered at the hands of police.

Further, it has only been within the last half-century that Blacks have been allowed to police White communities on a wide scale. Into the 1960s, Black officers were viewed as second class and assigned to patrol Black communities. "Separate but equal" meant that Black officers could not arrest White suspects. Police racial segregation was practiced in most large cities, including Miami and Houston. More than half of the people alive today were alive during a time when Black officers were *de facto* barred from policing White communities. For most Blacks, police oppression is far from a distant memory. A consideration of this history helps to explain why Black skepticism and disdain for police is a continuing phenomenon.

The Police at Work

One indicator of the breadth of police abuse is the number of famous Black men, allegedly immune from such discriminatory treatment, who report that they have been unfairly stopped and harassed by law enforcement officers. The list of well-known Black men who have "fit the profile" is impressive: Marcus Allen (athlete), Dee Brown (athlete), LeVar Burton (actor), Calvin Butts (pastor), Johnnie Cochran (lawyer), Christopher Darden (lawyer), Reginald Dorsey (actor), Tony Dungy (football coach), Michael Eric Dyson (professor), Earl Graves, Jr. (businessman), La-Van Hawkins (businessman), Al Joyner (athlete), Wynton Marsalis (musician), Michael McCrary (singer, Boyz II Men), Joe Morgan (athlete), Edwin Moses (athlete), Walter Mosley (author), Bobby Rivers (television personality), Will Smith (actor/rapper), Wesley Snipes (actor), Brian Taylor (athlete), Blair Underwood (actor), Tico Wells (actor), Cornel West (professor), Michael Wilbon (journalist), Jamaal Wilkes (athlete), Roger Wilkins (professor), and William Julius Wilson (professor).[26] Legendary trumpeter Miles Davis had a unique method for handling police harassment. To avoid being stopped and questioned by police, Davis would call and notify the Beverly Hills police department *before* leaving home.

Mae Jemison, the first Black female astronaut, had a remarkable run-in with police in her hometown. On the morning of February 24, 1996, Jemison was stopped by a Nassau Bay, Texas, police officer. The officer informed Jemison that she had made an illegal turn. After the officer discovered that Jemison had an outstanding traffic ticket, Jemison was arrested and handcuffed, and her head was pushed face down onto the pavement. She was also forced to remove her shoes and walk barefoot from the patrol car into the police station. After her release, Jemison filed a police brutality complaint against the White officer, Henry Hughes III. Hughes was cleared following an internal department investigation. Jemison's close-cropped Afro has caused some to speculate that she was initially stopped because the officer mistook her for a Black man.

The list of Black men who have "fit the profile" is even longer for less well known Black men. The Jonny Gammage case is a notorious recent example. Early on the morning of October 12, 1995, Gammage, 31, was driving home to suburban Pittsburgh. Gammage, a businessman driving a Jaguar, was pulled over by police for erratic driving. According to police statements, after exiting the vehicle, Gammage attacked all five officers. The officers restrained him by hitting him with flashlights and applying pressure with their batons. Gammage died following the encounter. The autopsy showed that he suffocated after one of the officers stood on his neck and pressed down with a metal club. Gammage's death was described as comparable to a nineteenth-century lynching. A month following his death, the two officers charged with manslaughter were acquitted by an all-White jury.

There are a host of other cases involving police harassment and police brutality against Black men, including Arthur Colbert, Joseph Gould, Malice Green, Don Jackson, Rodney King, Arthur McDuffie, Desmond Robinson, Brian Rooney, and Ron Settles.[27] Notably, two of these cases, those of Don Jackson and Desmond Robinson, involve off-duty Black police officers who were assaulted by another officer. Jackson's case is particularly compelling because he went undercover to expose the racism of the Long Beach, California, police department. In 1989, Jackson invited a television news crew to videotape his drive through a high crime area. He and another man traveled through the area at the posted speed. They were pulled over by two White officers and told their car had been weaving in traffic. Jackson politely questioned the basis of the stop but did nothing to escalate the encounter. After Jackson stepped out of the vehicle, one of the police officers bashed his head and arm through a plate-glass window. Jackson was ultimately charged with "resisting arrest." The videotape of the incident called into question the statements made by the officers in their case report. Both officers were charged with use of excessive force and filing a false police report.

Are all of the cases of police harassment and police brutality exceptions? After all, most police officers, of all races, carry out their professional duties without resorting to racial harassment, abuse, or brutality. Some people suggest that most officers do not violate the law and that, therefore, police abuse is not a serious problem. The fallacy of this claim is made clear by applying it to another context. In most years, a fraction of the total population is arrested for criminal activity. However, just as it is worthwhile to study those who are suspected of offending, it is worthwhile to study law enforcement officials who discriminate against Black citizens.

Police themselves have acknowledged that they practice racial targeting. The 1991 Christopher Commission Report found that more than 25 percent of Los Angeles police officers believe that some officers engage in racially discriminatory procedures. The same percentage of officers said that an officer's racial prejudice may result in the use of excessive force against a suspect.[28]

Measuring Police Abuse

A variety of studies examine the prevalence of police/Black citizen encounters. In a 1994 study that looked at whether Blacks are more likely to be harassed by the police or to know someone who has been, researchers found a "significant association" between being Black and being harassed by the police. Almost half of the Blacks interviewed had experienced harassment, while only 10 percent of the Whites had.[29]

The "out-of-place" doctrine gives police a legal justification for stopping and questioning Blacks at a disproportionate rate. The doctrine allows police to use a person's race as a basis for a stop if that person is in an area where another race predominates.[30] A number of courts have upheld the doctrine as a useful police practice to stem crime. The doctrine encourages police to view Black men as *de facto* guilty, without reference to legal indicators of criminal activity (e.g., reckless driving, speeding, making a drug sale). It permits Blacks to be stopped at a disproportionate rate since there are far more White neighborhoods than Black neighborhoods. We can only speculate as to the toll—spiritual, psychological, and physical—exacted upon a group whose freedom of movement is consistently challenged.

In 1996, the U.S. Supreme Court addressed the issue of pretextual vehicle stops. In *Whren v. United States*,[31] the Court was asked to determine whether it is constitutional for the police to use a minor traffic violation to stop a driver whom they suspect of criminal activity (hence, "pretextual"). Michael Whren and another Black man, James Brown, were stopped in a "high drug area" in Washington, D.C. The undercover officers became suspicious of drug activity after observing Brown pause at a stop sign for more than thirty seconds, fail to use his turn signal, and take off at a high speed. One of the officers saw Brown looking in the direction of passenger Whren's lap. At this point, the officers had probable cause to believe that there had been a violation of the D.C. Vehicle Code. After they pulled the car over, drugs were found, and the pair was arrested. In a unanimous decision, the Court held that as long as a traffic stop is based upon probable cause, the stop is valid. The individual officer's motive for the stop is irrelevant. In this case a traffic law had been violated, thus establishing probable cause. Obviously Brown violated the traffic code. However, because the police do not stop most people who engage in the same conduct, the question arises whether Brown was stopped because he was Black.

The direct and indirect experiences that Blacks have with the police affect their perception that the criminal justice system is skewed against them. Court decisions such as *Whren* enhance this view. A complete assessment of the role race plays in police stops requires the scrutiny of the actions of Black men *and* the actions of the police.

Many people would argue that it is unfair to blame the police for being suspicious of Black men. After all, Black men are disproportionately engaged in crime. It is reasonable, then, that the police disproportionately suspect them of criminal activity. Black men do commit street crimes at high rates—rates far exceeding their percentage in the U.S. population (6 percent). The important question, however, is, "Are Black men stopped and questioned by the police at a rate that greatly exceeds their rate of street crime?" If so, the high number of police stops cannot be legally justified.

The available research suggests that Black men are stopped and questioned at a rate much higher than the level of their involvement in crime. The few studies on this issue indicate that Black men are significantly more likely to be stopped than anyone else—at a rate far above their rate of arrest.[32] One way to determine this is to compare the rate of police stops for Black men with the rate of Black men who are involved in criminal activity. For example, assuming that one-third of all young Black men are involved in crime, we would predict that about one-third of them would be subject to police stops.

The available evidence indicates that more than one-third of all young Black men are stopped by the police. In fact, anecdotal research indicates that the majority of Black men have been stopped by the police. Statistically, Black men comprise only 6 percent of the population. More importantly, young Black men between the ages of 15 and 40 account for only 3 percent. What accounts for this group's high encounter rate with police? Black men should be subject to police stops to a degree that more closely matches their rate of offending.

NATIONAL DATA

As yet, no national data have been collected on the incidence and prevalence of police harassment and abuse. As part of the 1994 Crime Bill, the Department of Justice was directed to develop a method for collecting national data on police use of excessive force.[33] To meet this mandate, in 1996 the Justice Department pre-tested the "Police-Public Contact Survey."

The survey, to be administered to one hundred thousand households as part of the National Crime and Victimization Survey, will query residents about their contacts with police in the preceding year. The survey will collect demographic information (e.g., race, sex, geographic residence) and the circumstances of the police-citizen encounter (e.g., reason for the police-citizen contact; whether the officer conducted a frisk, pat-down, or used handcuffs; whether the officer used or threatened physical force; race and sex of officer; and whether the respondent provoked an encounter with the officer). (See Appendix A for the complete questionnaire.) The data from this annual survey promise to be a powerful tool in assessing the amount of police contact and abuse.

In 1997, Congressman John Conyers introduced the Traffic Stops Statistics Act of 1997.[34] The bill would direct the Attorney General to gather statistics on all routine traffic stops made by law enforcement officials. This would include data on the number of traffic stops, identifying characteristics of the persons who were stopped (e.g., gender, race, age), reason for the stop, whether contraband was found, and whether an arrest was made. Like the National Crime and Victimization Survey, the statistics collected under the Conyers bill would not reveal police or citizen identities. However, this bill would gather statistics directly from law enforcement officials.

The Justice Department maintains figures on the number of lawsuits it brings against police departments. However, these figures represent a fraction of the total number of police brutality cases. The lack of national statistics has forced researchers to rely on other indicators, including newspaper reports of police abuse, the number of judgments entered against police departments, the number of police departments under investigation for corruption, and the number of brutality complaints filed against police departments. What follows is a look at some cases involving allegations of police abuse and the issues they raise.

LAWSUITS

Since the mid-1990s, a barrage of lawsuits has been filed against state and local police departments. Many of these have alleged federal civil rights violations. In 1993, four Blacks filed suit against the Maryland State Police, challenging their use of profile stops. This lawsuit alleged that highway stops were being made solely on the basis of race. In 1992, the plantiffs were pulled over on Interstate-68 in Cumberland, Maryland. They were stopped because they fit a drug courier profile. One passenger,

Robert Wilkins, a Washington, D.C., lawyer, told the officer that he and his family were returning from a funeral in Chicago and that he had to make an early morning court appearance in D.C. The officer ordered everyone out of the car. Wilkins politely yet sternly objected. He questioned the basis for probable cause. Without answering, the officer informed them that they would be detained until they exited the vehicle. Eventually they got out of the car and a narcotics dog searched their vehicle. No drugs were found. Forty-five minutes after they had been pulled over and after a $105 speeding ticket had been issued to the driver, the family was released.

The American Civil Liberties Union, which represented the Wilkins family, discovered evidence of a race-based policy in effect for the Maryland Troopers. The policy was enacted to stem the flow of drugs into western Maryland. A confidential police memorandum referenced the increasing drug problem in the area and offered the following description of drug importers: "The dealers and couriers are predominantly black males and black females."[35] The implicit message was that the troopers would get the biggest bang for their buck by targeting Black drivers. The memo did not reference any other racial groups. The signal to the police officers was clear: because Blacks are responsible for much of the area's drug influx, they can be justifiably stopped, questioned, and searched. The race-based directive was problematic because it encouraged the police to suspect all Black drivers. Because "predominantly" is a vague term, each officer was allowed to have wide-ranging suspicion of Black motorists, depending upon his subjective interpretation of the term. "Predominantly" could mean that Blacks were responsible for anywhere between 51 and 99 percent of the drug imports. No evidence was offered to show that Black motorists are more likely to violate traffic laws or are substantially more likely to transport drugs through the interstate. The Wilkins case was settled for just under $100,000.

As part of the settlement, the Maryland State Police were instructed to maintain computer records of all motorist stops between 1995 and 1997. In 1995, Maryland troopers conducted 533 searches along the Interstate-95 corridor (a fifty-mile stretch of highway extending from Baltimore to the Delaware border). Seventy-seven percent (409) of the searches conducted by Maryland troopers involved vehicles driven by Black motorists, 18 percent involved White drivers, and 1 percent involved Hispanic drivers (Table 3.2). Drugs were found on 33 percent of the Black motorists who were stopped and 22 percent of the White motorists.

TABLE 3.2
Maryland State Police Data, 1995 (I-95 Stops)

I-95 Stops	Black	White	Hispanic	Other	Total
Number	409	97	20	7	533
Contraband found	33%	22%	10%	42%	—

SOURCE: ACLU of Maryland.

Table 3.3 provides a breakdown of Maryland Trooper searches by the Special Traffic Interdiction Force (STIF) unit. This all-White enforcement team was formed to intercept interstate drug transport. In 1995, STIF troopers conducted a total of 202 searches. Seventy-six percent (153) involved Black motorists. For all six STIF troopers, cars driven by Black motorists were the ones most frequently stopped. STIF unit members searched Black motorists at rates ranging from 40 percent of all stops to 100 percent of all stops (Table 3.3).[36] STIF troopers found drugs in 34 percent of the searches involving Black motorists and 13.5 percent of those involving White motorists. No drugs were found in their searches involving Hispanic motorists.

It is unclear why the Maryland State Police stopped Black motorists so frequently. As noted, no studies indicate that there are more Black motorists driving on the interstate and there is no evidence that Blacks are responsible for more than one-half of interstate crimes or interstate trafficking. A 1996 ACLU study shows that along Interstate-95 Blacks account for approximately 17 percent of the motorists and 17.5 percent of traffic law violators. The 1995–1996 figures highlight the intractability of race-based stops. Even after the settlement in the Wilkins case, with knowledge that their stops were being monitored, STIF troopers continued to stop and search Black motorists at a disproportionately high rate (more than 70 percent).

A look at the vehicle stops for the North Carolina Troopers in 1995 reveals a noteworthy racial pattern. The Special Emphasis Team (SET) was comprised of twelve North Carolina Troopers, ten White and two Black. Forty-five percent of all SET stops in 1995 were of Black males. This is double the number of Blacks stopped by troopers who were not members of the special drug unit. Though the SET officers denied any racial bias in their stops, the markedly different patterns represent more than a chance occurrence. A conclusive determination of whether the stops were racially biased is difficult to make because the North Carolina highway patrol does not have written SET training materials. Further, the training methods of

TABLE 3.3
Maryland State Police, Individual Trooper Stops, Special Target Interdiction Force,
Interstate-95 Stops, 1995

	Total Stops	% Black	% White	% Hispanic
Officer 1	38	84%	13%	0
Officer 2	55	87%	11%	2%
Officer 3	44	64%	23%	4%
Officer 4	30	90%	10%	0
Officer 5	30	40%	3%	10%
Officer 6	5	100%	0	0
Summary Data:	202 Stops			
	76% Blacks; 34% contraband found			
	18% Whites; 13.5% contraband found			
	3% Hispanics; 0% contraband found			

SOURCE: ACLU of Maryland data.

the Drug Enforcement Administration and Federal Highway Administration are not available to the public.

In November 1995, a lawsuit was filed against the Beverly Hills, California, police department. Black residents charged that the department employs race-based policies, in violation of their federal civil rights. The plaintiffs alleged that it is the "custom, policy, and practice" of the Beverly Hills Police Department to stop and detain Black motorists and pedestrians, solely on the basis of race. The plaintiffs stated they had been harassed by the police while walking, driving, or bicycling. The complaint alleged that Black men, ages 13 to 35, were being stopped and forced to answer questions regarding their destination, point of origin, domicile, and the nature of their trip. The eight plaintiffs stated that the police stops were without legal justification. Similar federal civil rights lawsuits have been filed in a number of other jurisdictions, including Chicago, Illinois; Eagle County, Colorado; Pittsburgh, Pennsylvania; Tinicum County, Pennsylvania; Gloucester Township, New Jersey; and Volusia County, Florida.[37]

INVESTIGATING THE POLICE

In the 1990s, police departments in several large cities found themselves under investigation. In New York, Philadelphia, and Los Angeles, departments faced allegations of department-wide corruption. In each of these cities, the primary targets of the police lawlessness were poor and working-class communities, comprised of mostly Black and Hispanic residents. In

Philadelphia, for example, five officers pleaded guilty to making false arrests, planting drugs, filing false reports, and robbing victims over a three-year period. Four of the officers were White, one was Asian. Over fifteen hundred cases were placed under investigation, and hundreds of convictions have been overturned. Forty-four plaintiffs, including individuals and organizations (e.g., the NAACP, the Police-Barrio Relations Project), sued the city of Philadelphia. By September 1996, the city of Philadelphia had settled with forty-two plaintiffs. Philadelphia has agreed to pay them almost $3.5 million in damages. As more suits are filed, the city of Philadelphia is expected to pay more money. Additionally, the city agreed to computerize all police report procedures and create an internal affairs office devoted to ethical behavior.

Conclusion: A Costly Enterprise

Numerous costs are associated with race-related police abuse. Blacks individually and as a community are psychologically harmed. While each case of police abuse or police harassment involves an individual officer and an individual citizen, the cases do not exist in isolation. For example, one Black man's painful encounter with the police is negatively reinforced when he learns that other Black men have had similar experiences with the police. The impact of police harassment is cumulative. Each negative experience creates another building block in the Black folklore about police.

It is unreasonable to expect that the net of the criminal justice system will capture only the guilty. We would expect that *some* Blacks who are not involved in crime would be mistakenly suspected of criminal activity. It is not reasonable, however, to expect that close to half of all Black men believe they have been wrongly suspected of criminal activity when less than one-third are involved in criminal activity. To more fully explore this issue, research on racial disparity must be expanded to include analyses of pre-arrest police contacts.

Police practices that allow law enforcement officials to act on negative Black stereotypes will continue to expand the gap between Black and White experiences and perceptions of police. For Blacks, race-based policies raise questions about the legitimacy of the police and further alienate them from the criminal justice system. Robert Wilkins, the successful plaintiff in the Maryland State Police case observed, "[There] is no compensation for the type of humiliation and degradation you feel when for no other reason than the color of your skin . . . you're charged and placed in a category of drug trafficker."[38]

Citizens who do not face the daily threat of being detained largely because of their race are unlikely to understand how burdensome these stops can be. To someone who is pulled over by the police once a month for no apparent reason other than his race, the stops take on an onerous feel. Race-based policies pit law enforcement against minorities and create an unbreakable cycle: racial stereotypes may motivate police to arrest Blacks more frequently. This in turn generates statistically disparate arrest patterns, which in turn form the basis for further police selectivity by race. What many Whites view as the police "doing their job" is viewed by many Blacks as harassment.

Beyond causing harm to Black men, race-based police stops also harm the larger society. There is the societal cost of perpetuating inaccurate stereotypes, which produces exaggerated levels of fear and more pronounced levels of scapegoating—such as racial hoaxes (detailed in chapter 5). Although Blacks are responsible for a disproportionate share of crime, they are not responsible for the majority of crime.

Police harassment of Black men operates as a denial of their civil rights. Jerome McCristal Culp Jr. explains:

> [T]he police and citizens have to figure out ways to allow me to have rights as a black male too. Every time there is a conflict between the rights of the majority and my rights as a stereotypical black male, my rights cannot always be subordinate, or else I have no rights at all.[39]

Treating Whites as if their constitutional rights are worth more has negative long-term consequences. Law enforcement is legitimately concerned with crime by Blacks. However, the strategies it employs should not end up causing greater racial damage, such as increased crime (see chapter 8).

Racial targeting and abuse by police is costly. U.S. taxpayers have paid tens of millions of dollars in police brutality lawsuits. Between 1992 and 1993, Los Angeles county alone paid more than $30 million to citizens victimized by police brutality.[40] In 1996, an all-White Indianapolis jury held the city liable for the police killing of an unarmed 16-year-old Black boy. The jury awarded $4.3 million.[41] These figures do not include legal fees—both those incurred by the cities charged with police abuse and the victims' legal fees, which losing parties are typically required to pay. Many of the nation's cities are in need of greater police services. The huge sums of money paid out in legal damages should instead be available to protect and serve the nation's citizens. Police abuse, harassment, and brutality exact a tremendous social and financial toll on society.

Many Blacks believe that their anti-police sentiments are justified by the racially discriminatory practices of the police. Particularly for young Black men, the police represent Public Enemy number one. Giving short shrift to the problem of excessive targeting of Black men hampers our efforts to reduce crime. For example, the perception that Black men are unfairly targeted by the police may make some Black jurors less likely to believe police testimony. It may also make some Blacks less likely to report crime and others less likely to cooperate with police investigations. Perhaps the issue of police abuse is downplayed because national data are not available. Also, the issue of disproportionality has blurred many people's ability to see the problem of racial discrimination. The reality of racial targeting can be dismissed, rejected, or trivialized. However, the problem is a real one and imposes enormous costs, both social and financial, on the criminal justice system.

4

Are We *Still* Talking about O. J.?

Post-acquittal Conversation

White female: How can you say you agree with the verdict when you believe O. J. killed them? Anyway, the case wasn't about race.

Black female: There was reasonable doubt. Race matters.

White female: The jury's verdict makes a mockery of the justice system.

Black female: How come you weren't this upset after the first Rodney King trial in Simi Valley, or for that matter after the acquittal of Claus von Bulow?

White female: Those cases were different. Isn't domestic violence important to you?

Black female: Of course. Are you saying that if I agree with the verdict that I support domestic violence?

White female: I give up!

The O. J. Simpson criminal case was a combination of time travel and science fiction. Unfortunately, as far as race relations go, the time travel was backwards. Public opinion appeared to vacillate between fascination and disgust during the eighteen-month-long saga. Throughout, the case was riveting, and even at its most disturbing it remained compelling. Everything about the Simpson case was writ large. It featured an ever-expanding cast of characters and themes that were constantly reinvented. There was the low-speed car chase that resembled a cavalcade for visiting dignitaries. Simpson's suicide note was read during the chase. The letter sounded like a cross between an acceptance speech and a high school yearbook signing. In it, Simpson "thanked" several people, including former football teammates and golfing buddies. He also thanked his first wife, Marguerite: "[T]hanks for the early years. We had some fun."[1] The bizarre note ended with Simpson placing a "smiley face" inside the "O" of his signature. Ironically, the chase, which signified the Heisman Trophy winner's downward spiral, took place while the two top-rated NBA teams fought for their sport's highest honors.

The criminal trial featured more incredible events. During the case a White defense attorney used the "N" word numerous times during a cross-examination. Interested parties and witnesses morphed into new roles. One witness was said to have close ties to the Mafia. One juror, Tracey Hampton, was said to have become suicidal during the trial. She was released from jury service and subsequently posed nude for *Playboy.* By the end of the case, Mark Fuhrman, one of L.A.'s finest, had become a poster boy for the Ku Klux Klan, and Geraldo Rivera, known for putting sleaze TV on the map, had reincarnated himself into a serious legal analyst.

This chapter poses some new issues about the Simpson case, focusing primarily on the criminal case and its aftermath. It explores the Black/White racial division in the case and questions whether the media accurately reported the gap. The discussion of "Black Protectionism" looks at possible explanations for the strong support Simpson received from the Black community. The chapter concludes with an examination of how the issue of race was discussed. As indicated, the discussion on race was limited to Black and White, overlooking large sections of the U.S. population.

Everlasting O. J.

The O. J. spectacle created one of the most successful cottage industries ever. More than forty books have been written about the case. Lawyers, jurors, ex-wives, ex-girlfriends, best friends, neighbors, victims' family members, police officers, and the defendant wrote their own accounts. Several landed on the *New York Times* best sellers list. Mark Fuhrman's book, *Murder in Brentwood*, reached the number one spot in March 1997. In a miraculously quick turn-around, Fuhrman, a convicted perjurer, managed, with the help of the press, to publicly rehabilitate himself. In 1997, Paula Barbieri, O. J.'s ex-girlfriend, signed a book deal for a reported $3 million. The trial autobiography of prosecutor Marcia Clark, which netted a signing bonus over $3 million, was published in May 1997.

The case, a television-marketing boon, was used to both reinvigorate and launch careers. Both trials created several "spin-offs" including *Burden of Proof* (hosted by Greta Van Sustern and Roger Cossack), *The Charles Grodin Show, Gerry Spence, Cochran & Company,* and *Lady Law* (this show, which was to be hosted by Marcia Clark, never aired). Though *Rivera Live* was not a spin-off, once the criminal trial began, it undertook a daily analysis of the case. Not everyone was lucky enough to have their own television show. Others, such as houseguest Kato Kaelin, have attempted to parlay their trial exposure into entertainment careers. Faye Resnick, Nicole Simpson's best friend, wrote a book about the case and, following the civil verdict, bared her body for *Playboy.*

Time, energy, and money spent discussing and dissecting the case were in evidence everywhere—the locker room, boardroom, street corner, talk radio, bedroom, and grocery store. The criminal trial literally tapped each of our senses. Few could erase the sight of Denise Brown crying on the witness stand or O. J. sitting at the defense table staring blankly ahead. Most of us remember sounds from the trial, including the 911 call by a petrified Nicole Brown Simpson, the three "thumps" that Kato Kaelin heard the night of the murders, and the Akita's "plaintive wail." Many people will remember almost feeling the black leather gloves that did not fit. Likewise, many will recall forensic chemist Greg Matheson's testimony, describing the smell of Ronald Goldman's blood-soaked clothing. Ultimately, the case left most of us with a sour taste in our mouths. The criminal case became a convenient springboard for airing our frustrations about race, police, crime, lawyers, and the media. We may have learned more than we wanted to know about ourselves and the state of U.S. race relations. More than our curiosity, the Simpson case piqued our anxieties.

"The Black/White Standoff"

The Numbers Game

Before, during, and after the trial, an endless barrage of poll data indicated a wide gulf between Blacks and Whites. We were told that Blacks and Whites had mirror-opposite opinions about the case. Surveys consistently showed that 70 percent of Blacks believed Simpson was innocent, while 70 percent of Whites believed he was guilty. The opinion polls heightened tensions between Blacks and Whites, and neither side was able to comprehend the other. At some point, the bewilderment turned to anger. Whites were angry with Blacks for not recognizing that Simpson was obviously guilty. Blacks were angry with Whites for not understanding the race issue and not considering the possibility that Simpson might have been set up. The result of this racial friction was "The Black/White Standoff." Media reports

TABLE 4.1
Black/White Simpson Poll Data
(Extrapolating Poll Data into Actual Numbers)

	Simpson "Guilty"	Simpson "Not Guilty"
Black	10 million [30 percent of Blacks]	22 million [70 percent of Blacks]
White	139 million [70 percent of Whites]	60 million [30 percent of Whites]
Totals	149 million [100 percent]	82 million [100 percent]

NOTE: These numbers are based on U.S. Census population estimates for 1996. The total population is 264 million, with Whites accounting for about 75 percent and Blacks about 12 percent.

about public opinion on the Simpson case stoked this fire by failing to address several issues, including:

- One could agree with the verdict and believe that Simpson committed the murders.
- The voices on either side of the racial divide were not equal in number.
- In actual numbers, more Whites than Blacks thought Simpson was not guilty (Table 4.2).
- There were many Blacks and Whites who had similar views on the Simpson case (Table 4.1).
- A sizeable number of Blacks thought Simpson was guilty (Table 4.1).
- Economic status was not factored into media representations of "The Black/White Standoff."

The media's crude depiction of the split between Blacks and Whites on Simpson's guilt implied that there was a group of Whites on one side with their opinions and an equal number of Blacks on the other side with opposing opinions. The media glossed over the fact that for every Black who thought Simpson was not guilty, there were six Whites who thought he was guilty. The power of the racial voices was not equal. Table 4.1 illustrates this point. A conversion of poll figures to actual numbers indicates that there were approximately 139 million Whites who believed Simpson was guilty, compared with approximately 22 million Blacks who believed he was innocent. The dueling choirs of angry, exercised voices were not evenly matched.

In reality, the "70-30 split" between Blacks and Whites indicates that, in actual numbers, Blacks who believed in Simpson's innocence represented a small fraction of public opinion (8 percent). The constant media focus upon those Blacks who thought Simpson was innocent helped create the image that "The Black Viewpoint" was slightly crazed and fanatical.

In the midst of the hype associated with "The Black/White Standoff," it was difficult to see that there were many Whites who believed that Simpson was not guilty. In fact, they outnumbered the number of Blacks who thought Simpson was not guilty by a 3:1 margin. This indicates that there were more Whites who agreed with the verdict than there were Blacks who agreed with it. The post-verdict split-television screen, which showed Whites shocked and Blacks elated, could just as accurately have been a split-screen with one side showing Whites who agreed with the verdict and the other side showing Whites who disagreed with the verdict. Table 4.2 illustrates this point. Approximately 60 million Whites believed Simpson was not guilty, compared with 22 million Blacks.

The media's overemphasis on how differently Whites and Blacks viewed the criminal case also masked the fact that many Blacks believed Simpson was guilty. The surveys indicated that one-third of Blacks polled believed Simpson was guilty—reflecting approximately 10 million Blacks (Table 4.1). It is understandable that the media focused on the majority Black viewpoint. It is not clear, however, why it gave so little attention to the remaining 30 percent. The perspectives of the ten million Blacks who thought Simpson had killed Nicole Brown Simpson and Ronald Goldman were effectively silenced. Although the media was frequently criticized for overreporting the Simpson case, some aspects of the case received little attention. During the eighteen-month saga, few media portrayals featured Blacks expressing the belief that Simpson was guilty.

Polls taken after the criminal verdict did an abysmally poor job of fleshing out racial viewpoints on the jury's decision. There were numerous reports that most Blacks were pleased with the verdict. The untapped data might have revealed that many Blacks, though in accord with the verdict, thought that Simpson had committed the murders. The opinion polls appeared to confound factual guilt and legal guilt. Actually, one could believe that Simpson was guilty and believe that the prosecution did not prove its case. The superficial reporting about the racial implications of the verdict and its aftermath were not surprising, given how racial issues were handled throughout the criminal trial.

TABLE 4.2
Black/White Simpson Poll Data
O. J. Simpson "Not Guilty" (Actual Numbers)

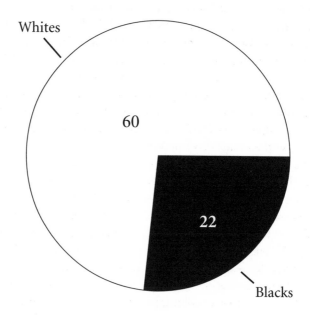

Whites

60

22

Blacks

In Millions

The media's insistence upon using race to explain reactions to the verdict precluded an analysis of other important variables. Specifically, what role did class status play in influencing viewpoints? A March 1995 Harris Poll showed that people with high incomes were more likely to believe Simpson was guilty. Sixty-five percent of people earning $50,000 or more per year believed that Simpson had committed the murders. Conversely, 41 percent of people making $7500 or less per year believed he was not guilty.[2] Unfortunately, this poll did not report findings on the interaction between race and class—e.g., whether high-income Blacks had a perspective on the case different from low-income Blacks. If there were national polls that examined the race-class relationship, they were not widely reported.

White Outrage

The depth of the White community's outrage over the Simpson verdict was exemplified by its public display of dissatisfaction with the verdict. It is hard to remember another time when Whites have been so outdone-angry-disappointed and let down by a public figure and public event. The outrage at the Simpson verdict is partly due to the fact that so many people watched the trial unfold in their living rooms.

Whites have distanced themselves from the verdict by both turning it into a joke and by characterizing "The Black Viewpoint" on Simpson as irrational. More than a year after the criminal verdict, jokes about the Simpson case were still a mainstay of the talk shows. Quips about Simpson's guilt and the jury's ignorance were regularly heard on David Letterman, Jay Leno, Conan O'Brien, Bill Maher, Dennis Miller, and Rosie O'Donnell. One of the more popular jokes that made the rounds after the acquittal was, "It's finally official. Murder is legal in the state of California."

White outrage also found a home on cable television. In what was accurately dubbed "The O. J. Show," *Rivera Live* focused almost exclusively on the criminal trial. Geraldo Rivera, whose appetite for all things related to O. J. was unmatched, regularly shared his opinions about the case and his belief in Simpson's guilt. Referring to the racial gap in the polls, he stated, "*Even* educated African Americans I have known and loved for years are rooting for [O. J. Simpson]. People who are so objective and analytical on almost any other topic, including race, seem to me irrational on this one."[3] Rivera's comments crystallize much of the anti-Simpson sentiment. His surprise that "even" Blacks who are educated believed Simpson was innocent implies that only blind race-loyalty could explain why an educated Black person could believe Simpson was not guilty. The *Charles Grodin Show* could be called "The O. J. Show, Part II." For more than two years, a visibly restrained Grodin used his TV platform to present long soliloquies on Simpson's guilt.

Mainstream print journalism's response to the Simpson acquittal is captured by the July 1996 *Weekly Standard*. The cover depicts a dark, sinister-looking caricature of O. J. The accompanying article, "Why He Still Haunts Us," begins, "Two years after murdering his ex-wife Nicole and Ronald Goldman. . . ."[4] Another example of anti–O. J. expression is Vincent Bugliosi's boldly titled best seller, *Outrage: Five Reasons Why O. J. Simpson Got Away with Murder.*

Before and after the verdict, the media continually mocked the idea that Simpson could be innocent. It uniformly promoted the view that the jury's verdict in the criminal case was irrational. The outcome of the civil lawsuits, filed by the families of Ronald Goldman and Nicole Brown, provided another opportunity to express anti–O. J. sentiments. Sixteen months following the acquittal, a mostly White jury found Simpson civilly liable for the deaths of Nicole Simpson and Ronald Goldman. A $33.5 million judgment was entered against him ($8.5 million compensatory damages and $25 million punitive damages). The "Black" (criminal) and "White" (civil) juries have been constantly compared with one another. For the most part, the criminal jury has been dismissed as biased, and the civil jury heralded as objective. The routine bashing of the criminal verdict was partly due to the fact that the public had more facts about the case than the jury.

The depth of White anger at Simpson, however, raises the issue of whether it is historically rooted. As discussed in chapter 2, White fear of Black male/White female sexual relationships has existed for centuries. States adopted harsh penalties to deter and punish White/Black sexual liaisons. Some people have suggested that some of the White hostility toward Simpson reflects the longstanding fear of race-mixing.

The mass anger and disgust at Simpson may not abate until he is relegated to pushing a shopping cart and mumbling to himself. Given the size of the civil damage award, this is not so remote a possibility. Early signs do not indicate that Simpson will be rehabilitated in the public mind. He has become the 1990s repository for fear and anger toward the criminal justice system. In particular, the murder of Ronald Goldman has come to represent the fear most Americans have of random acts of violence. The Rodney King beating represented the deep-seated fear that many Blacks have—fear that "justice" will be dispensed at the mercy of racist, White police officers. Similarly the Simpson case crystallized White fears—fear of Black-on-White crime, fear of justice run amuck, and the overarching fear of the Black man.

White fear may explain the wide-ranging reforms proposed in the wake of the criminal and civil verdicts, most aimed at diluting the power of criminal defense attorneys. Proposals included abolishing the unanimity requirement in criminal cases, limiting the number of defense attorneys, prohibiting jury sequestration, banning cameras from the courtroom, prohibiting jury consultants, and barring lawyers from using race-based appeals in closing arguments. One example of a law passed in direct response to the Simpson acquittal is a bill signed into law by California governor Pete Wilson. In September 1996, two weeks before the start of the civil case, Wilson signed a bill allowing personal diaries to be admitted as evidence in civil cases. On the heels of the civil verdict, California legislation has been drafted to have child custody revoked in cases where a parent has been found civilly liable for the wrongful death of the other parent.

The public has always been ruffled by unanticipated jury verdicts, but the reaction to the criminal case was unique in that the jurors were cast as mentally defective. Some suggested, only half-jokingly, that IQ tests should have been required for the jurors. No similar suggestion was made following the acquittal in the first Rodney King/LAPD trial—in which a mostly White jury acquitted four White officers. Underlying the criticisms of the criminal jury is the implicit view that the nine Black jurors coerced the three non-Black jurors to vote not-guilty. After the criminal trial, one of the White female jurors stated that she would have voted for conviction had she been aware of some of the evidence not admitted into trial. She has never said, however, that she was forced to vote for acquittal.

Black Indignation

The growing anger and disillusionment that many Whites expressed after the acquittal was evenly matched by the anger and disillusionment that many Blacks experienced. Black indignation is partly explained by Black protectionism, discussed in the next section. Whites were angry because of the verdict—angry that a guilty man could go free. Whites became frustrated with a criminal justice system that failed in spite of compelling, overwhelming evidence. How could the jury acquit Simpson, with his lengthy record of domestic abuse and no clear alibi? Further, what about the DNA evidence? Conversely, many Blacks could not understand why Whites were so upset, and they became angry that so many Whites were so angry. After all, what about the tainted blood evidence, no murder weapon, and the improbability of one person carrying out the murders? Most importantly, what about Mark Fuhrman?

Many Blacks who supported Simpson believed there was a Simpson media "blackout," which forced him to cancel public appearances. In one instance Simpson had planned to attend a card-trading show, and in another he had scheduled a post-verdict interview with NBC's Katie Couric. Both were canceled after complaints were lodged and protests were threatened. Some suggested that while O. J. was being silenced, anti–O. J. voices were loud and clear.

To many Blacks, White outrage at the Simpson verdict was inexplicable when contrasted with White reaction to an acquittal in another criminal case, the first Rodney King/LAPD trial. On May 1, 1992, two days following the acquittal in Los Angeles of police officers Stacey Koon, Laurance Powell, Theodore Briseno, and Timothy Wind, Pulitzer Prize-winning journalist William Raspberry wrote an editorial, "Where's the Outrage from White America." Raspberry said, "I'm waiting for responsible white leaders to tell me that [the] incomprehensible verdict outrages them as much as it outrages us."[5] Clearly, a case involving two brutal murders is not the same as one involving a near-fatal beating. Still, Whites were as vocal about the attack on White truck driver Reginald Denny during the Los Angeles riots as they were about the Rodney King beating. Polls taken after the Simi Valley verdict indicated that most Whites believed the police defendants were guilty of using excessive force. Why, then, were Whites so quiet, relatively speaking, about the Simi Valley acquittal and so outspoken about the Simpson acquittal?

In the months following the criminal case, polls showed that Blacks and Whites continued to have different views on its legitimacy. The fallout has caused some Blacks to retreat even further from the mainstream—evidenced by growing support for the Nation of Islam, increased interest in Black colleges and Kwanzaa celebrations, and the rising number of Black gated communities.

Some Blacks have responded to White indignation by reaching out to embrace Simpson. Since the verdict, Simpson has aligned himself with groups directly tied with or sympathetic to the Nation of Islam. Fear of poverty makes strange bedfellows. In August 1996, Simpson gave a talk at a Black church in Washington, D.C. The visit was sponsored by the Black Attorneys for Justice/O. J. Simpson Support Committee. One committee member, Malik Shabazz, attained notoriety in 1994 after making incendiary remarks about the power and motives of the Jewish community. More than two thousand people, most of them sympathetic to Simpson, paid ten dollars to hear him speak.

Transcendental O. J., Other "Colorless" Black Men, and Black Protectionism

Many Whites and not a few Blacks were puzzled by the widespread, unflagging support that Simpson received from much of the Black community. How is it that Simpson, who many said "is not really Black," came to represent so many Blacks and to symbolize Blackness? Many commentators observed that long before 1994 Simpson not only had divorced his Black first wife, he had divorced himself from the Black community. One theory that might explain the "strong love" for O. J. evinced by so many Blacks is Black protectionism.

The term Black protectionism is used to describe what happens when the credentials, past history, or behavior of a well-known, successful Black person is called into question. In these instances, the Black community's reaction is protective, almost maternal. The Black community builds a fortress around its fallen hero and begins to offer explanations and defenses. Whenever colorless Blacks fall into national disgrace and scandal, they are picked up and brushed off by the Black community. Like a good wife, Black people "stand by their man."

In recent years the Black community has seen a growing number of its members achieve mega-success. There is a small group of highly visible Black millionaires (e.g., Oprah Winfrey, Bill Cosby, Michael Jackson, Michael Jordan, Denzel Washington, Whitney Houston, and Shaquille O'Neal). Within the past generation there have been several Blacks who have risen to national prominence as politicians (e.g., Jesse Jackson, Ron Brown, Carol Moseley Braun) and military heroes (e.g., Colin Powell). The Black middle class has also grown. The relative newness of Black mega-success and achievement may partially explain Black protectionism. The next section examines the historical roots of Black protectionism, the rationales for it, to whom it applies, and how it works.

Transcendental O. J. and the Roots of Black Protectionism

O. J. Simpson, like Clarence Thomas, Colin Powell, and Michael Jackson had "crossed over." He, like they, had been accepted into polite White society. Simpson no longer belonged solely to Black people, he had transcended his race. How exactly is crossover status achieved? The seminal crossover indicator is that someone Black is embraced by a large, visible sector of the White community. By itself, being popular with Whites and Blacks is not enough to complete the crossover transformation.

Crossing over requires that the Black person take an affirmative step toward "color-free" status, such as proclaiming he is colorless or declining to attach significance to being Black. O. J.'s colorless aspirations are reflected in his following remarks:

> I was at a wedding, my [first] wife and a few friends were the only Negroes there, and I overheard a lady at the next table say, "Look, there's O. J. Simpson

and some niggers." Isn't that weird? That sort of thing hurts me, even though it's what I strive for, to be a man first.[6]

Claims of colorlessness and other dismissals of the relevance of race have been made by other prominent personalities, including Michael Jackson, Whoopi Goldberg, and golfer Tiger Woods.[7]

When someone Black receives widespread acceptance by Whites, it typically raises eyebrows among Blacks. Past experience has cautioned many Blacks to be suspicious of those Blacks whom Whites prop up as spokespersons, heroes, or role models. Influencing this suspicion is the question whether the Black person is someone who identifies with his Blackness or is someone who wishes to get as far away from it as possible. In this way, one's "authenticity" is measured. Denzel Washington, Whitney Houston, and Michael Jordan, widely adored and respected across color lines, are still viewed as "authentic." The bottom line on authenticity is whether the Black person "remembers where he came from." Some measures of this are the public comments the crossover person has made, if any, about being Black or about Blacks in general, their political affiliation, their charity work, and whether she or he is married to someone White.

Interestingly, transcendental racial status, or colorlessness has a fail-safe mechanism. It permits the "transcendor" (e.g., O. J.), to return home to the Black community whenever he is disrespected, accused of wrongdoing, or indicted by "the (White) system." The system can be any branch of government, corporate America, or the media. Numerous actions trigger the fail-safe response. These actions include charging a famous Black person with a criminal offense (e.g., O. J., Mike Tyson), unofficial allegations of criminal behavior (e.g., Michael Jackson), or perceived disrespectful treatment by the media (e.g., Clarence Thomas).

At this point, a logical question is, *why* would the Black community rally behind someone who has taken great strides to remove himself from it or done little to affirmatively remain a part of it? It goes without saying that the Black community would support "colorful" Blacks—those who embrace their Blackness or those who are not running away from it. Black protectionism, which operates like a homing pigeon, is rooted in the past and present. Blacks are mindful that many of the people they have upheld as leaders, including Martin Luther King, Jr., Malcolm X, Harriet Tubman, Jesse Jackson, Louis Farrakhan, and Fannie Lou Hamer, have been dismissed, ignored, or denigrated by Whites. For example, Jesse Jackson, who since the early days of Operation PUSH has been admired and respected by a sizeable percentage of the Black community, was not taken seriously by mainstream Whites, until he garnered seven million votes in the 1988 presidential primaries.

As noted above, the relatively small number of Black success stories may help explain the force of Black protectionism. From a population of more than thirty million, there exist few bonafide Black superstars. These few, whether they embrace their Blackness or not, are jealously guarded by the Black community. Discussing Black reaction to O. J. Simpson, communications professor Michael Eric Dyson notes:

> It can be viewed as the refusal of blacks to play the race authenticity game, which, in this instance, amounts to the belief that only "real" blacks deserve support when racial difficulties arise. But black responses to OJ can also be read less charitably. They can be seen as the automatic embrace of a fallen figure simply because he is black.[8]

Black protectionism likely arose during slavery when, in the interest of group survival, Blacks had to present a united front to White slave owners. A Black slave's minor infraction (e.g., returning late from an errand) could result in a major penalty. One of the harsher penalties a slave master could impose was to sell the slave, which would destroy the family unit. A minor offense could result in a whipping, torture, or execution. Denial of wrongdoing became a form of group protection against an irrational, racist system of formal and informal laws. A slave's acknowledgment to someone White that another slave had done something unlawful (e.g., learning to read) could forever seal the other slave's fate. The brutality of slavery created a strong bond between Blacks. Any slave who broke racial ranks and informed the slave master was viewed as selling out the race. Harry Edwards, University of California sociologist, supports a historical interpretation of Black support for Simpson:

> [Black support of Simpson] has not been so much an act of undying loyalty as an act of self-defense, a collective, almost intuitive appreciation of the historical fact that the black community is inescapably bound to its members—for better and worse—impacted by their actions and outcomes irrespective of their disposition toward the black community. Black people's inordinate empathy with O. J. Simpson is, then, mostly an artifact of cultural memory.[9]

Beyond its historical roots, Black protectionism appears to serve a present-day function. It creates a new, nondeviant way for Blacks to view themselves. University of Pennsylvania law professor Regina Austin states that oppressed people reject mainstream definitions of themselves and "create their own concepts of justice, morality and legality."[10] In this way, Black protectionism can be said to operate as a shield—to defend against stereotypical views of Black deviance and criminality. At other times, Black protectionism is worn like a badge of honor. For example, during the criminal case, many Blacks appeared to relish being "pro–O. J.," fully aware that this went against the status quo. Black protectionism is dynamic—the more Whites are perceived as closing in on the "target," the greater the community protection becomes.

The Deductive Logic of Black Protectionism

By design, Black protectionism guards Blacks against White assault. It operates even when the direct beneficiary of Black protectionism (e.g., Simpson) does not appear to appreciate the support. Black protectionism is a form of community redemption—not redemption in the traditional sense because it does not require that the person apologize or atone. The target person's actions are only marginally relevant to Black protectionism. The key factor is how the Black community views the response from the White community—specifically, whether the targeted Black is being mistreated by Whites, not whether he is a Johnny-come-lately to race.

Black protectionism is ostensibly a form of group self-interest. A superficial analysis might dismiss Black protectionism as a knee-jerk reaction at best or Black paranoia at worst. A look at how it works, however, suggests that it cannot be discounted so easily. When charges of misconduct are leveled against a well-known Black person, many Blacks ask themselves a series of questions, including:

- "Did he commit the offense?"
- "Even if he did commit the offense, was he set up?"
- "Would he risk everything he has (e.g., wealth, fame, material possessions) to commit this offense?"
- "Is he the only person who has committed this offense?"
- "Are White people who are accused of committing this offense given the same scrutiny and treatment?"
- "Is this accusation part of a government conspiracy to destroy the Black race?"

If it is determined that either the Black person did not commit the offense or that he may have committed the offense but was targeted because of race, Black protectionism goes into effect. Black protectionism is most easily triggered in cases involving well-off Blacks, because many would wonder why someone who has achieved the American dream would throw it all away. In the final analysis, the alleged actions of the Black person under scrutiny are measured against the actions of the state. If it is concluded that the state's actions are more culpable than the alleged wrongdoing, Blacks rally behind their fallen member. Marion Barry is an example of this. Blacks do not condone crack smoking; however, many Blacks viewed the government's tactics (using a former girlfriend as bait to lure Barry to a hotel room) as unfair entrapment. On balance, many concluded that government entrapment was a worse offense than the mayor of the nation's capital smoking a crack pipe.

For Whites, the analysis is much simpler—they begin and end with the first question, "Did he commit the offense?" For Whites, the consideration of other factors, such as whether the government's behavior was criminal or whether race played a role, does not affect the answer to the first question. As a result of how differently Whites and Blacks analyze the same set of facts, it is easy to understand how Whites conclude that Blacks are blinded by race loyalty. It is also easy to understand how Blacks conclude that Whites "just don't get it."

Clarence Thomas and Black Protectionism

The 1991 Clarence Thomas confirmation hearings offer a textbook example of Black protectionism. By virtue of affirmative action, Thomas had been permitted to opt out of Blackness. He sealed his colorless fate by preaching against affirmative action, denigrating his sister, arguing that Blacks are overly reliant on state aid, marrying a White woman, and dismissing Anita Hill as a potential love interest because she was "too dark."

However, once Hill's claims about Thomas became public and it appeared that Whites were lining up against him, Thomas "became" Black again. Many Blacks believed he was being unfairly treated—he was not only being "Borked,"[11] he was being lynched. In fact, Thomas described the Senate Judiciary Hearings as "[A] high-tech lynching for uppity Blacks who deign to think for themselves."[12] At that point, Thomas openly reclaimed his Blackness. In effect, his lynching metaphor was a trumpet call for Black support—or what journalist Clarence Page calls "Rally-Round-the-Brother Syndrome." For some people, the visual image of a Black man desperately trying to defend himself before an all-White, all-male Senate Judiciary Committee conjured up images of an actual lynching. Many Blacks suspected that a conspiracy was afoot. According to one theory, Anita Hill was being used by radical feminists and liberals to bring another Black man down. Another theory was that the Senate Judiciary Committee was badgering Thomas because it did not want to appoint a Black person to the Supreme Court.

Like Thomas, Simpson had to be backed into a corner before he publicly addressed the issue of race. Throughout the trial and for months following the verdict, the Black community's embrace of Simpson was one-sided. Simpson did not comment, thank, or even acknowledge the overwhelming support he received from the Black community. Nor did he publicly reflect on the racial implications and racial fallout from the verdict. His silence on the issue of race was remarkable in light of the fact that everyone else was so consumed by it.

Early in 1996, after Simpson realized he was no longer welcome in his former elite White inner-circle, he slowly began to speak publicly about race. He gave his first television interview to Black Entertainment Television, after protests led him to withdraw from a scheduled NBC interview. During the interview, Simpson insisted that most Whites agreed with the verdict. When journalist Ed Gordon asked Simpson whether he should move out of Brentwood because of neighborhood protests, his startling reply was, "Where am I supposed to go? Africa?"[13] During the interview, Simpson appeared painfully unaware of the depth of White outrage against him.

Since then, Simpson has acknowledged racial injustice in the court system and has said that "America is for the White." In his lectures, he speaks out against the media and charges it with racism. Simpson's post-verdict metamorphosis could be viewed as affirmative steps taken by him to re-enter the Black community. In direct contrast to earlier statements he made about being colorless, he now talks about being Black. One of his speeches was titled, "Is There Justice for Black People in America?" Simpson has commented that many people believe he is late to the race game, "I keep hearing everybody say, 'He's back.' Maybe there's a point there."[14] Some have speculated that his belated attempts to re-embrace Blackness are suspect. In 1996, *Washington Post* journalist Avis Thomas-Lester wrote, "I wonder when, before this latest money-making venture began [his speaking tour], O. J. was last inside a black church."[15]

Blacklash

Black protectionism has another interesting twist. While some transcendors are allowed to re-enter the Black community, others find that the cloak of Black protectionism is not a permanent one. The transcendor may later be exiled or ignored by the Black community. This appears to have happened with Clarence Thomas. Though most Blacks supported him during the confirmation hearings, the tide has since turned. Many who felt his treatment by the Senate Judiciary Committee was unfairly harsh and racist believed that he should be given a seat on the U.S. Supreme Court.

After six years on the Court, however, Thomas is now viewed by many Blacks as insensitive to issues important to the Black community (e.g., affirmative action, criminal procedure, and voting rights). It is one thing to be perceived as neutral about Black issues, it is quite another thing to be perceived as hostile, and Thomas appears to have crossed the line. In two widely publicized incidents, Thomas encountered vocal opposition from the Blacks when he was invited to speak before Black youth groups.[16] In a national survey of Black opinion, Thomas received the lowest rating of all the famous Blacks listed in the poll. Coretta Scott King and Jesse Jackson received the highest favorable ratings (82 percent). Johnnie Cochran, Colin Powell, Louis Farrakhan, and Benjamin Chavis all had higher ratings than Thomas.[17]

Are Black Women Protected?

Another important question raised by Black protectionism is whether its cloak extends to Black women. This is not an easy question to answer. First, women have far fewer avenues for attaining national stature than men. For instance, many Black superstars are athletes, and women, by and large, do not have access to the world of pro sports. Even those sports which have been slow to open up to Blacks, such as golf and tennis, are more likely to open up to Black men first. The same is true for the motion picture industry. There are few blockbuster movie roles for Blacks and most of these roles go to Black men. Second, well-known women are much less likely to become involved in public scandals. Given this, there exist fewer opportunities to invoke Black protectionism for Black women. It is difficult to imagine the Black community rallying behind a high-profile, colorless Black woman if she were accused of committing a serious crime. It is unlikely that the Black community would be as steadfast in its allegiance to a Black woman as it has been toward Clarence Thomas or O. J. Simpson.

At least two incidents involving Black women might have invoked Black protectionism. The first incident involved the nomination of Lani Guinier, constitutional law professor, to serve as the assistant attorney general for civil rights. President Bill Clinton withdrew her name after sizeable conservative opposition mounted against her. Though many Blacks were troubled by Clinton's actions, compared with the Clarence Thomas case, there was a low volume of Black protest.

The same is true for former Surgeon General, Dr. Joycelyn Elders. After making some controversial comments about sex education, she was summarily dismissed from her post. Again, though many Blacks were troubled by Clinton's actions, there was no groundswell of protest in support of Elders. If Black protectionism applies to Black women, it should have been invoked for Guinier and Elders. Both women have demonstrated a lifelong commitment to improving the conditions of their communities. If Black protectionism was not used to support these women, it appears unlikely that it would be for a "colorless" Black woman.

The Future of Black Protectionism

The theory of Black protectionism may partially explain the deep divergence between Black and White opinion on the Simpson case. Blacks understandably bring a different set of historical concerns to any racial issue than Whites. In one of his seminal essays, sociologist W. E. B. Du Bois wrote about the "double-consciousness" that Blacks must have. He described it as "this sense of always looking at one's self through the eyes of others."[18] Blacks are ever mindful of their history of oppression in this country and are acutely aware of the negative image that Whites have of them. Many Blacks have heard stories, passed down through generations, about the savagery of slavery and Jim Crow. Blacks are also aware that Whites as a group are not as interested in this history and how it affects race relations today. For many Blacks, their history as legally mandated second-class citizens, which is scarcely two generations old, is more than a historical footnote.

In contrast, Whites as a group rejected claims that America's history of racial discrimination bore any significance to the Simpson case. The relevance of this history may have been ignored, not out of maliciousness, but out of ignorance. This may explain why the White response to Mark Fuhrman was shock, while the Black response was "I told you so." In the end, Blacks and Whites use entirely different criteria to analyze racial incidents. If Blacks and Whites are going to bridge any more of the racial gap, Whites will have to understand not only Black protectionism, but also *why* it persists and the functions it serves.

"Black and White Only": The Dichotomy of Race

The American fascination with the tension between Blacks and Whites was never more apparent than during the Simpson criminal case. This interest was so intense that it overshadowed all other racial dynamics. During the trial, the racial pulse of the country was literally measured in Black and White.

One of the more problematic aspects of the criminal case, as far as media imagery goes, is how we were each forced into statistical boxes. From the early days of the trial, the polls indicated that Blacks overwhelmingly believed Simpson was innocent and Whites overwhelmingly believed he was guilty. Pollsters, aided and abetted by the media, only told us what Blacks and Whites thought—overlooking people of all other races. Not surprisingly, the media's racial pigeon-holing forced individual Blacks and Whites to become spokespersons for their entire race. Few newspaper or television polls taken during the trial were broken down by race, class, age, and region.

"Black" has been treated as a monolithic racial category that includes Blacks from anywhere in the world (e.g., Black Americans, Black Africans, and Black Caribbeans). It is possible that each of these groups, based upon their racial experience in this country and history, had a different opinion of the Simpson case due to their different historical experiences. Likewise, Whites were treated as a singular group. White opinions about the Simpson case might have varied by ethnicity, geography, or class. Notably, the media provided only crude data on Blacks and Whites. No doubt, for many of us, the media boxes that Blacks and Whites were forced into were unnerving.

The statistical boxes we did not see were equally unsettling. Race was dichotomized to mean "Black" and "White." Few, if any, major news stories reported the viewpoints of Asians, Latinos, or Native Americans. Although the Harris Poll collected survey data on Hispanics, these data received scant media attention. The media's racial blind-spot is no minor oversight, considering that approximately 15 percent of the U.S. population is neither Black nor White. U.S. Census estimates for 1997 report that Hispanics are 11 percent, Asians 3.5 percent, and Native Americans are less than 1 percent. Further, the U.S. Census estimates that Hispanics will soon replace Blacks as the largest minority group. Indeed, one hundred years from now, when historians study public opinion in the Simpson case, one of the more perplexing questions may be why there was such sparse documentation of Asian, Native American, and Hispanic viewpoints.

If the polls taken about the Simpson case had included a wider cross-section of the populace, we would have had a more colorful and more accurate picture of American racial dynamics. For instance, the different group experience that Blacks have had with law enforcement may explain why they are more suspicious of the criminal justice system. It is their group experience that caused many Blacks to question the prosecution's case against Simpson. Perhaps Hispanics, who also have strained relations with law enforcement, shared the same views. That information certainly would have been newsworthy. Rather than adopting the media's widespread conclusion that the reaction to the Simpson case was a "Black thing" or a "White thing," perhaps the best conclusion is that it was an "experiential thing."

Conversely, survey data might have shown that Hispanics were more closely aligned with Whites in their perceptions of the Simpson trial. It is also possible that Hispanics held viewpoints on the Simpson case dissimilar to both Whites and Blacks. One of the problems with making race a two-column category is that it causes us to mistakenly believe that there are only two viewpoints.

In addition to being ignored in poll data, Asian, Hispanic, and Native American pundits were also in short supply during the Simpson trial. Where were the Asian and Hispanic lawyers or journalists who could speak about the case? In 1996 there were 1,768 Hispanic newsroom journalists (3 percent), 1,088 Asians (2 percent), and 224 Native Americans (under 1 percent).[19] The Pacific region, which includes California, has the largest percentage of minority journalists. Further, more of the legal issues could have been discussed by the 248 Hispanic, 119 Asian, and nine Native American law professors.[20]

The city of Los Angeles, one of the most diverse cities in the country, is about 40 percent Hispanic and 10 percent Asian. Los Angeles County has the largest Hispanic population outside of Latin America. A few Hispanic voices managed to break through the Black/White O. J. debate: Mandelit del Barco (National Public Radio), Geraldo Rivera, and Richard Rodriguez (Pacifica News Radio, *News Hour with Jim Lehrer*). Speaking about the absence of "other" perspectives on the Simpson case, Rodriguez commented:

> As someone who thinks of himself as neither white nor black, I used to hear such talk as a kind of family quarrel. It went over my head. Today, I sense a weird nostalgia to such talk and a vanity. It is as though many whites and blacks cannot imagine an America peopled by anyone, except each other.[21]

The virtual absence of Asian commentary on the Simpson case is notable given that the presiding judge, Lance Ito, is Japanese American. The viewpoints of Asians, who have had a unique experience with the U.S. criminal justice system, one different from Blacks, Whites, and Hispanics, should have been heard.[22] Black and White journalists could not be expected to incorporate the perspectives of other racial groups. After the acquittal, a Chinese American college student said, "I feel like an invisible conduit. Both my Black and White friends feel like they can come up to me and express their rage and joy about the verdict. . . . But sometimes I just feel caught in the middle—that my perspective doesn't count."[23]

Diversity of opinions matters precisely because of the racial fallout from trials similar to the Simpson case. The post-verdict eruption was necessarily Black versus White, because it was the only picture the media represented. Not surprisingly, the fact that there was a Hispanic person on the Simpson jury got lost in public fervor over the "Black" verdict. That there were two Whites on the jury was also minimized. The majority of the conversation about the verdict has been about the decision of the "Black-dominated jury," "Black jury," or "predominantly Black jury."

One explanation for the Black/White divergence of opinion is that the tension between Whites and Blacks has not been effectively addressed. Many Blacks firmly believe that they have not been adequately compensated for slavery. Conversely, many Whites strongly assert that racism is a historical relic. Black/White racial friction is so long-standing and so deepseated that it remains difficult for Whites and Blacks to think more globally in terms of other races. The fact that Blacks have always been the largest minority group in the country may also explain the media's tunnel vision on race.

Media attempts to represent the views of a larger cross-section of the population would not have solved the Black/White racial schism. Still, its failure to offer a more nuanced picture of the racial issues raised by the case was a missed opportunity. Rather than throwing fuel onto an already explosive issue, a lot more could have been done during the trial to report not only how race affected opinion about the case but also how other factors played a role. Additionally, the media might have spent more time analyzing the overlap in opinion across races, and not just the Black/White racial gap. Finally, more attention should have been devoted to explanations for the racial divide.

Conclusion

If nothing else, the Simpson case reminded us that race not only matters but figures centrally. It reinforced the fact that Blacks and Whites have very different realities. For Blacks, this reality includes Black protectionism. For Whites, this reality includes White denial. The case also instructed us that we know very little about how Asians, Hispanics, and Native Americans view their racial circumstances and the criminal justice system.

The greatest threat of the Simpson case is that we will reduce it to a spectacle without learning from it. The case offers an opportunity to learn and re-learn America's racial realities. Thus far, in this post–O. J. era, we each continue to dig in our racial heels a little deeper and point our fingers outward, continuing to talk past each other. This is the biggest missing piece of the puzzle from the Simpson case: Will we do anything constructive with what we have learned?

5

The Racial Hoax as Crime

I am an invisible man. . . . I am a man of substance, of flesh and bone, fiber and liquids—and I might even be said to possess a mind. I am invisible, understand simply because people refuse to see me. . . . When they approach me they see only my surroundings, themselves, or figments of their imagination—indeed, everything and anything except me.   —Ralph Ellison, *Invisible Man* (1947)

In October 1994, Susan Smith, a White, South Carolina mother, told police that she had been the victim of a carjacking. She described her assailant as an armed, young Black male, 20 to 30 years old. According to Smith, the man drove off with her two sons, ages 3 and 14 months. In the days that followed, Smith appeared on national TV and pled for the lives of her boys, "Your momma loves you. . . . Be strong."[1] Based upon Smith's description of the assailant, the police drew and widely disseminated a sketch of a young Black man. Nine days after an extensive federal and state manhunt for the fictional Black carjacker, Smith confessed to murdering her sons.

In April 1992, Jesse Anderson, a White man, told the police that he and his wife had been attacked by two Black men in the parking lot of a suburban Milwaukee restaurant. Anderson's wife, who was stabbed twenty-one times in the face, head, and upper body, died following the attack. Anderson received superficial wounds during the attack. The Andersons were an upper-income couple with three young children. After a five-day search for the nonexistent Black criminals, Anderson was arrested and charged with his wife's murder. Several factors led the police to focus their investigation on Anderson, including lab results from hair samples and information that Anderson had called his wife's insurance company a month prior to her murder to inquire whether her $250,000 policy was in effect. Additionally, a store employee, who recalled that Anderson had purchased the distinctive knife used in the attack, positively identified him. Anderson was subsequently convicted of first-degree murder.

In November 1989, Charles Stuart told police that he and his wife, Carol, on their way home from a Lamaze birthing class, were shot and robbed by a Black man wearing a jogging suit. Carol Stuart and her unborn child died following the attack. Police invaded Mission Hill, a mostly Black neighborhood in Boston, in search of Carol Stuart's killer. After viewing a police line-up, Charles Stuart picked a Black man named Willie Bennett as the person who "most resembled" the attacker.[2] Based upon inconsistencies in Stuart's story and incriminating information obtained from his brother, Matthew Stuart, the police soon shifted their investigation to Charles Stuart. Shortly thereafter, Charles Stuart committed suicide. Police later determined that Stuart had planned the hoax as a scheme to cash in on his wife's insurance policy.

The actions of Susan Smith, Jesse Anderson, Charles Stuart, and others like them have made the words of Ralph Ellison prophetic. Fifty years ago, when Ellison wrote about the invisibility of the Black experience, he could not have envisioned that the negative image of Blackness would become so pervasive that *imaginary* Black people would be regularly invented as criminals. The Smith, Anderson, and Stuart cases are not aberrations. Table 5.1 lists sixty-seven racial hoaxes. A racial hoax occurs:

> When someone fabricates a crime and blames it on another person because of his race OR when an actual crime has been committed and the perpetrator falsely blames someone because of his race.

Hoax perpetrators are most frequently charged with filing a false police report. The number of racial hoaxes suggests that false report statutes do not operate as effective deterrents. New Jersey is the only state that has considered enacting legislation to criminalize racial hoaxes. Hoaxes impose social, psychological, economic, and legal costs on society. The actions of Susan Smith and others should be recognized for what they are, serious criminal offenses.

As the above definition makes clear, a racial hoax can be perpetrated by a person of any race, against a person of any race. However, the primary focus of this chapter is on those cases involving someone White who falsely accuses someone Black of a crime—a White-on-Black hoax. White-on-Black hoaxes are the most likely to receive media attention and the most likely to exact a high social and economic toll. Anyone, of any race, who perpetrates a hoax with a Black villain should face criminal punishment. A hoax where a Black person is singled out as the criminal deserves a special legal sanction. Racial hoaxes that target Blacks create a distinct, more acute social problem than hoaxes that target people of other races. Blacks in general and young Black men in particular are saddled with a deviant image. In fact, crime and young Black men have become synonymous in the American mind. As noted in chapter 1, these images have combined to create the *criminalblackman*. Given the pervasiveness of this stereotype, it is not surprising that so many people have manipulated this negative image to avoid criminal responsibility. Comedian Paul Mooney only half-jokingly comments on this phenomenon in his routine, "1-900-Blame-A-Nigger":

> Didn't some white man in Boston shoot his pregnant wife and then shot himself, crying, "Oh niggers did it." Always trying to blame some niggers. That's why I'm gonna start a new ad, "900-Blame-A-Nigger." So when white folks get in trouble, just call my agency. "[Hello] Blame-A-Nigger. I just pushed my mother down the stairs. I don't want to go to jail. Send a nigger over here."[3]

Racial hoaxes are devised, perpetrated, and successful precisely because they tap into widely held fears. The harm of the racial hoax is not limited to reinforcing centuries-old, deviant images of Blacks. Hoaxes also create these images for each new generation. The racial hoax should be recognized as a separate criminal offense, subject to a mandatory prison term.

Trends and Patterns

Table 5.1 provides case data for sixty-seven racial hoaxes perpetrated between 1987 and 1996 (see Appendix B for case summaries). As the table indicates, the majority of hoaxes involve Whites who fabricated crimes against Blacks.[4] Table 5.2 provides a breakdown of racial hoaxes involving Blacks and Whites. Most of the hoaxes were located through a search of LEXIS/NEXIS, an automated database that stores news articles. These sixty-seven cases represent only a fraction of all racial hoax cases, since most racial hoaxes are not classified or reported as such. For example, cases where a newspaper reports on a hoax but does not state the race of the perpetrator or victim are not included. More importantly, the overwhelming majority of criminal cases are investigated and closed by the police without ever making the news.

TABLE 5.1
Racial Hoaxes: Summary Data (1987-1996)

Name of Perpetrator	Year	Perperator: Race/Sex Victim: Race/Sex	Alleged Crime[a]	Duration of Hoax[b]	False Report Charge[c]	Police Stop[d]
ADAMS, Bradley	1995	P:W/M V: B/M	Murder	5 months	No	No
ANDERSON, Jesse	1992	P:W/M V: B/M	Murder	1 week	No	Yes
ANDERSON, Tisha & LEE, William	1995	P: B/F P: W/M V: W/M	Hate crime	1 month	Yes	No
ASBELL, Samuel	1990	P: W/M V: B/M	Attempted murder	1 week	Yes	Yes
AVENT, Anthony	1994	P: B/M V: W/M	Assault	1 week	No	No
BAISLEY, Adam & UNNAMED MINOR	1996	P: W/M V: B/M	Assault	1 week	No	No
BOLDUC, Daniel	1995	P: W/M V: B/M	Vandalism	1 week	Yes	No
BRAWLEY, Tawana	1987	P: B/F V: W/M	Rape, Hate crime	months	No	Yes
BYRDSONG, DeWayne	1995	P: B/M V: W/M	Hate crime	months	Yes	—
CAMPBELL, Toby	1995	P: W/M V: B/M	Robbery	1 week	Yes	Yes
CHERRY, Donald	1996	P: W/M V: B/M	Murder	1 week	Yes	Yes
CLEMENTE, Garrick	1995	P: B/M V: W/M	Hate crime	6 months	No	No
COLLINS, Sabrina	1990	P: B/F V: W/M	Hate crime	2 months	No	No
CRANE, Henry	1995	P: W/M V: B/M	Carjack	1 week	Yes	Yes
DARCI, Tanya	1989	P: W/F V: B/M	Kidnap	1 week	Yes	—
DROGAN, Thomas & PAPALEO, Louis	1993	P: W/M V: B/M	Assault	1 week	Yes	Yes
FRAKES, Dawn	1995	P: W/F V: B/M	Assault	2 months	Yes	No
GATELEY, Tina & KARAFFA, William	1993	P: W/M&F V: B/M	Attempted robbery, Assault	2 weeks	Yes	No
GAYLE, Matthew	1995	P: W/M V: B/M	Murder	3 Months	No	—

Name of Perpetrator	Year	Perpetrator: Race/Sex Victim: Race/Sex	Alleged Crime[a]	Duration of Hoax[b]	False Report Charge[c]	Police Stop[d]
GIBSON, Tonya; BUSH, Tynnush; HENLEY, Clayton; GIBSON, William; & SNYDER, Gary	1996	P: W/F, 4 W/M V: B/M	Attempted murder, Burglary	1 week	No	Yes
GILLIS, Kendra	1994	P: W/F V: B/M	Assault	1 week	No	No
GREEN, Joshua; PRATT, Daniel; & CROWLEY, Michael	1994	P: 3W/M V: B/M	Robbery	1 week	Yes	No
HARRIS, Persey VIGIL, Ann; & HARRIS, Caryn	1996	P: B/M, 2 B/F V: W/M	Vandalism	—	Yes	Yes
HARRIS, Robert	1996	P: W/M V: B/M	Murder	1 week	No	No
HEBERT, Jeffrey	1995	P: W/M V: B/M	Murder	1 week	No	Yes
HUENEKE, Brende	1995	P: W/F V: B/M	Robbery	—	Yes	—
JAMES, Sonia	1996	P: B/F V: W/M	Hate crime	3 months	Yes	—
JOHNSTON, Kathleen	1994	P: W/F V: B/M	Assault, Robbery	2 months	No	No
KASHANI, Miriam	1990	P: W/F V: B/M	Rape	1 week	No	No
LAMBIRTH, Mark	1995	P: W/M V: AI/M	Kidnap	—	No	No
LEWIS, Mark	1994	P: W/M V: B/M	Assault	—	No	No
LUPUS, Josephine	1994	P: W/M V: B/M	Robbery	1 week	Yes	No
MAGRONE, Lucille	1990	P: W/F V: B/M	Assault	5 months	Yes	Yes
MARTINEZ, Ramon; MENDEZ, Luis; & DEGROS, Joseph	1995	P: H/M V: B/M	Assault	1 week	Yes	No
MAXWELL, Janet	1993	P: W/F V: B/M	Kidnap, Rape	2 months	Yes	No
McCOOL, Cecil	1995	P: W/M V: B/M	Police misconduct	1 month	No	Yes
METCALFE, Milton	1993	P: B/M V: W/M	Assault, Hate crime	1 week	No	No
MILAM, Richard	1994	P: W/M V: B/M	Murder, Robbery	1 week	No	No

Name of Perpetrator	Year	Perpetrator: Race/Sex Victim: Race/Sex	Alleged Crime[a]	Duration of Hoax[b]	False Report Charge[c]	Police Stop[d]
MILLER, Phillip	1994	P: —/M V: B/M	Robbery	1 week	Yes	No
NICOLAS, Richard	1996	P: B/M V: W/M	Murder	1 week	No	No
O'BRIEN, Edward	1995	P: W/M V: B or H/M	Murder	1 week	No	No
PATTERSON, Brian	1996	P: W/M V: B/M	Murder	1 week	Yes	No
PITTMAN, Dennis	1996	P: W/M V: B/M	Carjack, Kidnap	1 week	No	No
POSNER, Maryrose	1994	P: W/F V: B/M	Robbery	1 week	Yes	—
PRINCE, Christopher[e]	1994	P: W/F V: B/M	Attempted rape, Burglary	1 year	No	Yes
RIVERA, Reggie[e]	1993	P: B/M V: W/M	Rape	1 year	No	No
ROUTIER, Darlie	1996	P: W/F V: W/M	Murder	2 weeks	No	No
RUSSELL, Judy	1988	P: W/F V: Indian/M	Assault	1 month	Yes	No
SARABAKHSH, Zhaleh	1995	P: Iranian/F V: W/M	Attempted murder	1 week	Yes	No
SHAW, Michael	1995	P: W/M V: B/M	Kidnap	1 week	Yes	Yes
SMITH, Susan	1994	P: W/F V: B/M	Carjack	2 weeks	No	Yes
SOLIMAN, Mounir	1994	—/M V: B/M	Robbery	1 week	Yes	No
STUART, Charles	1989	P: W/M V: B/M	Murder	10 weeks	No	Yes
TANCZOS, Lisa	1995	P: W/F V: B/M	Assault	6 months	Yes	Yes
VEACH, Paul	1995	P: W/M V: B/M	Kidnap, Robbery	1 week	Yes	No
VEITCH, Neva & CRAIG, David	1987	P: W/M&F V: B/M	Murder, Kidnap, Att. rape	2 years	No	—
WAGNER, Candice	1995	P: W/F V: B/M	Kidnap, Rape	2 months	Yes	No
WIGHT, Lisa	1996	P: W/F V: B/M	Attempted rape	3 weeks	No	Yes
YENTES, Michele	1989	P: W/F V: B/M	Rape	months	Yes	No

Name of Perpetrator	Year	Perpetrator: Race/Sex Victim: Race/Sex	Alleged Crime[a]	Duration of Hoax[b]	False Report Charge[c]	Police Stop[d]
YOUSHEI, Solomon	1995	P: Mid East/M V: B/M	Robbery	1 week	No	No
UNNAMED, Florida-1	1994	P: W/F V: W/M	Kidnap, Rape	1 week	—	No
UNNAMED, Florida-2	1996	P: W/F V: B/M	Rape, Assault	1 week	No	No
UNNAMED, Louisiana	1994	P: W/F V: B/M	Rape	1 week	—	Yes
UNNAMED, Maine	1994	P: W/F V: B/M	Assault	1 week	No	No
UNNAMED, New Jersey	1994	P: W/F V: B/M	Assault	—	—	No
UNNAMED, Virginia	1995	P: W/M V: B/M	Assault, Carjack	1 week	No	No
UNNAMED, Wisconsin	1996	P: W/F V: B/M	Rape	1 week	No	No

[a] Alleged Crime: Crime alleged by hoax perpetrator
[b] Duration: How long before police discovered the hoax ("1 week" indicates 1–7 days).
[c] False report charge: Whether hoax perpetrator was charged with filing a false police report
[d] Police stop: Whether an innocent person was arrested, detained, or questioned about the hoax.
[e] Name of Hoax Victim
— Information not available

TABLE 5.2
Racial Hoaxes Involving Blacks and Whites

Race	Number of Cases
White Perpetrator/Black Victim	47
Black Perpetrator/White Victim	11
White Perpetrator/White Victim	2
Black Perpetrator/Black Victim	0
Other Hoaxes[a]	7
Total	67

[a] "Other" includes cases involving a perpetrator or victim of another race, e.g., Native American or Hispanic, or cases where the race of either the perpetrator or victim is unknown. Notably, in four of these cases, the hoax perpetrator said he had been victimized by a Black man (Ramon Martinez et al., Phillip Miller, Mounir Soliman, and Solomon Youshei).

Several trends emerge from the racial hoax cases:

- 70 percent are White-on-Black hoaxes.
- Hoaxes are most frequently fabricated to allege assault, rape, or murder.
- More than one-half of the hoaxes have been revealed as fabrications in less than one week.
- Hoax perpetrators were charged with filing a false police report in approximately 45 percent of the cases.
- In almost 30 percent of the cases, an innocent person was stopped, questioned, or arrested for the alleged crime.
- Hoaxes are perpetrated by people of all races, classes, geographic regions, and ages.

White-on-Black Hoaxes

SORDID DETAILS

In a number of cases, the hoax was created with great attention to detail, sometimes bordering on a malevolent fantasy:

- In 1995, a White woman in Pennsylvania reported that she had been attacked by a thirtysomething, muscular Black man with a crew cut. She told police that the knife-wielding attacker used the weapon to play a game of tic-tac-toe on her arm. The woman claimed that the same man returned two months later to terrorize her (Lisa Tanczos).
- In 1990, a White female college student reported that another White female student had been raped at knife-point by two young Black men. The attackers were described as having "particularly bad body odor." Within days the woman admitted to making up the entire story (Miriam Kashani).
- In 1995, a 47-year-old White man told police that he had been robbed at gunpoint by a Black man, with "light-colored hair, 6–8-inch braids, a deformed pupil in one eye, acne scars on his cheeks, and one or two missing front teeth" (Paul Veach).
- In 1994, a White woman reported that while she was at an ATM, she and her 2-year-old daughter were approached by a Black man wielding a gun. The woman told police that the man, "put a gun to my child's head while he laughed" (Maryrose Posner).

These cases provide fleshed out examples of how different White people have visualized the *criminalblackman*. This image, generated by television, newspapers, radio, and American lore, translates into a menacing caricature. In each case, the person who devised the hoax added details to make their Black villain appear demonic. The fact that so many White-on-Black hoaxes are successful indicates society's readiness to accept the image of Blacks as criminal.

In a hoax case that defies classification, a White Louisiana woman told police she had been sexually assaulted by a Black man. She said her attacker had a tattoo of a serpent on his arm. A police sketch of the rapist was widely circulated in Baton Rouge. In a bizarre twist, *twenty-eight* other women notified the police that they too had been assaulted by the imaginary "serpent man." The high number of copycat victims appears to reflect more than the usual hysteria associated with criminals on the loose. Within days, the alleged victim confessed that she had made up the rape story (Unnamed, Louisiana).

POLICE AND JUDICIAL OFFICIALS

Another noticeable trend in the White-on-Black cases is the frequency of hoaxes that have been carried out by legal officials. Seven of the cases involve either police or court officers:

- In 1995, a Delaware state trooper reported that she had been shot by a Black teenager. She said her attacker was named "Willy" and described him as a light-skinned Black male, between 16 and 19, six feet tall, and weighing 160 to 170 pounds. After a two-month investigation, the officer admitted she had made up the story. The hoax was designed to cover up the fact that she had accidentally shot herself in the arm with her service revolver (Dawn Frakes).
- In 1990, a New Jersey prosecutor claimed that someone was trying to kill him. He reported that two Black men chased him and shot at his car. He later confessed to making up the attempted murder story (Samuel Asbell).
- In 1993, two New York police officers got into a physical fight over who would file a police report in a fire incident that both men had responded to. The altercation left both officers with extensive cuts and bruises. To hide their fight, the pair filed a police report stating that one of them had been assaulted by a Black man. At least six officers were involved in covering up the fight. Two weeks following the incident, an

officer who had witnessed the fight informed authorities of the hoax (Thomas Drogan and Louis Papaleo).

- In 1996, a White court deputy told police that a Black man had attempted to rape her in the hallway of a federal courthouse. Several Black male courthouse employees were questioned about the attack. After extensive questioning by the FBI, the alleged victim confessed to fabricating the attack (Lisa Wight).

VARIED REASONS: ALL-PURPOSE SUSPECTS

The majority of White-on-Black hoaxes are concocted to shift criminal responsibility, as in the Susan Smith case. A few racial hoaxes were perpetrated as insurance scams. In a 1996 case, Robert Harris told police that he and his fiancee had been shot and robbed on a quiet Baltimore street. Harris's fiancée died from her gunshot wounds. Harris described the attacker as a Black man, wearing a camouflage jacket and black-and-white pants. Based on the mistaken belief that he was the named beneficiary on his fiancée's $250,000 insurance policy, Harris had hired a White hit man to kill her. Another 1996 hoax involved a financial ploy. Dennis Pittman, a White man, reported that he had been carjacked by a Black man. He told police that he was forced at knife-point to drive his kidnapper from Philadelphia to Atlantic City. After intense questioning, Pittman admitted he had made up the story to avoid further car payments.

At least one hoax perpetrator claimed that she used the hoax to "send a message." Miriam Kashani staged a 1990 rape hoax and said she "had hoped the story as reported would highlight the problems of safety for women . . . [and] never meant to hurt anyone or racially offend anyone." Other hoaxes were devised for more mundane reasons, such as to get time off from work, to get attention from a spouse, to get sympathy, or to avoid punishment from parents. The following cases are representative:

- In January 1995, a White New Jersey man told police that he saw a Black man running into a wooded area carrying a small White child. Based upon his statement, an extensive air and land search was mounted. The next day, the man admitted to making up the story. Apparently the story had been concocted so he could get the afternoon off from work (Michael Shaw).
- In a 1993 case, a White woman told police she had been kidnapped from a shopping mall by three Black men. She said she was raped and forced to take drugs. She later confessed she had made up the story to

avoid getting into trouble for staying out past her curfew (Janet Maxwell).

MULTIPLE PERPETRATORS

The White-on-Black hoaxes frequently involved more than one perpetrator. This fact suggests that they cannot be dismissed as the work of a lone lunatic. In two cases, a group of Whites used the hoax to cover up an accidental shooting (Adam Baisley, Tonya Gibson, et al.). In another, a hoax was used to cover up a work-related scuffle (Thomas Drogan and Louis Papaleo). One White couple used a hoax to cover up domestic violence (Tina Gateley and William Karaffa), and in two cases a hoax was used to conceal a planned crime (Joshua Green et al., Neva Veitch and David Craig).

THE INTERRACIAL RAPE HOAX

Several of the Black-on-White hoaxes involve fabricated claims of rape. Most of these involve claims by a White woman that she was raped by a Black man. For many people, the mention of interracial rape taps age-old fears of Black men forcing themselves on innocent White females. Historically, protecting the virtue of White womanhood from defilement by Black men was placed on a legal pedestal. The fear of this act was the impetus for the lynch laws. Given this history, it is not surprising that so many White women have created Black male rapists as their fictional criminals.

Historically, rape was the most common criminal hoax played upon Black men. The case of the Scottsboro Boys is perhaps the best known example of Black men being used as racial scapegoats. In 1931, Victoria Price and Ruby Bates, two young White women, alleged that they had been assaulted and raped by nine "Negro boys." After swift pretrial procedures, eight of the Black boys were sentenced to death. The final case resulted in a hung jury. The press portrayed Bates and Price as symbols of Southern White womanhood. Eventually, Bates recanted her story.[5]

A racial hoax also triggered the 1923 Rosewood, Florida, massacre. A false claim by a White woman that she was raped by a Black man led Whites in an adjoining town to go on a killing rampage and burn down the all-Black Rosewood. According to official estimates, six Blacks and two Whites were killed. Unofficial estimates are that between 40 and 150 Blacks were killed. More than seventy years later, a court awarded Rosewood family descendants more than $2 million.

Black-on-White Hoaxes

The eleven Black-on-White hoaxes are an interesting counterpoint to the White-on-Black hoaxes. Most notable is that nine of them were framed as "hate crimes." The majority of the Black hoax perpetrators created a scenario in which they were victimized *because* they were Black. Apparently these hoax perpetrators believed that hate crime would be the most believable offense that a White person could commit against a Black person. The frequency of hate-crime hoaxes reflects the prevailing view—except for hate crimes, most of us have difficulty imagining someone White committing a random act of violence against someone Black.[6]

Black-on-White hate-crime hoaxes contrast sharply with White-on-Black racial hoaxes because the latter are typically created as random acts of Black violence. This reflects the public belief that Blacks run amok committing depraved, unprovoked acts of violence against Whites, while the only Whites who commit violent crimes against Blacks are racial extremists. Like the White-on-Black hoaxes, the motivations for Black-on-White hoaxes are varied. Some Black-on-White hoaxes are perpetrated as insurance scams, others are created to shift criminal responsibility, still others are fabricated to evoke sympathy.

The Tawana Brawley case is the most notorious Black-on- White hoax. In November 1987, Brawley, a 15-year-old Black girl from Wappingers Falls, New York, told police that she had been abducted and raped by six White men. Brawley said that the men were police officers. She also said she was smeared with feces, placed in a plastic bag, and left in a gutter. The story drew national attention. After convening for seven months, a grand jury declined to issue any indictments in the case. Although Brawley stands by her original account, the incident has been widely discredited as a hoax.

In 1990, Sabrina Collins, a Black college student at Emory University, said that she had received hate mail and that racial epithets had been scrawled on her dormitory wall. According to Collins, the attack so traumatized her that she was no longer able to speak. Two separate investigations into the case concluded it was a hoax.

The Reggie Rivera case is perhaps the most bizarre Black-on-White hoax. In this 1993 case, six Black men, all livery-van drivers in New York, alleged that they had been sodomized at gun point by Rivera, a White police officer. Following a year-long investigation, the Queens District Attorney concluded that the allegations were part of an elaborate revenge scheme against Officer Rivera. According to the district attorney's report, the six Black men were unlicensed livery drivers and were angry at Rivera because he had issued numerous tickets to vans in their area.

It appears that Blacks perpetrate hoaxes for many of the same reasons that Whites do—out of self-interest. The majority of Black-on-White hoaxes may have been created as hate crimes simply because hate crime is one of the few crimes that society can "see" a White person committing against a Black person.

Comparing Harms: Black-on-White v. White-on-Black Racial Hoaxes

A number of factors separate White-on-Black from Black-on-White hoaxes. First, as discussed above, Black-on-White hoaxes are almost always drawn as hate crimes. When Whites create imaginary crimes, they are unlikely to use hate crime as a ruse. Second, the White-on-Black hoax causes greater social damage and harm than the Black-on-White hoaxes. This is primarily because Black-on-White hoaxes are less likely to receive national attention. Third, in hoaxes involving an interracial crime, a White person who says she was victimized by a Black person is much more likely to be believed than a Black person who says she was victimized by a White person.

"AN AGGRIEVED COMMUNITY"

The social and legal response to hoaxes differs according to the race of the person alleging that a crime has occurred. For example, Charles Stuart's claim that he had been shot by a Black jogger led to a full-scale police invasion of Boston's Mission Hill. Blacks in Boston, as well as many Blacks nationwide, felt some sense of responsibility for the crimes committed by the fictional Black criminal. Although the Union, South Carolina, police department handled the Susan Smith case much differently, its Black community still felt betrayed by the hoax, as did many other Blacks. The same sense of community betrayal does not exist with Black-on-White hoaxes. There was no "White community" that bore comparable responsibility or group shame in the Tawana Brawley, Sabrina Collins, or Reggie Rivera cases. Nor was there a White community that was placed under siege after Brawley and Collins made their allegations.

In the Jesse Anderson, Susan Smith, Miriam Kashani, and Charles Stuart cases, there were calls for an apology to the Black community. This is evidence of how racial hoaxes are treated and perceived differently based upon the race of the perpetrator. The demands for an apology indicate that many Blacks believed the racial hoax had created a communal injury. While Susan Smith's brother offered an apology to the Black community, Ray Flynn, the Mayor of Boston during the Charles Stuart case, refused.

Because Black criminals are perceived as more menacing than White criminals, hoaxes created with a Black villain have different ramifications than hoaxes created with a White villain. Greater social harm results when someone White falsely accuses someone Black of a crime than when the reverse occurs. This is not to suggest that there is no social harm associated with Black-on-White hoaxes. Black-on-White hoaxes make it easier for Whites to dismiss claims of White racism. However, the greatest harm of White-on-Black hoaxes is that they create negative racial stereotypes for a new generation of young people. The Lucille Magrone case offers an example of this. In 1990, Magrone, a White woman living in upstate New York, sent out letters purportedly written by a Black man. The letters, sent to neighborhood Whites, threatened them with rape and murder if they did not move from the area: "You white people cannot live here. I will see you dead."[7] After Magrone's hoax was unmasked, one of her White neighbors stated:

> Small children in the neighborhood have been introduced to racism that was never there before. Now it is in their minds that black people are bad, that black people are trying to break in—that there's a bogeyman, a black bogeyman out there who is going to get [them].[8]

Another indicator that the criminal stereotypes of Blacks are having an impact on young people is the number of racial hoaxes that are perpetrated by teenagers. Almost a dozen cases involve young Whites who fabricated a crime against someone Black (e.g., Kendra Gillis, Edward O'Brien, and Toby Campbell). In one case, a 7-year-old White girl made up an assault charge against a Black man (Unnamed, Maine).

Whites who make up crimes against other Whites do not cause the same hysteria as Whites do when they fabricate crimes against Blacks. A comparison of the Susan Smith case with the Darlie Routier case is instructive. In 1996, Routier claimed that a White male intruder had entered her home and attacked her and her two boys. Both boys, aged 5 and 6, died following the brutal attack, and Routier was severely wounded. Within days, police began to suspect Routier in the deaths, and she was eventually charged with both murders. Although there was an outpouring of support for Routier following the attack, it was nowhere near the international support Susan Smith received.

CREDIBILITY

The public appears to be more willing to believe someone White who says they were victimized by someone Black than someone Black who says they were victimized by someone White. The Tawana Brawley and Reggie Rivera cases are examples of this. From the beginning, many suspected that the Brawley and Rivera incidents were fabrications. By contrast, the stories of Susan Smith and Charles Stuart cases were readily believed. The public swallowed their tales whole. The reluctance to believe the Brawley and Rivera cases, though, may be partly due to the fact that they involved criminal allegations against law enforcement officials.

Additionally, Black-on-White hoaxes often end without a clear resolution. In the Brawley case for instance, it was a grand jury's refusal to issue an indictment that officially labeled her claim a hoax. Similarly, in the Rivera case, the prosecutor's office concluded the incident was a hoax. No one has come forward in either case to state unequivocally that there was a hoax. Both cases were "closed" based upon the findings of an independent judicial body and not because someone confessed to a hoax. Unfortunately, in these cases Blacks and Whites remained divided. Many Blacks claimed there was a cover-up, and many Whites claimed there was a hoax.

Another reflection of the tension created by these cases is the amount of litigation they spark. In the Rivera case, the Police Benevolent Association filed a libel suit against the alleged victims' attorney. A year following the Rivera incident, Black civil rights leaders continued to hold weekly protests to demand a grand-jury hearing. Following the Brawley investigation, a $30 million defamation suit was brought against her and her advisers. A default judgment was entered against Brawley. A few years later, one of Brawley's lead attorneys was disbarred.

FALSE POLICE REPORT CHARGES

Black hoax perpetrators are more likely to be charged with filing a false police report than White hoax perpetrators. This, however, may be the result of other factors besides race. For instance, most hoaxes carried out by Blacks involve less serious crimes than those carried out by Whites. Half of the Black-on-White hoaxes involve vandalism. When someone uses a hoax to cover up a serious crime, such as murder, it is less likely that they will be charged with filing a false police report (e.g., Jesse Anderson, Jeffrey Hebert, Richard Nicolas, and Susan Smith).

Equating Black-on-White with White-on-Black hoaxes ignores the different social reaction to these hoaxes. Black men have always been perceived as a physical threat; however, until recently, that threat was portrayed in sexual terms. In the past twenty years, the image of the Black male as rapist has evolved into the image of the Black male as the symbolic pillager of all that is good. The *criminalblackman* stereotype persists, despite the fact that the majority of people arrested each year are White. The common perception of the Black male influences how Blacks and Whites, as individuals and as group members, are affected by racial hoaxes.

For Blacks as a group, racial hoaxes underscore White racism. For instance, many Blacks were initially skeptical of Susan Smith's story and troubled that so many Whites believed it so quickly. In particular, many Blacks wondered where a young Black man could possibly go with two small White children without raising suspicion.

White-on-Black hoaxes follow a standard pattern. First, law enforcement officials are called into action. They are asked to protect an innocent White person from further harm and to apprehend a widely perceived threat, a menacing Black man. Second, the incident arouses sympathy and results in calls for swift and stiff punishment. Third, even after the hoax is uncovered, the image of the *criminalblackman* lingers and becomes more embedded in our collective racial consciousness.

Other Noteworthy Cases

Research on racial hoaxes uncovered four cases that merit discussion although they do not fit into the above categories. In 1996, Donald Cherry, a White father of two, told police that his 2-year-old son had been killed by Black youths, following a traffic dispute. According to Cherry, following the traffic encounter, the youths fired shots at his car after he made an obscene gesture at them. Within one week, Cherry told police that he had not been involved in a traffic dispute, rather a drug deal gone bad. Cherry had driven across town to purchase crack cocaine. His small children were in the back seat of the vehicle. As it turned out, the suspect, who admitted to firing the shot, is Black. The case is unusual because Cherry attempted to portray himself as an innocent victim of random Black crime, thereby attempting to make the action by the Black youth appear more sinister.

In two separate cases, White assailants robbed White victims and told them to tell police that they had been robbed by someone Black. In a 1992 case, a gang of White thieves robbed a man and threatened to kill his family unless he told police that the robbers were Black. In a 1995 case, a White man robbed an elderly couple of $2,850 and told them to blame the crime on a Black man.[9] These cases mirror the rationale behind the racial hoax cases—to play on racial stereotypes and avoid criminal responsibility.

The fourth case involves Dallas Cowboys football players Michael Irvin and Erik Williams. In December 1996, Nina Shahravan, an Iranian woman, charged them with rape. According to Shahravan, she was forced to have sex with Williams while Irvin held a gun to her head. Less than two weeks later, the 23-year-old woman signed a confession stating her rape claims were a hoax. This case does not strictly classify as a racial hoax because it is not clear whether Shahravan singled out Irvin and Williams because they are Black, because they are famous, or both. Even so, the case raises the same troubling questions as the interracial rape hoaxes discussed above. By accusing Irvin and Williams of rape, Shahravan stirred up centuries-old images of Black men as sexually ravenous and promiscuous. In fact, because she charged two well-known Black men, her hoax may have caused more harm than lesser-known rape hoaxes. Initially Shahravan was charged with filing a false police report. This was upgraded to perjury, a felony that carries a maximum one-year prison sentence and $4000 fine. Since the incident, the Dallas police department has adopted a new policy requiring that only those suspects who have been officially charged can be identified by name.

Economics of the Racial Hoax

Beyond causing social injury, the racial hoax also exacts a financial toll. Untold resources have been wasted on efforts to locate fictional Black criminals. In Trenton, New Jersey, a city that has seen its share of racial hoaxes, the mayor commented:

> This kind of accusation [racial hoax] affects us all. It terrorizes a community and discriminates against a race of people. And it is the kind of crime that costs taxpayers thousands of dollars to launch massive, futile investigations.[10]

Indeed, the economic consequences of the Susan Smith, Jesse Anderson, and Charles Stuart investigations underscore this point. These cases involved days of manhunts, police investigations, and court proceedings. In the Smith case, several agencies were enlisted in the nine-day search. A precise accounting of the costs is not available, but is estimated in the tens of thousands. The

FBI and the South Carolina State Law Enforcement Division provided both manpower (e.g., air and ground searches) and technical services (e.g., computer equipment), along with county and city employees.

In some cases, the hoax perpetrator has been required to pay police costs. In 1989, Michele Yentes, a White college student, falsely claimed that she had been raped by a Black man. Police officials wasted hours looking into her claim. It was determined that the case cost more than $15,000 to investigate. Yentes, who confessed her story was a fabrication, was convicted of filing a false police report and ordered to pay the entire cost of the investigation.

A Legal Response: The Law and the Logistics

False Report Statutes

All jurisdictions have false reporting laws, but they are rarely applied to punish racial hoax offenders. Less than half of the hoax perpetrators were charged with filing a false police report. False reporting charges are most often filed in cases involving less-serious offenses. The fact that false report charges are not uniformly filed renders them an ineffective deterrent against future hoaxes. Further, most false report violations constitute misdemeanors, which also undercuts their deterrence value. On the one hand, adding a false report charge to a hoax such as Susan Smith's might appear to be overkill. At the other extreme, pursuing a false police report charge against Miriam Kashani (rape hoax) might seem like a waste of the prosecutor's time and resources.

The Law on Hate Crimes

Hate-crime statutes can be divided into two types. First, some statutes treat hate crimes as independent criminal offenses. These are referred to as "pure bias" statutes. The Minnesota statute at issue in *R.A.V. v. St. Paul*[11] is an example of this. In this 1992 case, the U.S. Supreme Court held that the state's bias-crime law selectively criminalized certain forms of hate speech, in violation of the First Amendment.

A second kind of hate-crime statute provides a "penalty enhancement" for crimes motivated by bias. Under these statutes, where the court finds that the offender has committed a crime against a person because of his race, it may impose additional penalties. In some states, for example, a person convicted of assault could face one year behind bars. However, if the assault was racially motivated, the penalty could be increased to two years. A number of states have adopted the Model Bias Crime provision, drafted by the Anti-Defamation League. The federal government has also enacted penalty enhancement legislation.

Penalty enhancement statutes have been upheld by the U.S. Supreme Court. In *Wisconsin v. Mitchell*[12] a Black defendant challenged the state's penalty enhancement statute. Mitchell, who had been convicted of assaulting a White boy, faced an increased prison sentence of five years because his crime was motivated by bias. Finding the state law constitutional, the Supreme Court noted that "bias-inspired conduct" is an appropriate arena for penalty enhancement because it is "thought to inflict greater individual and societal harm."[13] Further, the Court observed, such conduct is likely to provoke "retaliatory crimes, inflict distinct emotional harm on their victims, and incite community unrest."[14] A racial hoax law could be framed as either a pure bias-crime statute or as a penalty enhancement. Given that the Supreme Court has upheld bias-crime enhancement, this looks to be the safer constitutional route.

The Racial Hoax as Crime

CONSTITUTIONAL CONCERNS

The road to making the racial hoax a crime is, constitutionally speaking, a much smoother road than the one that earlier hate-crime legislation had to travel. This is primarily because First Amendment concerns do not pose a barrier to making the racial hoax a crime.[15] It is a long-standing principle of constitutional law that where speech involves imminent, lawless action, it is not accorded First Amendment protection. Thus, one does not have the right to yell "fire" in a crowded video store.[16]

When one uses a racial hoax to mislead law enforcement, a chain of predictable responses will follow from both law enforcement and the community. The speech element of the racial hoax triggers numerous actions, including the deployment of police officers to particular neighborhoods to locate potential suspects, creation of "wanted" posters, dissemination of information about the crime to the media, announcement of all-points bulletins, and meetings by the police and community groups to discuss what actions should be taken. The person uttering the words of a racial hoax has done more than simply speak. She has pointed her finger at a community of people, with the goal of thwarting justice. By design, the speech of the racial hoax is actually lawless conduct which is unprotected by the First Amendment.

LOGISTICS OF A RACIAL HOAX LAW: A LOOK AT NEW JERSEY

In 1995, New Jersey drafted legislation designed to punish racial hoaxes. It was drafted in direct response to two White-on-Black racial hoaxes. The proposed New Jersey law, "False Reports to Law Enforcement Authorities" includes the following provisions:

- FALSELY INCRIMINATING ANOTHER. A person who knowingly gives or causes to be given false information or a description of a fictitious person to any law enforcement officer with purpose to implicate another person because of race, color, religion, sexual orientation or ethnicity commits a crime of the third degree.
- FICTITIOUS REPORTS. A person who files a fictitious report is guilty of a crime of the fourth degree if the person acted with purpose to implicate another because of his race, color, religion, sexual orientation or ethnicity.
- RESTITUTION. In addition to any other fine, fee or assessment imposed, any person convicted of an offense under this section is to reimburse the governing body of the municipality for the costs incurred in investigating the false information or the fictitious report.[17]

The New Jersey legislation will serve as a reference for the following discussion on the proposed components of a racial hoax law.

The offender. Regardless of race, a hoax law should apply to anyone who perpetrates a hoax against someone Black. The earlier discussion and analysis support this approach. The damage done by a hoax that falsely incriminates someone Black is so great that there should be no exclusion as to who can be punished. Harm occurs irrespective of whether a hoax perpetrator is White or Black (notably none of the documented cases involve a Black-on-Black hoax).[18]

Community responses and injury may differ depending upon the race of the perpetrator. When a White offender points the finger at a Black person, it acts to further polarize Black and White communities. As a result, Blacks feel more vulnerable to indiscriminate police practices and Whites feel more vulnerable to crime by Blacks. Conversely, when the hoax perpetrator is Black and the victim is Black, it is probable that the alleged crime will not be taken as seriously. The police are unlikely to respond as quickly to a Black person claiming harm as they would to a White person claiming harm.

White-on-Black hoaxes receive a great deal of media attention. It is also less probable that a Black-on-Black hoax would be uncovered because such a fabrication would appear to reflect the status quo—the erroneous belief that the majority of crime is Black-on-Black. In fact, Whites comprise the majority of those arrested for crime in any given year. Furthermore, more than 80 percent of all crime involves a victim and offender of the same race. Both the Black-on-Black and the White-on-Black hoax should be sanctioned because they perpetuate the *criminalblackman* stereotype.

Law professor Mari Matsuda, in a compelling argument for criminalizing race-based hate speech, contends that only Whites can be offenders. She states that the harm of racist speech is greatest when the speech reinforces a "historically vertical relationship."[19] Likewise, professor Marc Fleischauer argues that penalty enhancement should only attach in cases involving a White offender. Without this "White only" rule:

> [M]inorities will be subjected to enhanced penalties at a disproportionate rate compared to Whites because it is the nature of society for the majorities to prosecute minorities more frequently and with more vigor than vice versa.[20]

The fact that *Wisconsin v. Mitchell*—the only hate crime sentencing enhancement case decided by the U.S. Supreme Court—involved a Black defendant supports Fleischauer's observations.

While Fleischauer and Matsuda make strong arguments, the race-of-the-perpetrator/race-of-the-victim line that they draw should not be applied to a racial hoax law. First, unlike the victim of racist hate speech, the victim of a racial hoax is not directly assaulted by the offender. Second, it is not just one person who is harmed by a racial hoax, but an entire community. Given the harm done by pointing a false finger at a Black person, anyone of any race who perpetrates a hoax against someone Black should be penalized. The New Jersey legislation does not make a distinction based upon race of the perpetrator.

Targets and victims. With regard to who is classified as a victim for the racial hoax, two questions arise. First, should a racial hoax law mandate an identifiable, named victim—a "Willie Bennett requirement"? Willie Bennett is the

Black man that Charles Stuart identified as the person who shot and robbed him and his wife. Since current false report statutes do not require an identifiable victim, there should be no such requirement for a racial hoax law. The goal of false report statutes is to punish intentional efforts to thwart law enforcement. Whether there exists an identifiable victim or not, the racial hoax causes harm. A penalty is also justified by the communal harm it causes.

Professor Frederick Lawrence, in a discussion on the breadth of harm caused by hate crimes, states, "The victim suffers for being singled out on the basis of race, and the general community of the target racial group is harmed as well."[21] As applied to the racial hoax, once a "victim" says "a Black guy did it," she has hurled a racial epithet that is actionable. Given the predictable responses of law enforcement, the hoax is a kind of physical harassment, solely on the basis of race. It is as if Susan Smith, Jesse Anderson, Miriam Kashani, Charles Stuart, and others called every Black man a "low life," "hoodlum," or "criminal" *because* of his race. The New Jersey legislation penalizes those who use a racial hoax to target a specific person because of his race ("False Incrimination") as well as those who use a hoax to create a nonexistent villain ("Fictitious Persons").

Assuming there exists a legally cognizable crime, a second question arises: Which racial groups should receive protection under a racial hoax law? A strong argument can be made for applicability only when there is a Black victim. Ideally, a racial hoax law would only be actionable when the finger has been pointed at someone Black. Fleischauer, in his discussion of Florida's hate-crime statute, argues that it would be constitutional to make minorities the only protected group.[22] He observes that one of the explicit goals of hate-crime legislation is to curb racism and empower minorities. To allow a racial hoax law to encompass both White-on-Black hoaxes *and* Black-on-White hoaxes unfairly accords the two equal weight. Beyond the individual harm a racial hoax may cause a targeted Black person, it brings harm to Blacks as a group and creates more tension between Blacks and Whites. A look at the hoax cases establishes that the harm of a White-on-Black hoax is not comparable to the harm of either a White-on-White or Black-on-White hoax. The New Jersey legislation is silent with regard to the victim's race—implying that a hoax victim may be of any race.

The Equal Protection Clause presents the biggest roadblock to the proposed construction of who qualifies as a victim under a racial hoax law. Such a distinction is legally justified because the White-on-Black hoaxes cause more harm than Black-on-White hoaxes. False reporting laws are an adequate penalty for Black-on-White hoaxes. White-on-White hoaxes, while they do occur, do not pose the same societal problems as those where the victim is Black. Considering the U.S. Supreme Court's race-neutral leanings, however, the safest route is to draft hoax legislation that would protect a victim of any race. This legal compromise, however, does not provide adequate protection to Blacks as a group.

Intent. A racial hoax law could be written to require either specific or general intent on the part of the perpetrator. A distinction could be made between whether the perpetrator acted "knowingly" or "purposely." If "knowingly" was required, the prosecution would only have to show that the hoax perpetrator was "practically certain" that law enforcement forces would respond and that some harm would occur as a result of his race-labeling. If "purposely" was required, prosecutors would have to prove that the hoax perpetrator had as his conscious objective causing the particular result—triggering a manhunt *and* harming a specific Black person or Blacks as a group. This higher standard of intent should not be required for a racial hoax law.

The New Jersey legislation appears to impose a general-intent requirement. Under the proposed law, one could be charged with false incrimination on the basis of race, where one "knowingly provides false information to a law enforcement officer with the purpose to implicate another because of race." [23] To avoid the problem of attempting to determine whether the hoax perpetrator intended to cause harm to Blacks as a group or to any particular Black person, specific intent should not be an element of a racial hoax offense. The very fact that a racial hoax has been employed means that existing stereotypes have been reinforced and racial dissension furthered. Law professor Charles Lawrence elaborates:

> Traditional notions of intent do not reflect the fact that decisions about racial matters are influenced in large part by factors that can be characterized as neither intentional—in the sense that certain outcomes are self-consciously sought—nor unintentional—in the sense that the outcomes are random, fortuitous, and uninfluenced by the decisionmaker's beliefs, desires, and wishes. [24]

Prosecutors should not be required to establish that a hoax perpetrator is a racist or that he intended to mislead law enforcement. As set forth in the proposed New Jersey law, it is sufficient that the perpetrator has blamed someone *because* of his race. The reasons behind the racial finger-pointing should be irrelevant.

Penalties and remedies. Perpetrating a racial hoax should be a felony offense because it is a serious crime and has ramifications beyond any one particular case. Further, a penalty must be imposed that would deter others from employing hoaxes. A state could decide to impose a criminal fine and prison time. Beyond a prison term, a racial hoax perpetrator should be required to pay restitution. The New Jersey provision requires restitution in the amount of law enforcement costs for wasted resources. Additionally, payment of court costs and restitution to any identifiable victims should be imposed.

In addition to imposing criminal penalties and restitution, the hoax offender should be required to publicly apologize for playing on racial stereotypes. An apology would be one step toward healing a racially divided community. Following Susan Smith's confession, there were numerous calls for an apology. Journalist William Raspberry commented, "This may be difficult for non-minorities to accept, but black people do feel specially violated by Susan Smith's lie."[25] Demands were also made for an apology in the Anderson, Kashani, and Stuart cases. At the same time the Black community is injured, so is the White community. An apology, therefore, is due the entire community.

Reporting requirement. In the same way that the law imposes reporting requirements for bias crimes, there should be reporting requirements for racial hoaxes. It is impossible to estimate the annual frequency of racial hoaxes because there is no database for this information. A national repository should be created that tracks information on racial hoaxes, including the race, sex, and age of the offender and victim; the underlying hoax offense; the number of days of the hoax; and the estimated cost of investigating the hoax. These data could be compiled as a part of the information collected for the Hate Crime Statistics Act.

Conclusion

The racial hoax should be subject to criminal penalty. With the exception of the New Jersey legislation, there has been a deafening legal silence about the ravages of the racial hoax. The legal analysis makes clear that a racial hoax law is constitutionally permissible. A racial hoax law provides a legal route for addressing this country's racial past, as it is played out today in perceptions of crime. As important, given that hate-crime statutes are similar to antidiscrimination laws, a racial hoax law is a natural and necessary extension of legally recognized racial harms. In sum, a racial hoax law acknowledges American racial history, the power of negative stereotypes based upon this history, and the need for legal redress.

Absent a specific legal intervention, people will continue to use hoaxes to play the race card and avoid criminal liability. In the absence of a law, we are in effect encouraging people to employ racial hoaxes. Enactment of racial hoax legislation would send a message, both real and symbolic, that the wide-ranging and deleterious impact of racial hoaxes will not be tolerated.

6

Science, Scientific Racism, and the Ethical Imperative

In September 1992, the University of Maryland planned a conference titled, "Genetic Factors in Crime: Findings, Uses, and Implications." The conference was supported by a $78,000 grant from the National Institutes of Health (NIH). A firestorm erupted when news of the planned conference hit the press. Some said the conference was a thinly veiled attempt at promoting racial eugenics. Others questioned the motivation of the federal government in funding the meeting. Still others expressed concern that so few minority scholars had been invited to attend. In response to the loud public dissent and also to some racist remarks made by a conference supporter, NIH de-funded the conference and placed it on hold. The same conference, reconstituted and renamed, was held in September 1995.[1]

The Maryland conference offers a textbook example of what can happen when racially sensitive issues are mishandled. Public discussion of research involving topics of general interest, such as race and crime, often becomes sharp, loud, and divisive. The issues of crime and race fascinate and confound the general public, academics, and politicians. This makes it especially important that accurate information is presented to the public, since unsupported racial hypotheses have great potential to cause harm.

The fallout from the scheduled Maryland conference attests to the need for ethical principles to guide public discussion and debate on race-and-crime research. Biased racial research is an unfortunate part of this country's history. This past includes the commission of crimes in the name of science, such as the eugenics movement and the Tuskegee syphilis experiment. This history imposes an affirmative duty on researchers today to take responsibility for the research claims put in the public domain. Specifically, researchers should have a duty to clarify and rebut inaccurate uses of their data, as well as false representations of the state of scientific knowledge. This ethical duty should extend to all research on race and crime, including relevant genetics research. The next section evaluates the current ethics standards and assesses the need to enact more ethical guidelines for social scientists.

Ethics Codes and the Duty to Rebut

Today, ethical principles for researchers are primarily directed at individuals and impose no duty upon the research community to respond to misuses or misreports of scientific data. For instance, the American Sociological Association (ASA) has an ethics code that details the parameters of sociological research, practice, and teaching. Under the code, the only check against misapplied research is the peer-review process, a form of academic self-regulation. The ASA guidelines place the burden upon individual researchers to conform to academic community standards: "In presenting their work, sociologists are obligated to report their findings fully and should not misrepresent the findings of their research."[2] While the ASA code instructs the researcher not to misrepresent his work, it does not require him or anyone else to point out that someone else has misrepresented his work.

The ethics code of the American Medical Association (AMA) places the onus on the researcher and her home institution to act ethically: "The ultimate responsibility for the ethical conduct of science resides within the institution . . . which conducts scientific research and with the individual scientist."[3] Both the ASA and AMA codes rely on self-regulation and are silent as to any duty to correct or clarify misrepresentations beyond the academic community. Significantly, the American Society of Criminology, the largest criminological association, with more than two thousand members, does not have an ethics code.[4]

Ethical Abuses: Some Examples

Considered together, the following four incidents make a strong case that current ethics codes offer the public inadequate protection from abuses and misuses of crime-and-race research. The first example involves a story that appeared in the *Washington Post*. In the article, Dinesh D'Souza, an American Enterprise Institute researcher, reported on a "white racist" conference he attended in 1995. At a talk during the conference, Michael Levin, of the City College of New York, explained why he believes that Blacks are less intelligent than Whites: "Black inferiority is overwhelmingly likely to be genetic. It is not the result of racism. Are white children taught to metabolize glucose differently than black children?"[5] Levin, whose work is supported by the pro-eugenics Pioneer Fund, has made it his life's work to prove that Blacks are genetically inferior to Whites.[6] His reasoning is as follows:

1. Glucose metabolism is an indicator of intelligence.
2. Glucose metabolism is a function of genetic makeup.
3. Glucose metabolism is a function of race.
4. Racial groups that have difficulty metabolizing glucose are genetically inferior to those racial groups that have less difficulty metabolizing glucose.

Several problems are posed by this deduction. The measurable gap in standardized-test scores between Black and White children (approximately fifteen points) does not scientifically justify a link between IQ scores and genetic makeup. Also, proof that Blacks have more difficulty metabolizing glucose than Whites does not prove that Whites are genetically superior. Levin's remarks constitute a hypothesis, not scientific fact, a point easily lost on the lay public.

The Bell Curve provides additional support for the need to impose greater ethical rules on the social science community. In their book, Richard Herrnstein and Charles Murray provide a detailed discussion of the fifteen-point gap between Black and White IQ test scores. Throughout the text, the authors present themselves as objective researchers, whose mission it is to shed light on undisputed scientific facts. For instance, in their chapter on crime, Herrnstein and Murray avoid the controversial subject of crime rates for Black men, opting instead to discuss crime rates for White men. The authors skillfully camouflage their racial determinism, until the end of the book when they argue for using IQ to determine social hierarchy. The uncritical reader is easily led to conclude not only that IQ and race are correlated, but that genetics, crime, and race are causally related.

Herrnstein and Murray's deductive reasoning proceeds along the following track:

1. IQ and race are correlated.

   How large is the Black-White Difference? The usual answer to this question is one standard deviation. In discussing IQ tests, for example, the black mean is commonly given as 85, the white mean as 100, and the standard deviation as 15 (p. 276).

2. IQ and street crime are correlated.

[B]y the end of the 1980s, most criminologists accepted not just that an IQ gap separates offenders and nonoffenders, but that the gap is genuinely a difference in average intellectual level or, as it is sometimes euphemistically called, "academic competence" (p. 242).

How big is the difference between criminals and the rest of us? Taking the literature as a whole, incarcerated offenders average an IQ of about 92, 8 points below the mean. The population of nonoffenders averages more than 100 points; an informed guess puts the gap between offenders and nonoffenders at about 10 points (p. 242). [For Herrnstein and Murray, "criminals" refers to violent offenders (p. 236).]

3. IQ explains the race-crime relationship.

In the national data, blacks are about 3.8 times more likely to be arrested relative to their numbers in the general population than whites. . . . [V]irtually all of the difference in the prevalence of black and white juvenile delinquents is explained by the IQ difference, independent of the effect of socioeconomic status [citing as authority sociologist Robert Gordon] (p. 338).

4. Race and genetics are causally related.

We may [use] "ethnic groups" instead of races if we wish—we too are more comfortable with *ethnic,* because of the blurred lines—but some ethnic groups nonetheless differ genetically for sure, otherwise they would not have differing skin colors or hair textures or muscle mass. They also differ intellectually on the average. The question remaining is whether the intellectual differences overlap the genetic differences to any extent.

Our reason for confronting the issue of genetic cognitive differences is not to quarrel with those who deny them. If the question of genetic differences in cognitive ability were something that only professors argued about among themselves we would happily ignore it here. We cannot do so, first because in the public discussion of genes and intelligence, no burden of proof at all is placed on the innumerable public commentators who claim that racial differences in intelligence are purely environmental (p. 297).

5. Therefore, race, crime, and genetics are causally related.
   [inferred]

There is no logical link between premises 1–4 and the conclusion. Herrnstein and Murray's analysis encourages the reader to deduce that because 1–4 have been empirically established, so has 5. They violate an elementary rule of statistics: correlation is not to be confused with causality. Their reasoning is flawed on a number of other grounds. First, Herrnstein and Murray use "Black" and "White" as if the terms had scientific and static definitions. A critique of biology and crime research by professor James A. Anderson applies to Herrnstein and Murray: "[Skin] color cannot explain crime rates. . . . In using the biological *difference* of skin color as if it were a biological *determinant* of social behavior, [researchers] participate in the practical accomplishments of racism."[7] As discussed in chapter 2, race has a socially constructed meaning, only partly related to genetic makeup. The one-drop rule—which classifies anyone with any trace of Black blood as "Black"—is proof of this. Herrnstein and Murray acknowledge this problem, yet proceed as though it were inconsequential.

Second, Herrnstein and Murray's analysis overlooks social correlates of crime. They pay little attention to economic factors (e.g., unemployment rate, inflation), criminal justice decision-making factors (e.g., proliferation of plea bargaining, race-of-victim effects, type of counsel, legislative changes), or political factors (e.g., federal crack-cocaine law). These factors may have as much to do with crime rates as IQ scores. Lastly, Herrnstein and Murray's analysis is limited to street crime. They do not consider white-collar or corporate criminality. Even if we accept their conclusions, the genes-IQ-crime-race link only "solves" a fraction of the crime problem. If low IQ is correlated with street crime, then what explains white-collar crime? Is the fact that white-collar criminals are disproportionately White a result of a White genetic defect?

A flood of academic and journalistic refutations followed *The Bell Curve*. Scores of newspaper articles, editorials, TV news stories, magazine articles, and several books weighed in on Herrnstein and Murray's treatise. Despite this, very little in the way of an organized response was heard from the scientific community. One response was published in the *Wall Street Journal*.[8] In a strong show of unity, fifty-two researchers published a statement titled, "Mainstream Research on Intelligence." The statement, written in support of the book, listed twenty-five "conclusions regarded as mainstream among researchers on intelligence."

There were numerous commentaries refuting *The Bell Curve*. Few of these, however, represented an official viewpoint from the scientific community. Rather, they reflected the opinions of individual journalists, academics, and scientists. While both the president of the American Sociological Association and the president of the Educational Testing Service published statements critical of Herrnstein and Murray's work, neither was published on behalf of their respective organizations.[9] The American Psychological Association (APA) provides a notable exception. The APA established a task force to report on the scientific issues raised in *The Bell Curve*.[10] The APA report, "Intelligence: Knowns and Unknowns," concluded that the relationship, if any, between race, genes, and IQ is unknown. In discussing the difference between average IQ score for Blacks and Whites, the report states, "There is certainly no such support for a genetic interpretation."[11] Unfortunately the report did not receive widespread publicity.

A 1995 speech by Florida State University psychologist Glayde Whitney provides a third example of why scientists should have an ethical duty to rebut and clarify. Whitney gave the keynote address at the annual meeting of the Behavior Genetics Association (BGA). Commenting on the strong correlation between the high murder rate in U.S. cities and the high percentage of Blacks who live in U.S. cities, Whitney said, "Like it or not, it is a reasonable scientific hypothesis that some, perhaps much, of the race difference in murder rate is caused by genetic differences in contributory variables such as low intelligence, lack of empathy, aggressive acting out, and impulsive lack of foresight."[12] The speech caused an uproar and many people left before the end of Whitney's remarks. Although some BGA executive board members found the speech offensive, the board decided that taking official action against Whitney would violate his free-speech rights. Whitney, a past-president of BGA, remained an official member of the executive board. Following the speech, Pierre Roubertoux, the incoming president, unsuccessfully attempted to persuade the board to sanction Whitney. Roubertoux was so disturbed by the executive board's inaction that he resigned from his post.

Although Whitney said he was presenting a hypothesis, he discussed it as if it were scientifically supportable. That Blacks have a disproportionately high rate of crime is hardly *a priori* proof that Blacks are genetically inferior. Whitney's tenure as president of BGA and his post on the executive board at the time of his remarks enhanced the legitimacy of his highly speculative research claims.[13]

The fourth incident, the passionate opposition to and fallout from the Maryland genes-and-crime conference, illustrates the need for an ethical imperative for researchers. Vocal opposition to the conference arose after the disclosure of comments made by Frederick Goodwin, former administrator of the Alcohol, Drug Abuse, and Mental Health Administration. Goodwin, one of the leading federal researchers on genetics and violence, was invited to speak to the National Institute of Mental Health (NIMH) Advisory Council.[14] In his talk, Goodwin compared the inner city to a jungle and described Black men as predatory and hypersexual, like rhesus monkeys. After noting that wild monkeys are hypersexual and that almost one-half are killed before adulthood, Goodwin stated:

> That is the natural way of it for males, to knock each other off. . . . Now, one could say that if some of the loss of social structure in this society, and particularly within the high impact inner city areas, has removed some of the civilizing evolutionary things we have built up and that maybe it isn't just the careless use of the word when people call certain areas of certain cities jungles, that we have gone back to what might be more natural.[15]

Following his remarks, the Congressional Black Caucus questioned Goodwin's ability to objectively conduct scientific research. Goodwin's subsequent apology to "anyone [he] may have offended" did not quell public outcry. He eventually resigned his post. Although many individuals voiced objections to Goodwin's remarks, there was no response from a branch of the science community. Some interpreted the science community's silence as accord with Goodwin and so opposed the Maryland conference.

In each of the above examples, a member of the research community made a controversial statement about race and crime that other social scientists knew to be questionable or false. The fact that the statements were made public underscores the need to impose an ethical duty to rebut for researchers.

Defining the Ethical Imperative

Each of the above incidents raises the same question: What professional responsibility, if any, should researchers have when science fiction is masqueraded as scientific fact? The ethics codes of academic organizations impose no special responsibility to respond. This means that the "voices of clarification" will be the angry retorts of *individual* scientists, and to the lay public such a debate may appear to be an ivory-tower version of "he said/she said." In fact, it is frequently advocacy groups (e.g., NAACP, Anti-Defamation League) that respond to misuses of data.[16] Political factors (e.g., an upcoming election) may determine whether the concerns of these groups will be taken seriously or treated as background noise. The fact that political organizations may bring misuses of scientific data to the public's attention should not let researchers off the ethical hook.

An ethical imperative has three minimum components:

1. A response by an official, recognized branch of the research community
2. A response by experts in the relevant fields
3. A public response

A response by an official, recognized branch of the research community. Officials of any research organization (e.g., president, executive board, or a subcommittee), such as the American Medical Association, could issue a statement of correction. The group could be a local or national organization. In the Michael Levin case, for instance, a subcommittee of the AMA could have issued a statement outlining what is known about the relationship between glucose metabolism and race. Likewise, the American Society of Criminology, which has members specializing in biology and crime, could have issued a statement.

A response by experts in the relevant fields. In the Glayde Whitney case, any group of sociologists, criminologists, or geneticists could have responded to his claims. The current ethics codes make such rebuttals voluntary. This places a heavy burden upon individual scientists. An individual researcher may not wish to engage in academic fisticuffs with a colleague who has gotten his facts wrong.[17] A researcher might reasonably fear that criticizing a colleague publicly could jeopardize his tenure, promotion, or research funding. Or he might not have the personality suited for a public confrontation. An organization does not have these same concerns. A statement issued to correct inaccuracies has more credibility coming from a recognized group than an individual.

A public response. The peer-review process is a limited check on questionable research claims. This process is mostly confined to academic journals, which have a specialized audience and a specialized discourse not easily accessible to the general public. To be effective, statements of clarification must be offered publicly and systematically. Statements could be in the form of a letter to a newspaper editor, a letter requesting clarification or correction (directed to the appropriate news medium), or a response to media inquiries on a particular issue.

The academic community failed to provide an adequate response in each of the above four incidents. And yet, clarifications and rebuttals that met the three requirements would have had a stamp of legitimacy and carried more weight than a statement by an individual researcher. Consider the assertions of Michael Levin, linking glucose metabolism to genetic inferiority. A letter to the editor of the *Washington Post* by a single sociologist who refuted Levin's claims would have had less scientific authority than a letter written by a subcommittee of the American Medical Association.

A response by an officially recognized group also would send a message that the scientific community is concerned about the misuse of racially sensitive research. The responses to *The Bell Curve* came closest to meeting the requirements of the ethical imperative. However, the academic community's refutation of Herrnstein and Murray's thesis did not constitute a public response. In the Glayde Whitney incident, there was no public response by any official wing of the academic community. Although there were public criticisms of the statements made by Frederick Goodwin, more effective responses would have been from those who could address the substance of his commentary.

The academic and political community's reaction to a misleading advertisement about the relationship between abortion and cancer provides an excellent example of how the ethical imperative should work. In January 1996, The Christ's Bride Ministries of Northern Virginia, a Tennessee based anti-abortion group, purchased advertisement space from the metropolitan transit systems in several cities, including Washington, D.C., Hartford, Baltimore, and Philadelphia. The ads stated, "Women who choose abortions suffer more and deadlier breast cancer." The signs listed a toll-free number, which informed callers that one-half of all women who have abortions get breast cancer. There were swift responses from several groups:

- The National Cancer Institute published a paper analyzing data from more than thirty studies on the relationship between cancer and abortion. The Institute concluded that the studies' findings were "inconsistent and inconclusive."
- The Assistant Secretary for the Department of Health and Human Services wrote a letter stating that the advertisement was "unfortunately misleading, unduly alarming and does not accurately reflect the weight of scientific literature. . . . We strongly object to the ad because it appears to be based on studies that are inconclusive, biased and poorly designed."[18]

- The National Women's Health Network, the National Black Women's Health Project, and the National Latina Health Organization joined to launch a campaign against the misleading advertisement.

As a result of the responses, several transit systems removed the advertisements. Following this, the Christ's Bride Ministries filed an unsuccessful First Amendment lawsuit against the Philadelphia transit system.[19] The responses by various public health organizations meet each of the three components of the ethical imperative—a public response by experts from a recognized branch of the research community.[20] The informed public discussion and debate that followed after the transit advertisements appeared attests to the value of input from research organizations. Without an informed dialogue, the public is left to rely on opinion rather than fact. The absence of an ethical imperative encourages public skepticism and cynicism about the accuracy of science and journalism.

As noted above, some organizations already have ethics codes. The ethical imperative would be directed at those organizations that represent researchers who conduct research bearing upon race and crime. This would include organizations such as the American Medical Association, American Psychological Association, American Sociological Association, American Society of Criminology, National Science Foundation, and the National Institute of Justice. Depending upon the size and resources of the organization, it could implement an ethics board, panel, or ombudsperson to respond to ethical issues related to race and crime. The association would be left to determine the appropriate action to take in particular cases. For instance, an organization might decide to write a letter to the editor, draft an editorial, issue a press release, or appoint a panel to review some of the issues. Alternatively, it could decide that no response is necessary.

The Scientists' Rebuttal and the Community's Best Interests

Some might think that the proposed ethical imperative is unnecessary since there are organizations that carry out the same function. For example, the Media Resource Service, a national, nonprofit referral service, puts journalists in contact with scientists. This referral, however, does not meet the first requirement of the ethical imperative: it does not elicit a response from an official, recognized branch of the research community.

Why should the research community be compelled to act? The academic community and the general public are harmed by the absence of an ethical imperative. The academic community suffers diminished credibility when it does nothing to deter the misuse of its research. Ironically, "empirical fiction" appears to be a lucrative trade. Charles Murray and Richard Herrnstein have sold tens of thousands of books partly based on research findings that are at best disputed and at worst discredited. Taking official action to address this problem would serve both symbolic and practical ends. It would signal the research community's concern with truth in the dissemination of scientific data and would deter researchers from misrepresenting data. As it stands, there is no official sanction for passing off fiction as empirical fact.

By failing to collectively respond to research half-truths, social scientists thwart their mission. Those who study the relationship between crime and race have the most to gain from heightened ethical standards. As long as the research community is perceived as hostile to minority communities, establishing a relationship will be difficult. The Black community in particular has been the minority community that has voiced the loudest opposition to race and crime research. Historically, this community has been both the target and subject of racist research. As a result of this history, many Blacks believe that scientific research is something done to them, rather than something done for them. By failing to correct the public record, the research community confirms the suspicions of many Blacks that Whites think they are socially and genetically inferior. Consequently, scientists cannot expect to earn the respect or support of communities that are harmed by its inaction.

In addition to enhancing the legitimacy of research within minority communities and deterring researcher abuses, enforcing an ethical imperative has other benefits. It takes one step toward addressing the harms of racial stereotyping. Increasing "stereotype vulnerability" is one harm that might result from failing to adopt an ethical imperative. Research on stereotype vulnerability examines the impact that negative group stereotyping has on individual group members, as reflected by standardized test scores.

Professors Claude Steele and Joshua Aronson have studied how expected low performance affects Black students' performance on standardized tests. They looked to see whether the results were different when Black students took examinations believing that they were being tested as "Black" students (members of a "low performance" group), as compared with how they perform when they believe they are being tested as individuals (not members of a "low performance" group). The presence of racial cues during the examination (e.g., the proctor announces that the test measures intellectual ability, and students are required to check a box indicating racial group membership) resulted in much lower test scores. Moreover, once the racial cues were removed, Black middle-class students scored on par with White middle-class students. Stereotype vulnerability is premised on the theory that the normal anxiety students experience is exacerbated for Black students because of the racial currents in society. Steele concludes that "after a lifetime of exposure to society's negative images of their ability, [Black] students are likely to internalize an 'inferior anxiety.'"[21] The racial currents that Blacks face include the not-so-subtle message of inferiority sent by books such as *The Bell Curve*.

If nothing else, the protests to the Maryland genes-and-crime conference show that community reaction can affect the availability of public research dollars. It behooves researchers to more actively address problems and issues of clarification. The potential impact is great given that the federal government annually awards millions of dollars for research on violence. Economic and political rationales aside, it is unethical to permit the research community to claim immunity from responsibility to rectify abuses or errors. Researchers are in the best position to refute and clarify misrepresentations of scientific data and research.

Some individual researchers may state that an ethical imperative would be too burdensome. After all, if they are not racist, they should not have to concern themselves with issues of racial sensitivity or a colleague's misrepresentation of data. Several panels at the Maryland genes-and-crime conference addressed the racial implications of the research. On one of these panels, Adrian Raine, a University of Southern California psychologist, stated that he was not a racist.[22] By inference, Raine's comment suggests that no ill motives can be attributed to him or his research because he is in the business (as any real scientist is) of pursuing Truth. No doubt Raine's antiracism claims are sincere. However, claims like these are irrelevant to the ethical imperative. Raine's absence of malice in pursuing genetics-and-crime research does not absolve him of responsibility when his research, or the research of other members of his research community, is misstated to imply unsupported conclusions.

Heightened ethical guidelines for race-and-crime research decrease the likelihood that people will propagate unproven negative racial stereotypes. Research that claims to prove Black inferiority exacerbates the negative images that Blacks have of themselves and that Whites, Latinos, Asians, and Native Americans have of Blacks. Misstatements of fact that are presented under the guise of academic scholarship may increase the Black community's susceptibility to conspiracy theories (see chapter 8). Many Blacks already mistrust official branches of government, including the criminal justice system. The research community's collective failure to correct racial misstatements blurs the lines between science and scientific racism. This country's history of racially biased research, conducted with the imprimatur of legitimate science, should serve as a constant reminder of the need to impose additional checks. Finally, scientists' failure to intercede sends a not too subtle message of encouragement for more of the same.

The Ethical Imperative and Free Speech

Shouldn't scientists be left alone to say whatever they like, even if it is inaccurate, even if it is intended to cause harm? The argument for the ethical imperative is not an argument for censorship. It is an argument for *talking back* instead of remaining silent. Glayde Whitney, Michael Levin, and like-minded others should be allowed to say whatever they think. However, when their statements are made in public and when they involve inaccurate research claims, the scientific community should have an affirmative duty to rebut them.

Some might dismiss the proposed ethics standards as a veiled attempt at "political correctness." While some use the term "p.c." to assail liberal hypersensitivity, it is only in its extreme forms that it becomes problematic. In the context of ethics and research, correctness *should be* the goal. Who would argue that the scientific community, especially given its dark history on racial research, should not be concerned with the politics of its work?

The ethics provisions of professional associations are an attempt at "correctness." The ethical imperative for race-and-crime research comports with the existing rationale for ethics codes: the belief that professionals should be bound by a code of conduct that outlines the parameters of their work. These guidelines address the tension between the interests of the research community, individual researchers, research subjects, and society in general. The end result is a blueprint for how scientists can best go about doing their work, producing optimum results with the least offense possible. The ethical imperative simply expands this mandate. More precisely, it seeks to determine what is "scientifically correct."

One might still question whether the ethical imperative is an attempt to impose a liberal agenda upon researchers. The duty to rebut applies to all information publicly disseminated, regardless of its political content. Thus far, it has been discussed in terms of statements made by right-of-center scientists. In addition, remarks made by Khalid Muhammad, Leonard Jeffries, and Frances Cress Welsing arguably fall within the ethical imperative.

Khalid Muhammad, a Nation of Islam minister, made some incendiary remarks in November 1993 at a Kean College lecture. Citing data from the 1830 Census, Muhammad stated that the majority of the Southern Jewish population owned slaves. Based on this data, he claimed that Jewish people played a major role in the African slave trade.[23] His remarks caused an uproar. Jewish groups, newspaper columnists, and the U.S. Senate stepped forward to denounce his speech as anti-Semitic. Many Jewish leaders disputed Muhammad's research and expressed concern that his harsh rhetoric would widen the chasm between Blacks and Jews. It appears that Muhammad's comments were only partly true. While many Southern Jewish people owned slaves, research indicates that they constituted a small percentage of the overall Southern White population and were not major slave traders.[24]

In 1991, comments made by Leonard Jeffries, chair of the now-defunct African American Studies department at the City University of New York, spoke about the role Jewish people played in the African slave trade. He stated that "rich Jews" helped manage the slave trade. Further, Jeffries asserted that Hollywood is conspiring with the Mafia to cause the "destruction of Black people."[25] Many people stepped forward to challenge these statements.

The writings of Frances Cress Welsing share features with the commentaries of Khalid Muhammad and Leonard Jeffries. Welsing's "color confrontation" theory posits that Whites are genetically inferior to Blacks because they lack melanin. Referred to as "pigment envy," Welsing's theory seeks to explain White oppression of darker-skinned peoples throughout the world and throughout history. She states that because White skin is recessive to dark skin, Whites fear going the way of the dinosaur. The fear of genetic annihilation has caused Whites to try to conquer and oppress all people of color:

> The white or color-deficient Europeans responded psychologically, with a profound sense of numerical inadequacy and color inferiority, in their confrontations with the majority of the world's people—all of whom possessed

varying degrees of color-producing capacity. This psychological response, whether conscious or unconscious, revealed an inadequacy based on the most obvious and fundamental part of their being, their external appearance. . . . Whites defensively developed an uncontrollable sense of hostility and aggression.[26]

The most obvious distinction between the incidents involving Herrnstein, Murray, and Levin and those involving Muhammad, Jeffries, and Welsing is the public's reaction. The statements made by Muhammad, Jeffries, and Welsing received negative mainstream coverage. Further, they were uniformly dismissed as hate speech. And yet, like the four cases detailed above, there was no organized public response from the academic community.

In some measure, the reach of the ethical imperative is determined by how widely a message is disseminated and how well it is received. In cases where research is reported through the mainstream media (e.g., major television networks, national newspapers) the duty to rebut and clarify is even greater. For example, the publication of *The Bell Curve* received an extraordinary amount of press. In addition to appearing on several talk shows, Charles Murray appeared on the cover of the *New York Times Magazine* the week the book arrived in stores. The book was reviewed in virtually every mainstream, alternative, national, and international publication. As a result of the press attention, there was a need for the research community as a group to respond to his disputed research claims.

Conclusion

The ethical imperative cannot solve the problem of racism in science. Increased ethical standards, however, could deter the more egregious abuses and misuses of scientific data, specifically those related to race and crime. It is in the best interests of the scientific community, as well as society in general, that researchers have a duty to rebut and clarify misrepresentations of crime and race research.

Existing ethics codes are simply inadequate because they do not address the specific ethical problems raised by race-and-crime research. The nature, scope, and history of research on race and crime mandate a higher standard of ethical scrutiny. Further, current ethics codes are directed at individual researchers. If a particular researcher is offended by inaccurate statements, he may choose to carry out an individual act of protest. Professional organizations should not confuse the constitutional issue of free speech with the ethical duty to rebut and clarify. The ethical imperative is not a choice between free speech and censorship. Even if individual researchers respond to every misrepresentation of race and crime research, their responses will lack the authority of an organizational response. Absent the imprimatur of a professional organization, a single response is merely one salvo in an ongoing debate between individual researchers. Without any sanctioning authority, the existing ethics provisions lack legitimacy.

Considering that crime and race are contentious subjects, it is especially important that research representing the state of our knowledge is not misrepresented. Many of the questionable race and crime "facts" that are offered for public consumption allude to Black inferiority and White superiority. These statements, comments, and research hypotheses, when they go unaddressed, constitute a kind of racial assault on Blacks (see chapter 8).

The examples discussed above establish that the misuses of scientific research are not sufficiently corrected by self-regulation. These cases show that the failure to impose a duty to rebut and clarify has the potential for creating far-reaching harm. The general public is affected when fiction is presented as science. Consequently, the credibility of the research community is marred each time its research is misrepresented. It does not matter whether a particular researcher intentionally or mistakenly misstates or misrepresents the research findings of others.

7

In Search of White Crime

No one focuses on White crime or sees it as a problem. In fact, the very category "White crime" sounds funny, like some sort of debater's trick.   —Richard Delgado, "Rodrigo's Eighth Chronicle" (1994)

Blacks, Latinos, Whites, Native Americans, and Asians alike visualize crime in Blackface. A person would have to live as a hermit to avoid seeing crime portrayed in shades of Black. One would have to avoid watching television, reading the newspaper, or engaging in public conversation. In addition to the image of Blackness commonly associated with crime, there is also a racial language: "Black-on-Black crime," "Black criminality," and "Black crime." This language, however, does not include terms such as "White crime" or "White-on-White crime."

Although the representation of crime in Black is a picture that has largely been sketched by the media, social scientists who study crime also portray crime in varied hues of Black. Like the general public, social scientists rely heavily on terms that spotlight crimes associated with Blacks. At the same time, however, they do not use similar labels to describe the crimes committed by Whites. The work of academics suggests that they are no better at putting a realistic color on the face of crime than the lay public.

This chapter looks at crime data by race, placing particular emphasis on White crime. The first section examines the amount of White involvement in the criminal justice system, as measured by arrests and prison confinements. Following this is a discussion of whether social scientists should use terms to highlight offenses by Whites, including "White crime" and "White criminality." There is also a consideration of whether the use of racial labels is influenced by the small number of Black criminologists. One downside of how we currently talk about crime and race is that it exacerbates "half-facts." The chapter ends with a detailed discussion of this problem, using James Q. Wilson's "Black crime causes White racism" thesis as an example.

TABLE 7.1
Black and White Arrests, Percent Distribution for All Crimes, 1991-1995 (Summary)

	Black	White
1991	29.0%	69%
1992	30.3%	67%
1993	31.1%	67%
1994	31.3%	67%
1995	31.0%	67%

SOURCE: *Sourcebook of Criminal Justice Statistics (1991-1995)*, Bureau of Justice Statistics.

The chapter concludes that half-facts skew our perception and thereby our understanding of the relationship between race and crime.

The Study of White Crime

Contrary to popular belief, arrests for crimes involving White offenders are the most common. As Table 7.1 indicates, this is not a new trend. Table 7.2, which provides a racial breakdown of arrests for 1995, shows that in three offense categories Whites account for approximately 80 percent of those arrested: driving under the influence (86 percent), liquor law violations (80 percent), and drunkenness (81 percent). For these offenses White arrest rates are on par with their percentage in the population. Table 7.2 also reports that Whites have high rates of arrest for several other offenses, including arson (74 percent), burglary (67 percent), loitering (76 percent), vandalism (73 percent), and sex offenses (75 percent).

Not only are Whites the majority of all those arrested, they also make up a sizeable percentage of the incarcerated population. In 1995, Whites comprised 49 percent of the total incarcerated population (Table 7.3). Of the approximately 1.2 million people in prison or jail, almost 700,000 are White. What is often left unsaid is that White criminal representation, though not disproportionate, is quite high. A public discussion about crime and race necessarily means discussing White crime. One outcome of the fact that race has become synonymous with Black is that White crime is rarely labeled.

Public Beliefs about Race and Crime

There is a widespread belief that Blacks both disproportionately commit crime and are responsible for the majority of crime. The first belief is true,

TABLE 7.2
Total Arrests, Distribution by Race, 1995

Offense charged	Total arrests					Percent distribution				
	Total	White	Black	American Indian or Alaskan Native	Asian or Pacific Islander	Total	White	Black	American Indian or Alaskan Native	Asian or Pacific Islander
TOTAL	11,386,627	7,607,522	3,523,409	129,843	125,853	100.0	66.8	30.9	1.1	1.1
Murder and nonnegligent manslaughter	16,691	7,245	9,074	134	238	100.0	43.4	54.4	.8	1.4
Forcible rape	26,519	14,739	11,234	260	286	100.0	55.6	42.4	1.0	1.1
Robbery	137,761	53,570	81,957	692	1,742	100.0	38.7	59.5	.5	1.3
Aggravated assault	437,686	260,778	167,857	4,152	4,899	100.0	59.6	38.4	.9	1.1
Burglary	291,901	195,486	90,421	2,765	3,229	100.0	67.0	31.0	.9	1.1
Larceny-theft	1,162,674	753,868	377,143	12,811	18,852	100.0	64.8	32.4	1.1	1.6
Motor-vehicle theft	148,899	87,159	57,060	1,743	2,937	100.0	58.5	38.3	1.2	2.0
Arson	14,931	11,083	3,543	150	155	100.0	74.2	23.7	1.0	1.0
Violent crime	618,657	336,132	270,122	5,238	7,165	100.0	54.3	43.7	.8	1.2
Property crime	1,618,405	1,047,596	528,167	17,469	25,173	100.0	64.7	32.6	1.1	1.6
Crime index total	2,237,062	1,383,728	798,289	22,707	32,338	100.0	61.9	35.7	1.0	1.4
Other assaults	973,672	613,098	338,038	11,985	10,553	100.0	63.0	34.7	1.2	1.1
Forgery and counterfeiting	91,782	59,630	30,336	509	1,307	100.0	65.0	33.1	.6	1.4
Fraud	319,904	204,473	110,920	1,559	2,452	100.0	64.0	34.7	.5	.8
Embezzlement	11,599	7,529	3,840	71	159	100.0	64.9	33.1	.6	1.4
Stolen property: buying, receiving, possessing	127,624	74,837	50,285	933	1,569	100.0	58.6	39.4	.7	1.2
Vandalism	232,387	170,647	55,611	3,139	2,990	100.0	73.4	23.9	1.4	1.3
Weapons: carrying, possessing, etc.	187,046	111,123	72,494	1,235	2,194	100.0	59.4	38.8	.7	1.2

Total arrests — Percent distribution

Offense charged	Total	White	Black	American Indian or Alaskan Native	Asian or Pacific Islander	Total	White	Black	American Indian or Alaskan Native	Asian or Pacific Islander
Prostitution and commercialized vice	81,050	49,334	29,866	439	1,411	100.0	60.9	36.8	.5	1.7
Sex offenses (except forcible rape and prostitution)	72,171	54,141	16,542	783	905	100.0	75.0	22.6	1.1	1.3
Drug abuse violations	1,143,148	709,704	421,346	5,286	6,812	100.0	62.1	36.9	.5	.6
Gambling	15,673	8,360	6,468	72	773	100.0	53.3	41.3	.5	4.9
Offenses against family and children	104,122	67,857	33,506	1,010	1,749	100.0	65.2	32.2	1.0	1.7
Driving under the influence	1,019,260	880,635	110,839	15,626	12,160	100.0	86.4	10.9	1.5	1.2
Liquor laws	433,585	345,127	75,137	10,212	3,109	100.0	79.6	17.3	2.4	.7
Drunkenness	526,742	425,514	86,608	12,749	1,871	100.0	80.8	16.4	2.4	.4
Disorderly conduct	560,809	352965	196,919	7,539	3,386	100.0	62.9	35.1	1.3	.6
Vagrancy	20,517	10,749	9,225	463	80	100.0	52.4	45.0	2.3	.4
All other offenses (except traffic)	2,915,568	1,840,568	1,012,616	30,274	32,110	100.0	63.1	34.7	1.0	1.1
Suspicion	9,055	4,697	4,302	35	21	100.0	51.9	47.5	.4	.2
Curfew and loitering law violations	114,702	86,902	24,445	1,519	1,836	100.0	75.8	21.3	1.3	1.6
Runaways	189,649	145,904	35,977	1,700	6,068	100.0	76.9	19.0	.9	3.2

SOURCE: FBI, *Uniform Crime Reports 1995*, U.S. Department of Justice (1996).

TABLE 7.3
Black, White Arrest and Incarceration Figures, 1995

	White	Black	Other	Total
Arrest	7,607,522 [67%]	3,523,409 [31%]	255,696 [2%]	11,386,627
Prison	469,300 [49%]	507,000 [49%]	15,300 [2%]	991,600
Jail	252,300 [52%]	223,900 [46%]	7,600 [2%]	483,800

SOURCES: *Uniform Crime Reports, 1995,* Bureau of Justice Statistics; *Sourcebook of Criminal Justice Statistics, 1995,* Bureau of Justice Statistics.

the second is not. The second belief, that Blacks commit most crime, is an extension of the first. Though distinct, these perceptions, one fact and one fiction, have become jumbled in the public mind. The public's inaccurate picture of the amount of Black crime is partly media driven. As detailed in chapter 1, television in particular focuses a great deal on street crime. Although each year two-thirds of the people arrested for street crimes are White, Blacks continue to represent the public face of street crime.

The public's perception's that crime is violent, Black, and male have converged to create the *criminalblackman.* By itself, this mythical criminal Black figure is scary enough. However, the figure has become ominous because we do not have anything to compare it with. There is no *criminalwhiteman.* There is every reason to believe that if more images of White criminals and White criminality were put in the media spotlight, the public image of crime would change. The damage of this Black stereotype, however, cannot be undone simply by highlighting White crime. The media and the academic community will also have to expose the *criminalblackman* stereotype as a misrepresentation.

Invisible Labels: A Look at the Research

Disproportionate rates of crime by Blacks do not explain why we rarely see crime represented in other colors. Our discussion of race and crime is not so much segregated as one-dimensional. Nobel Prize laureate Toni Morrison comments that the racial presentation of crime reinforces "racial half-truths. . . . Unless you can intelligently use the phrase 'White on White crime,' you can't use the phrase 'Black on Black crime.'"[1] A review of newspapers, law review articles, and social science articles indicates that when assigned a color, the picture of crime is almost always Black.

LEXIS/NEXIS, a computerized database that catalogs news stories from more than twenty-four hundred sources, lists fewer than fifty current articles that use the term "White crime," or "White-on-White crime." Notably, most of these articles reference White crime in comparison with Black crime—not as an independent phenomenon. In sharp contrast, more than one thousand articles use some variation of "Black crime." The grossly disparate use of the term "Black crime" cannot be completely explained by the different crime rates for Blacks and Whites. When discussing race and crime, legal analysts and journalists have a hard time seeing White crime. Of the thousands of law review articles catalogued by LEXIS/NEXIS, only a handful use the term "White-on-White crime" or "White crime."

One of these articles is "Rodrigo's Eighth Chronicle: Black Crime, White Fears—On the Social Construction of Threat," an article by law professor Richard Delgado, that examines White crime. The article explores why White crime has been neglected as an area of study. Delgado discusses the amount and costs of White crime. His research indicates that White crime is more costly than Black crime.

The virtual absence of articles on White crime suggests that in our singular and collective minds "White" and "crime" simply do not go together. In his book, *Two Nations,* professor Andrew Hacker observes, "[N]o one speaks of 'white crime,' since it would have too broad a compass."[2] "Black crime" could also be said to have too broad a compass since it is used to refer to a range of crimes, including crimes stereotypically associated with Blacks (e.g., carjacking), crimes involving a Black offender and Black victim, and crimes involving a Black offender and White victim.

In addition to journalists and law professors, criminologists have avoided explicit recognition of White crime. A review of four influential criminology journals between 1992 and 1996 revealed few journal articles explicitly devoted to "White crime."[3] White crime is being studied, yet it is not called White crime. The numerous academic articles that focus on the deviance of White adults and White youths avoid using terms such as "White criminality." The nonlabeling of White crime contrasts sharply with the pervasive labeling of Black crime.

Scores of academic articles refer to Black crime. In addition to those that use terms such as "Black crime," "Black criminality," and "Black-on-Black crime," many articles use ostensibly race-neutral words. These terms include, "inner city," "truly disadvantaged," "underclass," "poverty-ghetto," and "urban." Code words such as these widen the extent to which Black crime is labeled by social scientists.

The skewed focus on Black crime by journalists and academics may simply reflect society's skewed concern with street crime. By this reasoning, because Blacks are responsible for a disproportionate amount of street crime, they receive a disproportionate amount of attention by academics and the media. Such reasoning, however, rings only half true. Disproportionate offending by Blacks may explain why research centers upon Black crime, but it does not explain why so little media attention focuses on White street crime. Second, it does not explain why crime by Whites is rarely referred to as "White crime." Third, a look at the history of race and crime suggests that offenses committed by Blacks have always received extraordinary attention. This was true long before "disproportionality" became part of the public language on crime.

Crime in Whiteface: Some Examples

Several areas of research could be classified as "White crime." These include white-collar, rural, and suburban crime. White-collar crime, as defined by criminologist Edwin Sutherland, is "crime committed by a person of respectability and high social status in the course of his occupation."[4] Researchers have observed that Whites have a disproportionate opportunity to commit high-status offenses because they are more likely to hold high-status jobs. With the exception of fraud and embezzlement, data for white-collar offenses are not collected as part of the Uniform Crime Reports. Although white-collar criminality may never produce the same degree of fear as street crime, its impact upon society is substantial. Criminologists Francis Cullen and Michael Benson state: "[T]he costs of white-collar crime—the violence it entails, the money it transfers illegally, its damage to the moral fabric—may well outstrip the costs of traditional street crimes."[5] Some researchers estimate that white-collar crime costs ten times as much as street crime. It remains a mystery why there is no annual count of white-collar crimes. Cullen and Benson note that white-collar crime is downplayed because criminologists do not view it as real crime:

> Many criminologists secretly may believe what [James Q.] Wilson and the politicians are saying [that street crime is more serious than suite crime]. At the very least, their raised consciousness does not dispose them to place knowledge about white-collar crime on an equal footing with knowledge about street crime.[6]

RURAL AND SUBURBAN CRIME

If it is worthwhile to report that Blacks, who live mainly in urban areas, offend disproportionately in these areas, it is worthwhile to report that Whites, who mainly live in rural and suburban areas, offend in these communities at rates that approximate their percentage in the population. In rural areas, Whites comprise a disproportionately high percentage of the arrests for all crimes (Table 7.4). For arson, auto theft, burglary, embezzlement, and larceny, Whites account for approximately 80 percent of the arrests in these areas. There is a similar arrest pattern for Whites who live in suburban areas (Table 7.5). Whites account for approximately two-thirds of the suburbanites who are arrested for murder, rape, robbery, arson, DUI, and vagrancy.

HATE CRIMES AND ETHNICITY

Crimes driven by racial hatred did not end along with Jim Crow. In the last decade, hate-crime legislation has been enacted to curtail the rising number of race-related assaults against minorities. In 1995, the majority of people arrested for hate crimes were White.

In response to the media and research emphasis on Black crime, Andrew Hacker observes that little research attention focuses on the differences between White ethnic groups. He proposes conducting research that compares the success and failures of the fifteen White ethnic groups denoted by the U.S. Census. Hacker observes, somewhat tongue in cheek, that if some researchers can insist on examining Blacks and low achievement, the same can be done with Whites. His research indicates that French-Canadian and Dutch Whites are much less likely to complete college than Russian and Scottish Whites.[7]

Calling Names

Race and criminal law are inextricably linked, and therefore, the phenomenon of Black crime cannot be discussed without a discussion of the phenomenon of White crime. If Black crime is labeled, then White crime should be labeled. Race labels could be imposed for all crime. For instance, when journalists refer to crime in rural areas, it could be labeled White crime. In this way, "rural" crime would be used to denote race in the same way that "inner-city" crime is used. Another example would be to catalog the crimes of White militia groups as White crime.

Another option, to eliminate labels altogether, is unrealistic since they are already in widespread use. Further, if race labels were discouraged,

TABLE 7.4
Total Rural County Arrests, Distribution by Race, 1995

Offense charged	Total arrests					Percent distribution				
	Total	White	Black	American Indian or Alaskan Native	Asian or Pacific Islander	Total	White	Black	American Indian or Alaskan Native	Asian or Pacific Islander
TOTAL	855,703	671,837	145,916	24,626	13,324	100.0	78.5	17.1	2.9	1.6
Murder and nonnegligent manslaughter	1,311	799	457	46	9	100.0	60.9	34.9	3.5	.7
Forcible rape	2,244	1,679	467	70	28	100.0	74.8	20.8	3.1	1.2
Robbery	2,634	1,208	1,296	61	69	100.0	45.9	49.2	2.3	2.6
Aggravated assault	28,000	20,023	6,842	1,007	128	100.0	71.5	24.4	3.6	.5
Burglary	26,499	21,157	4,093	930	319	100.0	79.8	15.4	3.5	1.2
Larceny-theft	43,243	33,567	7,907	824	945	100.0	77.6	18.3	1.9	2.2
Motor-vehicle theft	7,568	6,065	1,005	326	172	100.0	80.1	13.3	4.3	2.3
Arson	1,262	1,078	144	26	14	100.0	85.4	11.4	2.1	1.1
Violent crime	34,189	23,709	9,062	1,184	234	100.0	69.3	26.5	3.5	.7
Property crime	78,572	61,867	13,149	2,106	1,450	100.0	78.7	16.7	2.7	1.8
Crime index total	112,761	85,576	22,211	3,290	1,684	100.0	75.9	19.7	2.9	1.5
Other assaults	71,811	53,733	14,926	2,010	1,142	100.0	74.8	20.8	2.8	1.6
Forgery and counterfeiting	7,457	5,689	1,633	98	37	100.0	76.3	21.9	1.3	.5
Fraud	49,404	36,400	12,439	449	116	100.0	73.7	25.2	.9	.2
Embezzlement	794	666	99	11	18	100.0	83.9	12.5	1.4	2.3
Stolen property: buying, receiving, possessing	6,972	5,498	1,289	170	15	100.0	78.9	18.5	2.4	.2
Vandalism	16,207	13,405	2,105	492	205	100.0	82.7	13.0	3.0	1.3
Weapons: carrying, possessing, etc.	11,284	8,633	2,190	297	164	100.0	76.5	19.4	2.6	1.5

Total arrests

Percent distribution

Offense charged	Total	White	Black	American Indian or Alaskan Native	Asian or Pacific Islander	Total	White	Black	American Indian or Alaskan Native	Asian or Pacific Islander
Prostitution and commercialized vice	244	199	34	5	6	100.0	81.6	13.9	2.0	2.5
Sex offenses (except forcible rape and prostitution)	6,043	5,218	596	176	53	100.0	86.3	9.9	2.9	.9
Drug abuse violations	67,664	53,218	596	176	53	100.0	79.4	17.6	1.8	1.1
Gambling	470	279	68	2	121	100.0	59.4	14.5	.4	25.7
Offenses against family and children	11,419	8,592	2,372	331	124	100.0	75.2	20.8	2.9	1.1
Driving under the influence	158,075	129,363	19,442	5,058	4,212	100.0	81.8	12.3	3.2	2.7
Liquor laws	35,788	32,433	1,543	1,504	308	100.0	90.6	4.3	4.2	.9
Drunkenness	33,607	29,352	2,924	1,272	59	100.0	87.3	8.7	3.8	.2
Disorderly conduct	26,042	20,593	4,306	961	182	100.0	79.1	16.5	3.7	.7
Vagrancy	378	269	101	8	—	100.0	71.2	26.7	2.1	—
All other offenses (except traffic)	227,029	172,165	44,823	6,932	3,109	100.0	75.8	19.7	3.1	1.4
Suspicion	444	353	88	2	1	100.0	79.5	19.8	.5	.2
Curfew and loitering law violations	1,566	989	86	96	395	100.0	63.2	5.5	6.1	25.2
Runaways	10,244	3,673	712	231	628	100.0	84.7	7.0	2.3	6.1

SOURCE: "Crime in the United States, 1995," U.S. Department of Justice (1996).

TABLE 7.5
Total Suburban Area Arrests, Distribution by Race, 1995

Offense charged	Total arrests					Percent distribution				
	Total	White	Black	American Indian or Alaskan Native	Asian or Pacific Islander	Total	White	Black	American Indian or Alaskan Native	Asian or Pacific Islander
TOTAL	3,921,773	2,974,856	901,650	20,303	24,964	100.0	75.9	23.0	.5	.6
Murder and nonnegligent manslaughter	3,778	2,396	1,335	22	25	100.0	63.4	35.3	.6	.7
Forcible rape	8,254	5,714	2,432	42	66	100.0	69.2	29.5	.5	.8
Robbery	30,111	14,663	15,126	120	202	100.0	48.7	50.2	.4	.7
Aggravated assault	142,160	101,062	39,300	769	1,029	100.0	71.1	27.6	.5	.7
Burglary	102,707	78,352	23,135	468	752	100.0	76.3	22.5	.5	.7
Larceny-theft	404,343	281,254	116,595	1,976	4,518	100.0	69.6	28.8	.5	1.1
Motor-vehicle theft	44,302	31,477	12,132	243	450	100.0	71.1	27.4	.5	1.0
Arson	5,461	4,662	732	26	41	100.0	85.4	13.4	.5	.8
Violent crime	184,303	123,835	58,193	953	1,322	100.0	67.2	31.6	.5	.7
Property crime	556,813	395,745	152,594	2,713	5,761	100.0	71.1	27.4	.5	1.0
Crime index total	741,116	519,580	210,787	3,666	7,083	100.0	70.1	28.4	.5	1.0
Other assaults	330,840	243,794	83,077	1,891	2,078	100.0	73.7	25.1	.6	.6
Forgery and counterfeiting	31,099	21,987	8,754	105	253	100.0	70.7	28.1	.3	.8
Fraud	124,724	88,376	35,394	357	597	100.0	70.9	28.4	.3	.5
Embezzlement	3,836	2,588	1,189	11	48	100.0	67.5	31.0	.3	1.3
Stolen property: buying, receiving, possessing	44,868	30,598	13,599	191	480	100.0	68.2	30.3	.4	1.1
Vandalism	81,271	67,462	12,770	457	582	100.0	83.0	15.7	.6	.7
Weapons: carrying, possessing, etc.	57,993	41,653	15,652	192	496	100.0	71.8	27.0	.3	.9

| | Total arrests | | | | | Percent distribution | | | | |
Offense charged	Total	White	Black	American Indian or Alaskan Native	Asian or Pacific Islander	Total	White	Black	American Indian or Alaskan Native	Asian or Pacific Islander
Prostitution and commercialized vice	9,336	6,888	2,320	26	102	100.0	73.8	24.9	.3	1.1
Sex offenses (except forcible rape and prostitution)	23,412	19,525	3,591	117	179	100.0	83.4	15.3	.5	.8
Drug abuse violations	350,649	261,719	86,380	1,109	1,441	100.0	74.6	24.6	.3	.4
Gambling	2,128	1,159	889	8	72	100.0	54.5	41.8	.4	3.4
Offenses against family and children	54,452	36,347	17,768	159	178	100.0	66.8	32.6	.3	.3
Driving under the influence	463,646	419,102	38,703	2,379	3,462	100.0	90.4	8.3	.5	.7
Liquor laws	130,836	117,683	11,004	1,238	911	100.0	89.9	8.4	.9	.7
Drunkenness	167,451	147,852	17,074	1,880	645	100.0	88.3	10.2	1.1	.4
Disorderly conduct	168,158	125,406	40,785	1,033	934	100.0	74.6	24.3	.6	.6
Vagrancy	3,928	2,764	1,111	26	27	100.0	70.4	28.3	.7	.7
All other offenses (except traffic)	1,020,789	726,507	284,723	4,889	4,670	100.0	71.2	27.9	.5	.5
Suspicion	3,277	2,711	535	28	3	100.0	82.7	16.3	.9	.1
Curfew and loitering law violations	29,932	25,779	3,685	197	271	100.0	86.1	12.3	.7	.9
Runaways	78,032	65,376	11,860	344	452	100.0	83.8	15.2	.4	.6

SOURCE: FBI, *Uniform Crime Reports 1995*, U.S. Department of Justice (1996).

some researchers and journalists might rely more frequently on code words, which would not solve the underlying problem.

Perhaps the biggest concern with our current use of racial labels for Black crime is that it implies that there exists something about crime that is race-specific. Without a comparable language that describes and defines White crime, the implication is that there is something about Blackness that "explains" criminality. Thus, the current practice of labeling Black crime might lead some people to the incorrect conclusion that Black people are genetically predisposed to commit crime.

Those Who Study Race and Crime: A Look at the Numbers

By all accounts, fewer than fifty Blacks in the nation have received doctorates in criminology or criminal justice. In 1995 forty-one people received graduate degrees in criminology. Twenty-nine were White (70 percent), eight were Black (19 percent), one was Native American, and one was Asian. Between 1986 and 1995, Whites received 78 percent of the 337 doctorates in criminology. Almost one-half went to White men. Blacks received approximately 14 percent of the doctorates awarded over the same ten-year period (Table 7.6).

There is no threshold number of Black criminologists that would be enough. Fifty, however, may be too few to substantially impact how crime and race are discussed, analyzed, and researched. The small number of Blacks in criminology, the behavioral science that focuses predominantly on street crime, is problematic in view of the disproportionate rates of Black arrests, conviction, and incarceration. Studies indicate that to some degree a researcher's race is correlated with his ideology and areas of research interest. If so, the racial makeup of the profession is relevant. A look at journalism and law, two other arenas that affect research and public discussion on the criminal justice system, also reveals a pattern of Black underrepresentation. An increase in the number of Black criminologists might hasten the development of theories to explain Black crime and shift the focus from Black crime to White crime.[8]

Implications and Future Possibilities

The issue of whether racial labels should be attached to crime and criminals raises several questions. First, when would a racial label be appropriate? If

TABLE 7.6
Criminology Doctoral Degrees Awarded to Black and White Students,
1986-1995 (U.S. Citizens Only)

	Black Men/Women (Total)	White Men/Women (Total)	Total
1986	0/2 (2)	16/5 (21)	24
1987	1/0 (1)	13/5 (18)	23
1988	4/4 (8)	15/7 (22)	32
1989	1/4 (5)	17/6 (23)	29
1990	1/1 (2)	20/15 (35)	38
1991	3/1 (4)	8/10 (18)	26
1992	3/0 (3)	17/10 (27)	33
1993	1/3 (4)	15/10 (25)	31
1994	4/2 (6)	19/8 (27)	36
1995	6/2 (8)	11/8 (19)	41
Totals	24/19 (43)	151/84 (235)	313[a]

[a] "Total" column includes thirty-five doctoral graduates for whom race is unknown.
SOURCE: National Science Foundation, et al. (1996).

disproportionality is used as the standard, then White crime labels and Black crime labels have to be used. Another possible standard is that whenever a crime involves an offender and a victim of the same race, it will bear a racial label. Thus, crimes involving White offenders and White victims would be called "White-on-White crime" or "White crime." Intraracial crime involving Latinos, Native Americans, Blacks, or Asians would be similarly labeled. This still does not resolve the question of how to label interracial crimes—e.g., Asian offender/Latino victim.

The issue of labeling crimes by race is problematic beyond the straightforward concern about fairness and accuracy. Historically, crimes committed by Blacks were singled out as the ultimate example of deviance. As detailed in chapter 2, this was particularly true for crimes involving Black offenders and White victims. A Black person who committed an offense was subject to a harsher penalty than a White person who committed the same offense. Today, the widespread practice of highlighting crimes by Blacks and overlooking those by Whites may reflect this history.

By every yardstick, the general public has a distorted picture of the racial makeup of crime in the United States. As a result, academics and journalists have a heightened responsibility to present a picture of crime and race that bears some semblance to reality. Sociologist C. Wright Mills cautioned, "All social scientists, by the fact of their existence, are involved in the struggle between enlightenment and obscurantism. In such a world as ours, to practice social science is, first of all, to practice the politics of truth."[9] If Mills is correct, social scientists have an obligation to shed light on the phenomenon of White crime. This obligation also requires us to discuss crime and race in ways that do not perpetuate inaccurate stereotypes.

Too often, the disproportionate rate of Black crime is used as the whipping boy for U.S. racial ills. The next section critiques professor James Q. Wilson's thesis that Black crime causes White racism. As detailed below, Wilson's conclusions are wide of the mark in analyzing how race, racism, and crime are interlinked.

Fearful, Angry White People: James Q. Wilson's "Black Crime Causes White Racism" Thesis

One of the biggest roadblocks to an informed discussion about crime and race is the perpetuation of half-facts. Half-facts are statements or propositions about crime that are discussed in a vacuum, divorced from their context. James Q. Wilson's discussion of the relationship between White racism and Black crime provides an interesting example of this phenomenon. The argument that White racism is at the root of the problems faced by Black America has been assailed by others as well.[10] Wilson, a professor of political science at the University of Southern California, is considered one of the nation's premier thinkers on crime.

Wilson's basic thesis, which appeared in a 1992 *Wall Street Journal* editorial, is that if Blacks would stop committing so much crime there would not be so much White racism. His thesis, developed in subsequent writings, is that White racism and White fear of Black and Latino men are justified because Black and Latino men have high rates of crime.[11] It is fear, Wilson contends, not racism that accounts for the negative perceptions that White people have of Black and Latino men. In fact, Wilson states, "fear can produce behavior that is indistinguishable from racism."[12] His tacit conclusion is that the current level of White racism is acceptable, so long as it coexists with the current level of Black and Latino crime. At first read, Wilson's argument sounds vaguely tenable or at least difficult to dismiss. However, a careful consideration of his underlying premise indicates that his thesis raises more questions than it answers.

At core, Wilson suggests the following one-directional relationship:

Black crime rates ⟶ White racism

Two major assumptions undergird Wilson's hypothesis. First, the Black crime rate is the primary source of White racism. Second, solving the Black crime problem rests primarily with the Black community.

White Fear and White Racism

According to Wilson, "The best way to reduce racism real or imagined is to reduce the black crime rate to equal the white crime rate."[13] He points out that Black men offend at a rate six to eight times greater than the rate for Whites. Accordingly, it is reasonable to expect that White racism will persist until Blacks and Whites offend at an equal rate. Awaiting such a drop in the Black crime rate is neither the best nor the quickest way to reduce White racism. Ignoring the interconnection between crime, poverty, and education, Wilson commands Blacks to rise above their circumstances before they can ask for a reduction in White racism. This is a tall order.

Not only does Wilson imply that the Black crime rate is the sole source of White racism, he also places the onus of eradicating White racism upon Blacks. Even if the Black crime rate were reduced to equal the White crime rate, how would this affect the *amount* of White racism? Is Wilson suggesting that if Black and White crime rates were equal, White racism would disappear completely? Drop by one-half? Wilson implies that White racism will wither away or decline substantially if the rate of Black crime were equal to the rate of White crime. Wilson provides neither theoretical nor empirical support for this sweeping assertion. In fact, he could not, as there are no such data available.

Wilson also offers an incomplete analysis of the role of fear. His hypothesis suggests that fear is a one-dimensional variable. White fear, however, has at least four related, though distinct, components: the fear of crime, the fear of losing jobs, the fear of cultural demise, and the fear of Black revolt. Wilson overlooks the fact that the generalized White fear of Black crime encompasses these other fears.

Studies show that the closer Whites live to Blacks, the more fearful they are of crime. This fear is justified since Whites who live near Blacks also face the greatest threat of victimization by Blacks.[14] Although levels of neighborhood integration may explain why Whites who live in urban areas are fearful of Black crime, it does not justify the general, nationwide White fear of Blacks. Most Whites do not live close to Blacks—not surprising given that Blacks are a small percentage of the population. Furthermore, given the fact that more than 80 percent of all crime is *intra*racial, White fear of Black crime is inexplicably high. It may be that Whites translate their discomfort about race relations into attitudes about crime.[15]

In 1993, Jesse Jackson remarked that he was saddened that Black crime had reached such epidemic proportions, that when he walks down the street at night he is actually relieved to discover that the person coming toward him is White.[16] Several White commentators (e.g., John DiIulio, George Will) have pointed to Jackson's comments as "proof" that White fear of Black crime is justified.[17] However, each fails to recognize that, statistically, the greatest crime threat to Jesse Jackson *is* another Black man. On the other hand, the greatest crime threat to someone White is another White person, since most crime is intraracial. At least Jackson's fears are factually based.

There exists an economic component to White fear of Blacks. This fear is commonly couched in affirmative action terms. There has been a lot of talk about "qualified" Whites losing jobs, government contracts, or university admissions slots to "unqualified" Blacks. Many Whites believe that Blacks pose a serious threat to their economic well-being. Affirmative action is perceived as a threat by many Whites, who fear losing their privileged status. While many Whites have legitimate fears about the state of the economy, blaming Blacks for downsizing and global economic decline misses the mark. Andrew Hacker notes that Whiteness has been devalued and "for the first time in this country's history, [Whites have been] made to feel they no longer come first."[18] The media's response to this fear has created more heat than light. It has failed to report the obvious: it is statistically impossible for Blacks, who make up less than 13 percent of the population, to take all the jobs, college admissions spots, and government contracts.

Another type of fear that Whites have of Blacks is cultural. Some Whites view Black culture as the antithesis of American culture. This fear manifests itself when Black culture crosses over into White culture such as music, clothing, hair styles, speech patterns, and posture. The loudest cries of cultural decline can be heard when White youths mimic and adopt aspects of Black culture. Specifically, calls for school dress codes, record-label warnings, standard English, and music morality are sounded when Black culture contaminates Whites. The creation of moral panics to marginalize a racial or ethnic group from the mainstream is not new.[19]

Other fears include the fear of losing majority status and the fear of a Black revolt. The fear that Blacks will become the majority race and in turn use their power to pay Whites back for centuries of slavery was expressed as early as 1751.[20] In 1996, two-and-one-half centuries later, conservative pundit

William F. Buckley commented that many Whites favor abortion to ensure that Blacks do not overpopulate the country. Andrew Hacker, referring to the fear of "racial revenge,"[21] states, "There is a fear in White America of this second nation, this Black nation. There is fear of rebellion."[22] Some have speculated that this fear drives popular support for abolishing welfare and affirmative action.

As the above makes clear, most of the fears that Whites have of Blacks are not rational. Wilson's dichotomous treatment of White fear obscures its dimensions and its irrationality. For Wilson, White fear is a typical, therefore justifiable, response to Black crime. Wilson's analysis glosses over the fact that while it may be commonplace for Whites to fear Blacks, it is not necessarily reasonable. Fear is not always a rational emotion; however, to use fear to justify racism, which Wilson does, the fear must be grounded in reality. A great deal of White fear—of crime, of economic loss, of cultural demise—has been a knee-jerk response to media stories. By all indicators, Wilson is correct when he says that Whites are fearful of Blacks, yet his analysis jumps past the fundamental question of the logic of White fear. Why does this matter? Whether or not White fear is justified, whether White fear is used to cloak prejudice, has *everything* to do with determining the relationship between White racism and Black crime. A generalized, empirically insupportable White fear of Black crime cannot be used to excuse White racism.

The problem with allowing White fear to justify White racism is driven home when we consider Black fear of Whites. Although rarely acknowledged publicly, many Blacks are fearful of Whites. This sentiment was expressed by some of the focus group participants detailed in chapter 1. Black fear of Whites may stem from the fact that Whites are at the helm of every American institution. The office of the President, Congress, the Supreme Court, and the private sector all show a White face. Black fears of White power and its abuses, however, do not justify Black racism against Whites. Are Blacks "excused" from being racist because they fear Whites? Wilson says no.[23] Wilson characterizes Black outrage at the verdict in the 1992 LAPD/Rodney King trial as "appalling racist bigotry." How is it that Wilson allows Whites to blindly leap from fear to racism, yet this same leap is impermissible for Blacks? Wilson's "White only" fear-racism link speaks volumes.

White Racism or Black Crime Rates: Which Came First?

Wilson offers little historical support for his assumption that high Black crime rates trigger White racism. Considering the fact that American slavery brought Blacks to this country in chains, it would be a safe bet that White racism existed centuries before disproportionate rates of Black crime. One need only review the slave codes and Black codes for blatant examples of White racism written into early American criminal law for proof of this. Wilson's thesis conveniently ignores this history.

Derrick Bell provides an interesting counterpoint to Wilson's thesis. In his book *And We Are Not Saved*, Bell considers what would happen if Black crime magically disappeared. Using a hypothetical, Bell describes a scenario in which magic stones have been discovered. Once ingested, the stones eliminate all desire to engage in crime. The stones, whose power only works for Blacks, are distributed throughout the country. However, now that "blacks had forsaken crime and begun fighting it, the doors of opportunity, long closed to them because of their 'criminal tendencies,' were not opened more than a crack."[24] Though there was no longer a crime excuse, this did not reduce the barriers to racial equality. Bell's hypothetical, based upon historical fact, is much closer to reality than Wilson's suggestion that White racism surfaced only in response to high Black crime rates.

Whose Fault Is It Anyway?

Wilson draws an interesting configuration. He assigns Whites a passive role in the Black crime/White racism dynamic. Simply put, he blames Blacks for White racism. Wilson has asserted that Blacks unfairly use racism as an excuse for criminal activity. According to Wilson, racism that is "imagined" by Blacks will disappear if the Black crime rate declines. Wilson never tells us what "imagined" racism is. The reader is left to surmise that this is racism that only exists in the minds of Blacks. How is it that a reduction in the Black crime rate will cause a reduction in imagined racism? Wilson does not tell us this either. Rather than holding Whites accountable for their racism, Wilson allows them to claim victim status—they are victimized by Black crime. Wilson allows the blame for White racism to be placed entirely on Black shoulders. Yet, he charges that Blacks unfairly place all the blame for the Black crime rate upon Whites. This smacks of a double standard.

Another troublesome aspect of Wilson's argument is that it encourages us to think along racially segregated tracks about crime and other societal problems. His argument that Blacks are responsible for Black crime and White racism is part of the larger racial finger-pointing that persists—

none of which reduces the crime rate or diminishes racial divisions. The net result is that Blacks blame Whites for their lack of progress and Whites blame Blacks for all social ills. As detailed in the first part of this chapter, the overemphasis on Black crime makes it difficult to see that "race and crime" is not synonymous with Blacks and crime. More must be done to present the public with an accurate racial picture of crime, including White crime.

8

Affirmative Race Law

The American system of criminal justice may never be completely free of racial influence. This is undoubtedly true for other social institutions as well. This country's history of chattel slavery and legalized racial subordination, ending just over a century ago, would predict nothing less. We would not expect the twentieth-century vestiges of slavery—e.g., Jim Crow legislation—to disappear in the brief forty years since *Brown v. Board of Education* and the passage of civil rights legislation. An evaluation of today's criminal justice system indicates that race is no longer the explicit linchpin of criminal law. What is left to measure, however, is whether racial discrimination persists in other, more subtle forms. The sixth fairness principle used to evaluate the equity of a justice system requires that criminal justice system checks and balances exist to mitigate against racial bias by the legal system (see chapter 2).

There are three components to an analysis of whether our justice system adheres to this principle. First, there must be a look at whether there are unexplained racial disparities. If so, the next step in the analysis is to determine whether the system creates opportunities to correct them. A second and more difficult issue is whether the law recognizes and adequately sanctions racial harms. This assessment is difficult because it requires an analysis of whether *more law* is necessary to balance out new and persistent forms of racial discrimination.

In addition to these two measures, analyzing whether the sixth fairness principle is met also requires evaluating the *current racial climate*. This means an examination of the degree to which Blacks still face social discrimination—how they are treated as individuals and group members. Ultimately, the inquiry is whether the combination of existing law, absence of law, and racial climate allow the justice system to run roughshod over Blacks. If so, then today's legal system operates as an agent of social injustice in a muted, though comparable, manner as the slave codes, Black codes, and Jim Crow.

This chapter examines the legal and racial components of the justice system and concludes that the sixth fairness principle is not met. Existing laws act to further racial disparity, and more laws are needed that sanction racial harms. "Affirmative race law" is the term given to legislation that seeks to address overt and covert racial discrimination. Affirmative race law acknowledges American racial history and acts as a bulwark against existing racial subordination and discrimination. Failing to adopt more affirmative race law promises a range of potentially negative consequences, including alienation, criminal violence, community unrest, health risks, and paranoia.

Racial Disparities under Existing Law: Two Examples

Explicit racial double standards have been excised from the American criminal law. Yet, race still affects today's criminal justice system. For example, police department policies that target particular crimes and particular communities may result in unintended racial disparities in arrest and conviction rates. Police crackdowns on drug sales are an example of this. It is widely acknowledged that it is easier for police to uncover drug activity in open-air drug markets than in office suites. People engaged in drug trafficking on the street are thus more likely to be arrested than those who operate from an office. For a number of reasons, minorities engage in street-level drug dealing more than Whites, and Whites engage in office-level drug dealing more than Blacks. A police department's decision to target street-level drug offenders may be based upon efficiency and not race. It also may be based upon a decision to target violence associated with street-level drug offending. Whether driven by these or other concerns, such policies result in arrest patterns and sentences that are racially disparate. This means that police policies and practices can result in one kind of law enforcement for Blacks and another for Whites. The federal crack-cocaine law is a more specific example of this problem.

Crack v. Powder Cocaine

In 1986, immediately following the death of college basketball star Len Bias, Congress enacted the federal crack cocaine law. It was believed that Bias, who had just signed a million-dollar contract to play for the Boston Celtics, died from an overdose of crack cocaine. Later it was learned that he died from ingesting powder cocaine.[1]

TABLE 8.1
Crack v. Powder Cocaine under Federal Law

	Quantity	Sentence
Powder cocaine	500 grams	5 years
Crack cocaine	5 grams	5 years

Crack cocaine is made by mixing powder cocaine with baking soda and water. These ingredients are heated until the water evaporates and all that remains are crack-cocaine rocks. The federal crack statute mandates a five-year prison term for possession of five grams of crack cocaine. Under the same federal law, possession of five hundred grams of powder cocaine is required for a five-year prison term. Prison sentences are mandatory under the federal law. In 1995, 88 percent (12,300) of the people serving sentences under this law were Black.[2] Because the penalty for possession of crack cocaine is one hundred times harsher than the penalty for possession of powder cocaine, the federal law is described as having a "100:1 disparity" (Table 8.1).

In *U.S. v. Clary*,[3] Edward Clary was convicted under the federal crack law. Clary, who is Black, was convicted of possessing 67.6 grams of crack and faced a mandatory ten-year prison term. He argued that the law was racially discriminatory, in violation of the U.S. Constitution. After reviewing the history of U.S. drug laws, the district court agreed with Clary. It found that drug use that is perceived to be threatening to middle-class Whites tends to result in harsh legislative penalties—particularly where the threat is racialized. For instance, in the early 1900s, widespread animosity toward Asians led to the 1909 Smoking Opium Exclusion Act. The Harrison Act of 1914 was enacted to allay White fears of being harmed by Black heroin addicts.

In addition to reviewing the social and political impetus for drug legislation, the court evaluated the medical evidence. The court found little medical support for the harsh legislative distinctions between powder and crack. The court determined that Congress had enacted the law for symbolic reasons, not because crack is one hundred times more lethal than powder cocaine. The *Clary* court concluded that racial disparities in the federal crack law were driven primarily by White fear of Black crime. On appeal, the decision was reversed.

Racial disparities in the application of the federal crack law have triggered diverse voices of dissent. In 1995, after reviewing the history of the federal law, its goals, and its application, the U.S. Sentencing Commission recommended that Congress equalize the sentences for crack and powder. The Commission was specifically created to review federal law and eliminate unwarranted sentencing disparity.

The Commission's review of the federal crack law revealed that more Whites use crack cocaine than Blacks and that the medical research does not support the 100:1 disparity. The Commission concluded that the distinctions between crack and powder are primarily social, not physiological. For example, the distribution and marketing of crack are more likely to involve violence, due to "turf" wars and open-air drug sales, than the sale of powder cocaine. In the final analysis, the Sentencing Commission found that the federal law was the "primary cause of growing racial disparity between sentences for Black and White federal defendants."[4]

Congress voted 332-82 to overrule the recommendation of the Sentencing Commission. President Bill Clinton upheld the Congressional vote, thus making it the first time a president rejected the recommendations of the Sentencing Commission.

In *U.S. v. Armstrong*[5] the Supreme Court had a chance to address the crack statute's inequities, or minimally to express alarm about the 100:1 disparity. The Court declined to do either. After reviewing claims that Black crack defendants were being tried in federal court while White crack offenders were being tried in state court (which imposes lighter penalties), the Court found insufficient evidence of selective prosecution.

After Congress voted against equalizing crack and powder cocaine sentences, federal prisoners initiated riots at five correctional facilities. Fires were set, windows and furniture were damaged, and several inmates and prison staffers were injured. The riots led to a nationwide lock-down of federal prisons.

The most unique response to the powder and crack inequities has come from federal judges. Judges at both ends of the political spectrum have actively opposed the statute, arguing that the mandatory sentences do not allow enough judicial elbow room. The law forces judges to impose tough sentences, without due consideration of mitigating circumstances. Some judges have resigned in protest, and others have refused to follow the guidelines.[6] Some of the communities hardest hit by crime associated with crack have also protested the 100:1 disparity.

In November 1996, two psychologists published research results that challenged the medical arguments for the disparity. After reviewing two decades of research on cocaine, they concluded that a 2:1 disparity between crack and powder is medically supportable. The researchers found that some distinction is justified because crack produces a quicker, more intense high and because its cheap price makes it more widely accessible than powder cocaine.[7] In April 1997, the Sentencing Commission altered its position and called on Congress to reduce the crack and powder disparity from 100:1 to 5:1. Three months later Attorney General Janet Reno recommended that Congress consider narrowing the disparity to 10:1.

The Death Penalty and the Race-of-the-Victim Effect

In the landmark case of *McCleskey v. Kemp*,[8] a Black man was convicted of killing a White police officer and sentenced to die. Warren McCleskey argued that the Georgia death penalty was racially biased, in violation of the Equal Protection Clause. The defense introduced the results of a study that analyzed more than two thousand Georgia homicide cases. The research indicated that the victim's race was the most significant factor in determining whether someone convicted of capital murder would be sentenced to death. In 22 percent of the cases involving a Black offender and a White victim, the defendant was sentenced to death. In stark contrast, only 1 percent of the cases involving a Black offender and a Black victim resulted in a death sentence.[9]

Despite these findings, the U.S. Supreme Court upheld the Georgia death penalty. To establish a violation of the Equal Protection Clause, a capital defendant has to prove that there was racial discrimination in his particular case—e.g., that the judge or jury members were motivated by racial bias in their decision to impose a death sentence. Though the Court indirectly acknowledges the existence of unexplained racial disparity, it finds that statistics alone are insufficient to establish a constitutional violation. The Supreme Court failed to offer a convincing rationale for rejecting empirical proof of racial discrimination. In civil cases, such as Title VII race discrimination suits, statistics are routinely used. In practical effect, the *McCleskey* Court sets an impossible standard for proving that the death penalty is racially discriminatory. Today, very few Whites—e.g., jurors, judges, and lawyers—would publicly admit that race affected their legal decision-making. Furthermore, the decision overlooks the fact that race discrimination may not be intentional. All of us are influenced by the negative stereotypes of minorities, and this likely has some impact on the criminal justice system. The *McCleskey* decision is disappointing because the Court failed to address the fact that racial discrimination has newer, subtler forms that cannot be rectified by an intentional discrimination standard.

The federal cocaine statute and the operation of the death penalty challenge the notion that the criminal justice system has sufficient checks against race discrimination built into it. The racial disparities inherent in both of these laws have eluded justice system checks. The federal law remains despite objections by federal judges, doctors, prisoners, and the U.S. Sentencing Commission. It has remained despite its dire social consequences, including the loss of voting rights for huge numbers of Black men.[10] Likewise, attempts to adopt the Racial Justice Act, a clear check on racial discrimination in capital sentencing, were soundly defeated. The Act would have required states to monitor their death sentences to assess what role, if any, race played. In February 1997, the American Bar Association (ABA) issued an unprecedented call for a moratorium on capital punishment. The ABA resolution was motivated by concerns that the death penalty is being administered in an unpredictable, haphazard manner. The ABA's vote for a moratorium, like the Racial Justice Act, if heeded, would have operated as a check and balance on racial disparities in capital sentencing.

Racial Redress

The above discussion indicates that existing laws need more corrective measures to reduce racial disparities. The discussion that follows considers the impact of the absence of legislation and how this can operate as a form of race discrimination. To address these "invisible" harms, more affirmative race laws are needed. A law that makes it a crime to perpetuate a racial hoax, detailed in chapter 5, would be an example of an affirmative race law. Until the criminal justice system enacts more laws that recognize racial injustice, it is unlikely that its legitimacy will be enhanced. Legal gaps in the law's recognition and punishment of racial harms legitimate the view that the law is biased against Blacks. Reparations are another, controversial, example of affirmative race law.

Reparations

For most people, the issue of Black reparations for slavery touches a raw nerve. This reaction, however, is not new. The movement for Black reparations touched off controversy when it was first considered following the Civil

War. Congressman Thaddeus Stevens introduced a bill that would provide each newly freed slave with "forty acres and a mule" as reparations for slavery. The bill was passed but was later rescinded by President Andrew Johnson. Johnson ordered that all lands revert to their pre–Civil War owners.

Since the late 1800s, there have been several movements for Black reparations. Over the last one hundred and thirty years, this movement has taken different shapes and has been called by different names. Historically, Whites have been of at least two minds on reparations. Some have supported reparations in conjunction with the removal of Blacks from America—as a way to solve the "Negro Problem." In the 1940s, for example, a White Mississippi congressman called for organizations to provide money to establish Black American colonies. In contrast, some Whites have viewed reparations without any strings attached as a necessary measure.

One argument against reparations is that the "spirit" of reparations has been incorporated into post–Jim Crow legislation. According to this argument, laws such as the Civil Rights Act, the Voting Rights Act, and affirmative action effectively amount to reparations. This argument, however, is ahistorical. Civil rights legislation was enacted to enforce constitutionally protected rights. Likewise, affirmative action was adopted because Blacks and women were being shut out and denied jobs solely on the basis of race and sex—a clear violation of the Equal Protection Clause. These legislative actions, however, did not directly address the crimes of slavery but its vestiges.

Though public support for reparations has mostly ebbed, Blacks have remained steadfast in their belief that there should be monetary compensation for slavery. It is this longstanding belief that explains the continued quest for reparations, pursued through various legal channels. For almost a decade, Congressman John Conyers has introduced Black reparations legislation. These bills mandate that Congress establish a Commission to Study Reparations which would look at the institution of slavery, the impact of *de jure* and *de facto* discrimination and discrimination against free Blacks, and assess the lingering negative effects of slavery on Blacks today.

In 1995, rumors circulated that there was a "Black tax" credit. According to the rumor, Blacks were entitled to take a $43,000 federal tax deduction. This amount was purported to be today's equivalent of forty acres and a mule. More than twenty thousand Blacks filed for the deduction. No such deduction had been approved. To deter others from similar filings, the IRS assessed five-hundred-dollar penalties against people claiming this deduction.[11]

Cato v. United States[12] involved a civil action for reparations filed in federal court. The 1995 civil case sought $100 million for a host of racial injuries caused by slavery, including "forced, ancestral indoctrination into foreign society; kidnapping of ancestors from Africa; forced labor; breakup of families; removal of traditional values; and deprivations of freedom." The lawsuit also requested that the U.S. government issue a formal apology for slavery. The case was dismissed by the Ninth Circuit Court of Appeals. The court found, among other things, that the time limit for bringing the claim had expired.

For many Blacks, the absence of racial compensation is compounded by the fact that some of the harms committed against other minority groups have been acknowledged and minimally redressed. For example, in 1988 the federal government paid twenty thousand dollars apiece to sixty thousand Japanese Americans, who were forcibly interned during World War II. The reparations included a formal apology from the U.S. government. In 1980, eight Sioux Indian tribes were awarded $105 million for land that had been taken away from them in 1877.[13]

In August 1996, a federal lawsuit was filed for reparations on behalf of more than two thousand Latin Americans of Japanese descent who were deported to America during World War II. By presidential order they had been forcibly interned in the United States. In addition to the request for the same reparations that were granted to interned Japanese Americans in the United States, the plaintiffs sought punitive damages.[14]

The grassroots movements for reparations indicate that many Blacks still believe that the offenses of slavery have not been adequately redressed. It is plausible that Blacks would view reparations as unnecessary if the playing field were level today. For Blacks, the belief that the justice system discriminates against them is likely buttressed by the fact that other racial groups have been compensated for their racial injuries.

Many argue that reparations are not feasible because it is impossible to determine who is "Black." "Black," however, could be defined according to the one-drop rule, a direct descendent of the slave codes. Or, any of the racial classifications used by official government agencies (e.g., U.S. Census Bureau) could be employed. It should be noted that legislators frequently have to determine who falls within a particular class so that they may determine who is entitled to legal protection. In the case of reparations, this determination would be difficult but not impossible.

For some, the call for reparations is less compelling as time passes. While some believe it is too late for reparations, others view the failure to make good on the promise of reparations as proof that the United States is unwilling to redress the most basic of harms.

If nothing else, it would seem that the U.S. government would step forward and formally apologize. Symbolism aside, some think that payment of Black reparations would exacerbate racial tensions between Blacks and Whites because Whites would view it as reverse discrimination or an implication that Whites today have done something personally to harm Blacks. While some may share this sentiment, it is not a sound argument against reparations. First, every attempt by Blacks to achieve equality has been met with widespread resistance from Whites. One need only consider the responses to various movements for racial justice—e.g., abolition of slavery, dismantling of *de jure* racial segregation, affirmative action, and voting rights. White resistance, therefore, comes with the terrain. Furthermore, failing to redress the ravages of slavery may increase levels of racial tension experienced by Blacks.

Invisible Harms

An analysis of whether there are adequate checks and balances to correct for racial discrimination in criminal justice requires a look at how Blacks fare socially. As this section demonstrates, one of the present-day realities of Black life is the persistence of racial affronts. Many Blacks feel the sting of racism on a regular basis. Racial affronts are usually no more than minor annoyances. Some, however, whether intentional or unintentional, are deeply painful. A look at the prevalence of racial assaults provides an indicator of the racial climate.

Microaggressions and Macroaggressions

"Microaggressions," a term used to describe racial assaults, are "subtle, stunning, often automatic and non-verbal exchanges which are 'put downs' of Blacks by [Whites]."[15] Examples include a White person who refuses to hold an elevator for a Black person, a White person who will not make direct eye contact with a Black person while speaking to him, a White person who enters a business office and assumes that the Black person she sees is a secretary or a janitor, a cab driver who refuses to pick up a Black passenger, a White person who refuses to give directions to someone Black, and a White sales clerk who offers assistance to a White patron in line behind a Black patron. Even President Bill Clinton acknowledges the harms caused by microaggressions. In his March 29, 1997, weekly radio address, Clinton stated:

> Let's be honest with ourselves: racism in America is not confined to acts of physical violence. Every day African Americans and other minorities are forced to endure quiet acts of racism—bigoted remarks, housing and job discrimination. Even many people who think they are not being racist still hold the negative stereotypes and sometimes act on them. These acts may not harm the body, but when a mother and her child go to the grocery store and are followed around by a suspicious clerk, it does violence to their souls. We must stand against such quiet hatred just as surely as we condemn acts of physical violence.[16]

Microaggressions are not the only racial assaults that Blacks are forced to contend with. In addition to personal affronts, Blacks face group affronts. These are termed "*macro*aggressions": attacks, insults, or pejorative statements made against Blacks by Whites. They differ in two key respects from microaggressions. Unlike microaggressions, they are not directed toward a particular Black person, but at Blackness in general. Further a macroaggression may be an action taken by a private individual or official authority.

Some macroaggressions become major news stories. When this happens, they become part of our national racial consciousness. If they are played out on a national stage, they have a far greater potential for harm, more than microaggressions. The message of the macroaggression is unequivocal: Blacks are inferior. Sometimes macroaggressions are intended as "jokes"; others are "mistakes"; most, however, are malicious assaults. The following nationally reported macroaggressions are illustrative:[17]

- In 1995, Rutgers University president Francis Lawrence inadvertently commented that Blacks are genetically inferior.[18]
- In 1991 and 1992, on Martin Luther King's holiday, two White men drove around St. Louis spraying Blacks with a fire extinguisher. The men sprayed more than fifty Blacks with water and Koolaid.[19]
- During Black History Month in 1995, hate mail was left in the mailboxes of U.C. Berkeley minority law students. The letter read in part, "Rejoice you crybaby niggers. It's affirmative action month. . . . When I see you in class it bugs the hell out of me because you're taking the seat of someone qualified."[20]

- In 1995, the attorney general of South Carolina, reversing an earlier opinion, decided that the confederate flag should fly atop the state capitol. He reached this decision despite longstanding protests that the flag is an inappropriate reminder of slavery.[21]
- In 1995, a century after federal adoption of the Thirteenth Amendment (outlawing slavery) the Mississippi legislature voted to ratify and incorporate it into the state constitution.[22]
- The Minnesota Educational Computing Corporation produced a computer game called "Freedom!" In this game, sold to elementary schools, players begin as illiterate Southern slaves, referred to as "boy." At one point during the game, a White man appears on the computer screen, holding a gun on the slaves. The game was available in the Tempe, Arizona, school district. Playing the computer game was the "reward" a Black fifth-grader received for his high class performance.[23]
- In 1995, five White male high school students in Greenwich, Connecticut, placed a coded message in their yearbook. The message spelled out, "Kill All Niggers."[24]
- In 1995, merchants in a Georgia town posted a criminal "offenders" sheet, which listed only the names of Black patrons.[25]

Macroaggressions reinforce negative stereotypes of Blacks as either criminals, illiterates, or intellectual inferiors.

Macroaggressions also exacerbate racial tensions. In many instances they are perpetrated by someone who is motivated by racial hatred. The fallout from each macroaggression follows a consistent pattern: the macroaggression occurs and people take sides. Some people will argue for tolerance. Those with this view usually suggest that there was no racial assault and even if there was, it was unintentional. Still others will suggest that there is no cause for alarm because the assault was committed by a fringe, outsider group. Other people will take the view that the assault was racially offensive and requires immediate action. At some point, the macroaggression gets lost in the discussion, as people on either side critique the strategy and tactics of the opposing side.

Consider the macroaggression involving Rutgers president Francis Lawrence. Following his remarks, there were student protests and demands for his resignation. The Rutgers community was racially divided. Many Whites pointed to Lawrence's administrative record as proof that he was "pro-minority" and argued that one mistake should not jettison his presidency. In response, Black students said that if Lawrence believes that minorities are genetically inferior to Whites, then he is not "pro-minority." Lawrence's apology did little to assuage the pain and anger many Black students felt. One Black student commented, "If Lawrence is racist, it's his business, but if Lawrence is a racist and represents me, it's my business."[26] A college basketball game had to be suspended after 150 students staged a sit-in during half-time. Tensions, still simmering two months after published reports of Lawrence's remarks, led 250 students to stage a demonstration outside his home. White students criticized Black students for their protest tactics. Black students criticized White students for downplaying the racial issues raised by Lawrence's remarks.

Some macroaggressions leave little room for misinterpretation. After hate letters appeared in the mailboxes of some minority law students at the University of California at Berkeley, a rally against racism was held. The rally attracted more than two hundred people. The ensuing campus debate centered on whether racial incidents such as the hate letter represent the attitudes of a fringe group of Whites or the majority.

While not all macroaggressions are the subject of protest rallies, they invariably result in some level of dissension or unrest. Both the Georgia "Blacklist" case and the South Carolina confederate flag case resulted in community protests. The parents of Brian Vinson, the Black child who was humiliated after playing "Freedom!" filed a federal civil rights lawsuit against the school district and the computer-game manufacturer, alleging that the game caused Brian severe emotional distress.

Absence of Affirmative Race Law and the Increased Probability of Antisocial Responses

What will happen if more affirmative race law is *not* adopted? There are a range of possible outcomes, including alienation, disdain, anger, and criminal violence. Alienation, a form of social isolation, may be the most common response. Developing affirmative race law is minimally necessary to build Black trust in police, courts, and corrections. The distrust that many Blacks have of the criminal justice system has a number of ramifications. For instance, it strains the relationship between the police and Black communities and may mean that Blacks will be less likely to assist police in crime solving. This is particularly troubling since Blacks are disproportionately likely to be crime victims.

Absence of Affirmative Race Law and Criminal Offending

Affirmative race law is premised on the fact that the low level of trust Blacks have in the criminal justice system may manifest itself in antisocial behaviors, including criminal violence. Violence may be the way that someone responds to racial injustice. An angry, physical response may be the only way the person can be heard. The following incidents illustrate this point.

In an article by law professor Patricia Williams, she recounts a racial incident in which she was denied entrance to a clothing store by a White clerk. Williams, who is Black, states, "I was enraged. At that moment I literally wanted to break all the windows in the store and take lots of sweaters."[27] Williams responded to the racial slight by making a creative public complaint. She typed up a detailed account of the incident, made it into a poster, and attached it to the window of the United Colors of Benneton store where she had been denied entry. In discussing her feelings of outrage about the incident, Williams comments on the direct, causal link between racism and crime. Williams confides, "My rage was admittedly diffuse, even self-destructive, but it was symmetrical."[28] Williams says that her emotional reaction matched the offense against her and that her response was not only reasonable but predictable. In her case, she had a legal, productive medium through which she could express her anger. Further, the combination of her education and public stature allowed her to publicize the incident—which likely produced some measure of vindication.

Such public channels, however, are not available to most Blacks who are subjected to continuing racial assaults. For young Black men in particular, who may be embarrassed and angered by the sting of racism, there is no such outlet. There are numerous incidents that describe how racial assaults can escalate to violence. For instance, in January 1995, four Black teens in Kentucky were arrested for killing a White man. The man was purportedly killed because he hung a confederate flag in the back of his truck.[29]

The macroaggression involving the Greenwich, Connecticut, yearbook slur also resulted in a physical confrontation. Shortly after the incident, one of the White youths responsible for the coded message was attacked by four Black youths. Although the incident was investigated as a hate crime, police declined to file charges, citing insufficient evidence.

In November 1995, a Black man set out to murder Stacey Koon, one of the police officers convicted in the Rodney King beating. On the eve of Koon's release from a halfway house, after less than three years behind bars,

Randall Tolbert stormed into the correctional facility. He took three hostages when he was unable to locate Koon. Tolbert was killed in a shootout with the police. Tolbert was upset that Koon had served a light sentence in the King beating and also took offense that Koon had been placed in a halfway house in a Black Los Angeles neighborhood. Tolbert's brother commented, "It was like they were trying to slap us in the face by putting [Koon] here."[30]

In February 1995, a White rookie police officer shot and killed an unarmed Black youth in a Paterson, New Jersey, drug bust. In response to the shooting, one young Black man commented, "The [Black] youth of Paterson we don't want to be violent, but we want justice served. . . . [I]f justice is not served, then there will be repercussions."[31] The young man's statement is consistent with Williams's rage and Tolbert's violence. His comments express his view that the New Jersey police acted beyond their legal authority, that the system will not redress this wrong, and that he had no legal way to voice his discontent and be heard.

Community Responses to the Failure of Law

There have been several cases involving a racial assault that have resulted in widespread community protests. In October 1996, after the police-shooting death of a young Black man, a Black community in St. Petersburg, Florida, erupted in hours of violence. Sixty homes and businesses were burned down and damage was estimated in the millions. A month earlier, the Black community in Pittsburgh reacted angrily to the acquittal of a police officer tried in the beating death of Jonny Gammage.

The reaction that followed the acquittal in the first LAPD/Rodney King trial produced the greatest violence in response to a criminal verdict this century. In April 1992, a jury comprised of eleven Whites and one Hispanic returned not-guilty verdicts for all four officers charged in the King beating. The acquittals sparked days of rioting in Los Angeles. There were outbreaks of violence in several other cities across the country. In Los Angeles alone, more than fifty people were killed, hundreds of people were injured, dozens of businesses were burned down, and countless stores were looted. Estimates of property damage were in the billions.

The above examples offer clear links between racial assaults and criminal responses. Incidents of police brutality and harassment create further disillusionment within minority communities. In 1997, the U.S. Commission on Civil Rights completed its review of the conditions in St.

Petersburg that led to the rioting. A federal civil rights investigator charged the St. Petersburg police with exacerbating racial tensions. After noting that the department had a gross pattern of misconduct, he urged "special training because [the police] represent the spark that could bring about more-disturbances."[32]

For some Blacks, disillusionment with the justice system may become anger, and anger may become rage. Rage may become crime. The concern is whether this rage will cause retaliation, either in the form of intraracial or interracial violence. The latter could take the form of Blacks committing crime in White communities or the targeting of White law enforcement officials.

Physical Tolls

Recent studies have established that exposure to race discrimination and racism may have health consequences. In a 1995 study, Duke University researchers designed a study to measure whether exposure to racist encounters has an effect on heart rates for Black women. Black participants were placed in a setting where controversial racial comments were made and discussed. Participants heard comments including, "It is necessary for police to use force with Blacks, given the inherent hostile and aggressive tendencies Blacks are known to have." Researchers found that after being exposed to racist comments, the participants' heart rates and blood pressure accelerated. They also found that participants had a range of reactions to the racist comments, including cynicism, anger, resentment, and anxiety. The researchers noted that each of these emotions is associated with stress hormones. The findings indicated that the chronic stress of racism may contribute to increased rates of heart disease among Blacks.[33] In another study, published in 1996, two medical researchers looked at the impact of race discrimination on blood pressure. The study is based upon interviews with more than four thousand Blacks and Whites. They found elevated blood pressure levels for those Blacks exposed to multiple incidents of race discrimination and higher levels for those who internalized rather than confronted race discrimination.[34]

The next section examines another, less obvious effect of the law's failure to redress racial harm. "Conspiricizing" addresses how the appeal of genocide theories may increase when the justice system is perceived as illegitimate.

"Conspiricizing"

The Black community has elevated theorizing about government-sanctioned conspiracies to an art form.[35] All manner of conspiracies have been offered to answer the question, "What's wrong with this picture?" More to the point, why are Black people in such bad shape? Circulating in the Black community are conspiracy theories offered to explain a host of inexplicable racial conditions. The ones with the most potency are those related to genocide. These include:

- Plots to infect the Black community with infectious diseases, including the acquired immune deficiency virus
- Plots to contaminate the Black community through food or commerce
- Plots to destroy the Black man
- Plots to infiltrate poor Black communities with crack cocaine

For years, rumors have circulated that the U.S. government created the acquired immune deficiency virus. According to this conspiracy theory, the virus was placed in Black communities in the United States and African countries to wipe out the world's Black population. Another related theory is that the government already has a vaccine for the virus but has not made it widely available. The popularity of this theory is buttressed by the government-sanctioned Tuskegee syphilis experiment in the 1950s. In this case, close to four hundred Black men with syphilis were recruited to participate in a medical treatment experiment. The men thought they were being treated. Instead, White doctors were using the Black men as guinea pigs, watching and studying the progression of the syphilis.

Various conspiracy theories have circulated that certain companies with large Black markets sell contaminated goods or are connected to White-supremacist groups. Businesses including Church's Chicken, Coors Beer, and Snapple Beverages have been the focus of some of these rumors.

Perhaps the most popular conspiracy theory is that there is a government plot to destroy successful Black men. These theories reach their zenith when criminal allegations are leveled against entertainers, athletes, and politicians (e.g., Mike Tyson, Marion Barry, Clarence Thomas, Michael Jackson, and O. J. Simpson). Many Blacks believe that the FBI was behind the assassination of Malcolm X. Some have speculated that the FBI solicited the Nation of Islam to murder Malcolm X. Others have suggested that Martin Luther King's assassination had the fingerprints of the U.S. government.

For more than a decade, it had been rumored that the crack-cocaine epidemic was engineered by the U.S. government. The crack scourge has had a particularly devastating effect on poor, Black communities—sending many of its members to prisons or to graves. In August 1996, this conspiracy theory was given new legs. Gary Webb's three-part series for the *San Jose Mercury News* indicates a link between the CIA and crack cocaine. According to the article, the Nicaraguan contras were allowed to smuggle crack cocaine and guns into the inner cities. This was done to help the contras raise money to overthrow their government.[36] The Congressional Black Caucus, the Rainbow Coalition, and other Black organizations and individuals called for a thorough federal investigation. Attorney General Janet Reno and National Drug Czar Barry McCaffrey have stated that the CIA was not directly involved with introducing crack into poor communities. An official investigation concluded there was no conspiracy.

A recent incarnation of the genocide conspiracy theory is that rap music has been allowed to proliferate as a way to perpetuate negative images of Blacks. According to this theory, Black rappers are encouraged to portray Black men as street hustlers and thugs and Black women as ever-ready sexual objects. Some have questioned whether the government and record executives have enlisted gangster rappers to engage in a form of "psychological warfare."[37] This argument is reminiscent of other conspiracy theories in which Blacks, knowingly or unwittingly, participate in anti-Black conspiracies with Whites.

Many White eyes glaze over when someone Black insists that the government is out to destroy Blacks. These claims are often dismissed as paranoid ramblings or as an unfair attempt to shift blame. However, each time a conspiracy is proven to have some basis in fact, it increases the likelihood that Blacks will believe the next conspiracy theory that circulates.[38] The most recent news about the government's role in introducing crack into Black communities, combined with historical evidence (e.g., Tuskegee experiment), underscore the legitimacy of conspiracy theories. It is not surprising that the belief that the government is engaged in an aggressive assault on the Black community is strengthened each time a conspiracy myth turns out to be a conspiracy fact. The prevalence and credence attached to these conspiracies indicate high levels of social alienation. Many of these theories are directly traceable to the law's failure to provide adequate Black redress.

Critique of Affirmative Race Law

Affirmative race law can be critiqued on a number of grounds. First, some might suggest that it is impractical, especially in today's political climate. In the past decade there has been a steady retrenchment on civil rights for minorities (e.g., affirmative action). It is, therefore, unlikely that politicians would embrace laws designed to explicitly address subtler forms of discrimination against Blacks.

Another concern raised by affirmative race laws is their usefulness. Specifically, how far do they go in addressing the problems of racial discrimination in the justice system? It is true that the law cannot reasonably be relied upon to solve the problem of racial injustice. However, more laws can be enacted and applied to more effectively combat these problems.

A third concern is that affirmative race laws would create greater interracial tension. Accordingly, rather than legitimizing the fact that Blacks are discriminated against, adopting and enacting more affirmative race law will reinforce for Whites that Blacks are always "crying wolf." It might even increase the probability of "White riots." That is, Whites would be more likely to "leave the cities, go to Idaho, or Oregon, vote for [Newt] Gingrich . . . and punish the blacks by closing their day care centers and cutting off their Medicaid"[39]

Assuming that each of the above criticisms is legitimate, the harm that will result from the failure to adopt more affirmative race law far outweighs any harm that will result from adopting more affirmative race law. As the discussion in this chapter makes clear, there are numerous harmful outcomes—political, sociological, physiological and criminological—should we fail to recognize and remedy racial injustices. Law professor Randall Kennedy, who as a general rule rejects color-conscious remedies for race discrimination, acknowledges that more must be done. In his recent book, Kennedy states, "[A]ction will have to be taken to rectify injustices that nourish [Black] feelings of racial aggrievement. To improve the effectiveness of police and prosecutors, high priority should be given to correcting and deterring illegitimate racial practices that diminish the reputation of the law enforcement establishment."[40] The explicit aim of affirmative race law is to rectify injustices. Whatever resentment occurs as a result of enacting more affirmative race laws will be offset by the reduction of other forms of racial tension.

Conclusion

The criminal justice system fails to meet the sixth fairness principle which mandates systematic checks and balances on racial disparities. As a result, it cannot be said to operate in a racially fair manner. An analysis of how existing laws correct for racial bias and how the law redresses racial harms suggest that more legal intervention is necessary—especially when considered in the context of the hostile social climate that Blacks face (e.g., microaggressions and macroaggressions). Affirmative race law is offered as one way to address these problems. This form of law is premised on the notion that racial harms are largely invisible and the failure to recognize them may have a number of negative outcomes, including alienation, violence, community unrest, negative health consequences, and greater adherence to genocide theories.

Afterword

The public representation of Blackness is a distorted one. The media as well as the academic community are largely responsible for this caricature. Blacks are routinely portrayed as marginal, deviant members of society. The exceptions to these portrayals have been insufficient to alter the public's perception. These deeply rooted images are clearly holdovers from slavery. Our public language on race and crime make it difficult to combat these stereotypical images. Specifically, research methods for measuring racial discrimination in the criminal justice system (relying only on the formal stages), a gross underemphasis on White crime, and the failure to require that scientists publicly rebut incorrect statements on race and crime research combine to reinforce skewed, negative impressions of Blacks and Blackness. Some of these concerns may abate as more minorities enter the social science, law, and journalism communities.

The O. J. Simpson case has provided an ongoing national stage to air our racial viewpoints on crime. Among the more salient lessons we can take away from the criminal case is that Blacks and Whites have a perception of the criminal justice system that is tied to their direct and indirect experiences. Other racial groups also have experience-based perceptions of the justice system. Hopefully, more researchers will take on the charge of studying Latinos, Asians, and Native Americans and criminal justice.

The negative opinions that Blacks express about the justice system are partly rooted in the fact that the law continues to provide inadequate redress for racial harms. The law is no racial panacea. However, it could be used more effectively to provide racial redress. Its failure to provide consistent racial remedies may result in greater racial unrest, peaking in violence.

Part of our problem in examining race, crime, and justice is our generally ahistorical analysis of the role the law has played as an agent of repression. The slave codes, Black codes, and Jim Crow attest to this. Blacks will remain steadfast in their distrust of the justice system until the law is used more affirmatively to redress racial wrongs. Addressing racial disparities requires scrutiny of existing law as well as a willingness to ponder what additional laws are necessary. The current criminal justice system offers insufficient checks and balances to correct unexplained racial disparities.

It is odd that in current debates on crime and race we focus little attention on the historical workings of American criminal law. This painful history is roundly dismissed as irrelevant to the operation of the criminal justice system today. However, an analysis of this history indicates that there are aspects of past discrimination that persist today. This history and its vestiges affect current thinking on race, crime, and criminal justice. Any discussion of the legacy of slavery is often characterized as "playing the race card," and consequently not taken seriously. (This sentiment is embodied by statements like, "Slavery ended over a hundred years ago," "I didn't own slaves," or "You weren't a slave.") American racism and criminal justice, which involved the systematic denial of basic human rights to Blacks for more than three hundred years, simply cannot be dismissed as irrelevant to today's criminal justice system.

The contradiction of an ahistorical analysis of race and crime should be readily apparent. For example, two of this country's political founders, Thomas Jefferson and Abraham Lincoln, are regularly lauded for their political savvy and impact upon the principles and future of this nation. At the same time, however, their ideology and actions on slavery are conveniently overlooked. The selective application of historical facts creates a kind of "intellectual chaos" and cannot help us move forward in resolving critical issues regarding the relationship between race, crime, and criminal justice.

Appendix A
Police-Public Contact Survey

FORM **PPCS-1(X)**
(3-28-96)

U.S. DEPARTMENT OF COMMERCE
BUREAU OF THE CENSUS
ACTING AS COLLECTING AGENT FOR THE
BUREAU OF JUSTICE STATISTICS
U.S. DEPARTMENT OF JUSTICE

NOTICE – Your report to the Census Bureau is **confidential** by law (U.S. Code 42, Sections 3789g and 3735). All identifiable information will be used only by persons engaged in and for the purposes of the survey, and may not be disclosed or released to others for any purposes.

We estimate that it will take from 5 to 15 minutes to complete this interview with 10 minutes being the average time. If you have any comments regarding these estimates or any other aspect of this survey, send them to the Associate Director for Management Services, Room 2027, Bureau of the Census, Washington, DC 20233.

POLICE-PUBLIC
CONTACT SURVEY

Sample

Control number

	PSU	Segment	CK	Serial
J				

FIELD REPRESENTATIVE – *Only administer this supplement to persons aged 12+ in 7th Enumeration Households*

A. Field representative code `001`

B. Respondent
Line number `002`
Age `003`
Name

C. Type of PCCS interview `004`
1 ☐ Personal (Self)
2 ☐ Telephone (Self)
3 ☐ Personal (Proxy)   } *Skip to Intro 1*
4 ☐ Telephone (Proxy)
5 ☐ Noninterview – *FILL ITEM D*

D. Reason for noninterview `005`
1 ☐ Refused PCCS
2 ☐ Not available for PCCS
3 ☐ NCVS noninterview
4 ☐ Other – *Specify* 🗷

FIELD REPRESENTATIVE – *Read introduction*

INTRO 1 **Now think back to the last 12 months. I want to ask you a few questions about any contacts you may have had with the police during the last 12 months, that is since _____, 1995. By police I mean, for example, city, county, state police or federal police, housing or transit police, or any other type of law enforcement officer. This does not include private security guards. Also, please do not include contacts with police officers whom you may see on a social basis or who may be related to you or to contacts that occurred outside the U.S.**

E. CONTACT SCREEN QUESTIONS

1a. During the last 12 months, did you have any contact with a police officer? `006`
1 ☐ Yes
2 ☐ No – *END INTERVIEW*
3 ☐ Don't remember – *END INTERVIEW*

1b. Were any of these contacts with a police officer(s) in person, that is face-to-face? `007`
1 ☐ Yes
2 ☐ No – *END INTERVIEW*

1c. How would you best describe the reasons for these in-person contacts with the police over the last 12 months?

As I read some reasons, tell me if any of the contacts occurred once or more than once.

(Mark all that apply)

		ONCE	MORE THAN ONCE	NOT AT ALL
You saw a police officer –				
(a) to report a crime	`008`	1 ☐	2 ☐	3 ☐
(b) to ask for assistance	`009`	1 ☐	2 ☐	3 ☐
(c) to let the police know about a problem in the neighborhood	`010`	1 ☐	2 ☐	3 ☐
You saw a police officer because you were involved in a traffic incident in which –				
(d) you received a traffic or parking violation	`011`	1 ☐	2 ☐	3 ☐
(e) you were involved in a traffic accident	`012`	1 ☐	2 ☐	3 ☐
(f) you were a witness to a traffic accident	`013`	1 ☐	2 ☐	3 ☐
Police asked you questions about –				
(g) a crime in which you had been a victim	`014`	1 ☐	2 ☐	3 ☐
(h) a crime in which you had been a witness	`015`	1 ☐	2 ☐	3 ☐
(i) a crime they thought you were involved in	`016`	1 ☐	2 ☐	3 ☐
(j) what you were doing in the area	`017`	1 ☐	2 ☐	3 ☐
You saw a police officer for any of these other reasons –				
(k) the police had a warrant for your arrest	`018`	1 ☐	2 ☐	3 ☐
(l) casual encounters with police	`019`	1 ☐	2 ☐	3 ☐
(m) community meetings with police	`020`	1 ☐	2 ☐	3 ☐
(n) some other reason – *Please specify* 🗷	`021`	1 ☐	2 ☐	3 ☐
(o) no specific reason	`022`	1 ☐	2 ☐	3 ☐

CHECK ITEM A — FIELD REPRESENTATIVE – *Is box 1 or 2 marked in category (i) in item 1c?*
☐ Yes – Ask item 1d
☐ No – Skip to CHECK ITEM B

E. CONTACT SCREEN QUESTIONS – Continued

1d. You reported that the police asked you questions about a crime they thought you were involved in. Did they frisk you or pat you down?

`023` 1 ☐ Yes
2 ☐ No

CHECK ITEM B FIELD REPRESENTATIVE – *Is box 1 or 2 marked in category (j) in item 1c?*

☐ Yes – *Ask item 1e*
☐ No – *Skip to item 1f*

1e. You reported that the police asked you questions about what you were doing in the area. Did they frisk you or pat you down?

`024` 1 ☐ Yes
2 ☐ No

1f. During any of these in-person contacts, did a police officer handcuff you?

`025` 1 ☐ Yes
2 ☐ No –*Skip to item 2a*

1g. For which of the contacts you reported did a police officer handcuff you?

(Mark all that apply)

FIELD REPRESENTATIVE – *Read only categories marked 1 or 2 in item 1c.*

`026` 1 ☐ To report a crime
`027` 2 ☐ To ask for assistance
`028` 3 ☐ To let the police know about a problem in the neighborhood
`029` 4 ☐ Other reason – *Specify* ⟋

`030` 5 ☐ Received a traffic or parking violation
`031` 6 ☐ Involved in a traffic accident
`032` 7 ☐ Was a witness to a traffic accident
`033` 8 ☐ A crime in which respondent had been a victim
`034` 9 ☐ A crime in which respondent had been a witness
`035` 10 ☐ A crime they thought respondent was involved in
`036` 11 ☐ What respondent was doing in the area
`037` 12 ☐ Police had a warrant for respondent's arrest
`038` 13 ☐ Casual encounters with police
`039` 14 ☐ Community meetings with police
`040` 15 ☐ Some other reason
`041` 16 ☐ No specific reason

2a. In any of these contacts with a police officer, did any officer warn you that he or she would use physical force such as: a nightstick or baton, a firearm, a chemical spray, a flashlight, a police dog, or any device other than handcuffs to restrain you or to take you into custody?

`042` 1 ☐ Yes
2 ☐ No

2b. In any of these contacts with a police officer, did any officer actually use any form of physical force against you including using any of the items just mentioned?

`043` 1 ☐ Yes
2 ☐ No

CHECK ITEM C FIELD REPRESENTATIVE – *Is box 1 (Yes) marked in item 2a or 2b?*

☐ Yes – *Ask item 3*
☐ No – *END INTERVIEW*

3. How many times did the police actually use or threaten to use force against you during the last 12 months?

`044` 000 ☐ None
001 ☐ Once ⎱ *Skip to item 4a*

More than once – **How many times?** ⟋

☐☐☐ *Read INTRO 2*

INTRO 2 **You say that police used force against you more than once during the last 12 months. Please limit your answers in the following questions to any contact in which you received an injury or which you consider to have been the most serious.**

4a. Did you know that the person was a police officer at the time of this incident?

`045` 1 ☐ Yes – *Ask item 4b*
2 ☐ No – *Skip to item 4c*

4b. How did you know that the person was a police officer at the time of the incident?

(Mark all that apply)

`046` 1 ☐ Wore a uniform
`047` 2 ☐ Showed respondent a badge or identification ⎱ *Skip to item 5*
`048` 3 ☐ Arrived in a police vehicle
`049` 4 ☐ Told respondent
`050` 5 ☐ Other – *Specify* ⟋

Skip to item 5
`051` 6 ☐ Don't know – *Skip to item 5*

FORM PPCS-1(X) (3-28-96)

E. CONTACT SCREEN QUESTIONS – Continued

4c. Why didn't you know that the person was a police officer at the time of the incident?
(Mark all that apply)

052	₁☐ Did not wear a uniform
053	₂☐ Did not show respondent a badge or identification
054	₃☐ Did not arrive in a police vehicle
055	₄☐ Never told respondent
056	₅☐ Other – *Specify* ↗

_____

_____

| 057 | ₆☐ Don't know |

5. Was the police officer in this incident a *(read answer categories)* –

| 058 | ₁☐ member of a city or county police department, sheriff's department, or state police department? |

₂☐ Federal law enforcement officer such as the FBI, the DEA, Immigration/INS, Customs, military police, or a Park Ranger?

₃☐ an officer from some other police agency such as housing police, transit police, or campus police?

₄☐ Don't know what kind of police agency

6a. During the incident, did the police officer, do any of the following *(read answer categories)*?
(Mark all that apply)

059	₁☐ Hit or punch you
060	₂☐ Kick you
061	₃☐ Hold you by the arm
062	₄☐ Push you
063	₅☐ Use a chokehold
064	₆☐ Use some other form of force – *Please specify* ↗

| 065 | ₇☐ None |

6b. During the incident, did a police officer, warn use or actually use any of the following weapons *(read answer categories)*?
(Mark all that apply)

066	₁☐ Nightstick or baton
067	₂☐ Flashlight
068	₃☐ Police dog
069	₄☐ Chemical or pepper spray
070	₅☐ Firearm
071	₆☐ Something else – *Please specify* ↗

_____

| 072 | ₇☐ No weapon was used – *Skip to item 7* |

CHECK ITEM D — FIELD REPRESENTATIVE – *ASK the following for each weapon that is marked in item 6b.*

How was the weapon used by the police officer. Was it used only to threaten or restrain you or was it actually used on you?

		THREATEN RESPONDENT ONLY	*RESTRAINED RESPONDENT ONLY*	*ACTUALLY USED IT ON RESPONDENT*
a. Nightstick or baton	073	₁☐	₂☐	₃☐
b. Flashlight.	074	₁☐	₂☐	₃☐
c. Police dog	075	₁☐	₂☐	₃☐
d. Chemical or pepper spray.	076	₁☐	₂☐	₃☐
e. Firearm (such as a handgun, rifle or shotgun)	077	₁☐	₂☐	₃☐
f. Other weapon	078	₁☐	₂☐	₃☐

CHECK ITEM E — FIELD REPRESENTATIVE – *Is box 2 or 3 marked for category e (firearm) in CHECK ITEM D?*

☐ Yes – *Ask item 6c*
☐ No – *Skip to item 7*

6c. You said that a firearm was actually used against you. Did the police officer shoot the firearm during this contact?

| 079 | ₁☐ Yes |
| | ₂☐ No – *Skip to item 7* |

6d. Were you shot by the officer during this contact?

| 080 | ₁☐ Yes |
| | ₂☐ No |

E. CONTACT SCREEN QUESTIONS – Continued

7. Did you do any of the following during the incident *(read answer categories)*?

(Mark all that apply)

081	1 ☐ **Threaten the officer**
082	2 ☐ **Assault or attack the officer**
083	3 ☐ **Argue with the officer**
084	4 ☐ **Interfere with the officer while he/she was interviewing, investigating, or arresting someone else**
085	5 ☐ **Possess a weapon such as a firearm, knife, or club**
086	6 ☐ **Block an officer's exit or entrance or interfere with his or her movement in any way**
087	7 ☐ **Attempt to escape, hide, or evade the officer such as by fleeing or being involved in a high-speed chase**
088	8 ☐ **Resist being handcuffed**
089	9 ☐ **Resist being placed in a police vehicle**
090	10 ☐ **Ask bystanders to become involved in the incident**
091	11 ☐ **Try to protect someone else from an officer**
092	12 ☐ **Do anything else that might have provoked the officer to use or warn you about the use of force –** *Please specify* ⬈

_____

_____

| 093 | 13 ☐ **Did nothing** |

8a. Had you been drinking or using drugs before this incident?

| 094 | 1 ☐ Yes |
| | 2 ☐ No – *Skip to item 9* |

8b. Which was it, drinking, using drugs, or both?

095	1 ☐ Drinking only
	2 ☐ Drugs only
	3 ☐ Both drinking and using drugs

9. Was it daytime or nighttime when the incident occurred?

| 096 | 1 ☐ Daytime |
| | 2 ☐ Nighttime |

10. How many officers were present during this incident?

| 097 | ☐☐☐ Number of officers present |
| | 0 ☐ Don't know number of officers |

F. CHARACTERISTICS OF OFFICER(S)

CHECK ITEM F FIELD REPRESENTATIVE – *Is the number in item 10 more than 1?*

☐ Yes – *Skip to item 11c*
☐ No – *Ask item 11a*

11a. Tell me about the officer with whom you had the contact.

Was the officer White, Black, or some other race?

098	1 ☐ White
	2 ☐ Black
	3 ☐ Other – *Specify* ⬈

_____

4 ☐ Don't know

11b. Was the officer male or female?

| 099 | 1 ☐ Male ⎫ *Skip to item 12a* |
| | 2 ☐ Female ⎭ |

11c. Tell me about the officers with whom you had the contact.

Were the officers White, Black, or some other race?

100	1 ☐ All white
	2 ☐ All black
	3 ☐ All of some other race
	4 ☐ Mostly white
	5 ☐ Mostly black
	6 ☐ Mostly some other race
	7 ☐ Equally mixed
	8 ☐ Don't know race of any/some

11d. Were the officers male or female?

101	1 ☐ All male
	2 ☐ All female
	3 ☐ Mostly male
	4 ☐ Mostly female
	5 ☐ Equally mixed
	6 ☐ Don't know

FORM PPCS-1(X) (3-28-96)

G. INJURIES

12a. Were you injured as a result of this incident?

`102` ₁☐ Yes
       ₂☐ No – *Skip to item 12d*

12b. What type of injury was it *(read answer categories)***?**

(Mark all that apply)

`103` ₁☐ **Gunshot wound**
`104` ₂☐ **Broken bones or teeth knocked out**
`105` ₃☐ **Internal injuries**
`106` ₄☐ **Bruises, black eye, cuts, scratches, swelling or chipped teeth**
`107` ₅☐ **Other –** *Please specify* ↗

12c. What type of care did you receive for your injury?

`108` ₁☐ No care received
       ₂☐ Respondent treated self (e.g. bandage)
       ₃☐ Emergency services only
       ₄☐ Hospitalization
       ₅☐ Other – *Specify* ↗

12d. To your knowledge, was any police officer injured in this incident?

`109` ₁☐ Yes – *Ask item 12e*
       ₂☐ No   } *Skip to item 13*
       ₃☐ Don't know

12e. What type of injury was it *(read answer categories)***?**

(Mark all that apply)

`110` ₁☐ **Gunshot wound**
`111` ₂☐ **Broken bones or teeth knocked out**
`112` ₃☐ **Internal injuries**
`113` ₄☐ **Bruises, black eye, cuts, scratches, swelling or chipped teeth**
`114` ₅☐ **Other –** *Please specify* ↗

`115` ₆☐ Don't know

12f. What type of care did the officer receive for his/her injury?

`116` ₁☐ No care received
       ₂☐ Emergency services only
       ₃☐ Hospitalization
       ₄☐ Other – *Specify* ↗

       ₅☐ Don't know

H. OFFENSES

13. As a result of this contact with the police, were you charged with any of the following crimes *(read answer categories)***?**

(Mark all that apply)

`117` ₁☐ **Resisting arrest**
`118` ₂☐ **Assaulting an officer**
`119` ₃☐ **Unlawful flight from the officer**
`120` ₄☐ **Obstructing justice**
`121` ₅☐ **Other –** *Please specify* ↗

`122` ₆☐ Don't know
`123` ₇☐ No charges

14. Following this contact with the police, were you charged with any (other) crimes such as *(read answer categories)* **–**

(Mark all that apply)

`124` ₁☐ **Murder?**
`125` ₂☐ **Rape?**
`126` ₃☐ **Sexual assault?**
`127` ₄☐ **Robbery?**
`128` ₅☐ **Assault?**
`129` ₆☐ **Burglary?**
`130` ₇☐ **Theft or larceny?**
`131` ₈☐ **Motor vehicle theft?**
`132` ₉☐ **Trafficking in drugs?**
`133` ₁₀☐ **Possession of drugs?**
`134` ₁₁☐ **Possession of firearm or concealed weapon?**
`135` ₁₂☐ **Gambling?**
`136` ₁₃☐ **Some other offense?–** *Please specify* ↗

`137` ₁₄☐ No charges

I. CITIZEN ACTIONS TAKEN

15. Looking back at this incident, do you feel the police behaved properly or improperly?

|138| 1☐Properly – *END INTERVIEW*
2☐Improperly
3☐Don't know

16a. Did you take any formal or informal actions, such as filing a complaint or lawsuit, claiming that unnecessary or excessive force was used against you by police in this incident?

|139| 1☐Yes
2☐No – *END INTERVIEW*

16b. Have your actions only been informal, such as a telephone call to the police department to complain about the incident, with no official written complaint or lawsuit filed with any public agency?

|140| 1☐Yes – *END INTERVIEW*
2☐No

16c. With whom have you actually filed formal written complaints or initiated formal actions *(read answer categories)*?

(Mark all that apply)

|141| 1☐Civilian Complaint Review Board
|142| 2☐Law enforcement agency employing the officer
|143| 3☐Local prosecutor's office
|144| 4☐The FBI or the U.S. Attorney's office
|145| 5☐Filed a lawsuit against the law enforcement agency or the local government
|146| 6☐Filed a lawsuit against the officer involved in the contact

17. In your own words, how would you describe the incident and how it happened. What started the incident? What happened next?

_____

_____

_____

_____

_____

_____

_____

_____

_____

_____

_____

_____

_____

_____

_____

_____

_____

_____

_____

_____

_____

_____

_____

_____

_____

FORM PPCS-1(X) (3-28-96)

Source: U.S. Department of Justice, 1996.

Appendix B

Racial Hoaxes: Case Summaries (1987–1996)
*(Alphabetical Listing)**

Bradley Adams

In February 1995, Molly Sullivan was killed. Her boyfriend, Bradley Adams, blamed the murder on an unknown group of Black men. Adams was arrested five months following the murder. He later admitted that Sullivan, who suffered from a degenerative muscle disease, died after he sat on her chest. Bradley was convicted of murder and sentenced to seventy years in prison.

Jesse Anderson

In April 1992, Jesse Anderson, a White man, told the police that he and his wife had been attacked in the parking lot of a suburban Milwaukee restaurant. Anderson said two Black men stabbed him and his wife. His wife was stabbed twenty-one times and died following the attack. Anderson received superficial wounds. Following a week-long search for the fictional criminals, Anderson was arrested and charged with murder. He had devised the hoax to cash in on his wife's $250,000 insurance policy. Anderson was convicted of first-degree murder. In 1994, he was murdered in prison along with serial murderer Jeffrey Dahmer, causing some to speculate that he was killed because of the racial upheaval his hoax caused.

Tisha Anderson and William Lee

In December 1995, Tisha Anderson, a Black woman, and her White boyfriend, William Lee, told police they had received death threats. They also said that their apartment had been defaced with racial slurs. It was subsequently determined that the pair had staged the hate crimes to get out of their apartment lease.

* For a detailed discussion of racial hoaxes, see chapter 5, "The Racial Hoax as Crime."

Samuel Asbell

In January 1990, Samuel Asbell, a White New Jersey prosecutor, told police that he had been chased by two Black men. Asbell, who said that the chase had reached speeds up to one hundred miles per hour, said that the assailants had fired at his car with an automatic rifle. After a police investigation established that the attack could not have happened the way Asbell described it, Asbell admitted that he had shot at his own car. Following this, Asbell said he had been under stress and checked himself into a psychiatric clinic.

Anthony Avent

In 1995, Anthony Avent, then a player for the Orlando Magic basketball team, told police that he had been stabbed by three White men on an Orlando street. Avent is Black. His injuries required thirty stitches. Avent later recanted his tale, telling police he made up the story to protect the identity of a friend, with whom he had had a fight. The Orlando Magic fined Avent three thousand dollars.

Adam Baisley

In 1996, Adam Baisley and three other White teenagers decided to skip school and have a party. At the party, a gun was passed around. It accidentally discharged, and a bullet hit one of the boys in the cheek. After the shooting, the boys cleaned up the area with bleach. They told police that a Black man, wearing a dark sweatshirt and carrying a semiautomatic handgun, had committed the crime. The boys later admitted that they had lied.

Daniel Bolduc

In April 1995, Daniel Bolduc, a White police officer from Hartford, Connecticut, filed a police report in which he stated that three Black men had smashed the windshield of a vehicle. Bolduc's report stated that the vehicle was a police car that was permanently out of service. When it was determined that the police report was false, Bolduc was suspended for one day and placed on sick leave, pending psychological exams.

Tawana Brawley

In 1987, Tawana Brawley told police that she had been abducted and raped by six White men. Brawley, a Black 15-year-old, said that the men were police officers. According to Brawley, she was smeared with feces, placed in a plastic bag, and left in a gutter. No criminal indictments were issued in the case, which is widely believed to have been a hoax.

Dwayne Byrdsong

In 1995, Dwayne Byrdsong of Coraville, Iowa, fabricated a hate crime. Byrdsong, who is Black, painted his Mercedes Benz with racial slurs, including "Go Back to Africa" and "KKK." The Black community mobilized to collect funds for Byrdsong, who is a minister. Byrdsong was convicted of filing a false police report.

Toby Campbell

In 1995, Toby Campbell, a White 7-11 convenience store clerk in South Carolina, told police that he had been robbed. Campbell said that two Black men had robbed him at knife point. According to Campbell, the robbers took a dozen cartons of cigarettes. He provided detailed descriptions of the two Black men, including that one man wore earrings showing a marijuana leaf and a bull. Campbell later admitted that he had stolen the cigarettes.

Donald Cherry

In 1996, Donald Cherry told police that following a traffic dispute Black youths shot and killed his 2-year-old son, who was seated in the back of his car. Cherry, who is White, later admitted that he had gone to purchase drugs and gotten into a dispute with the dealer over payment. When Cherry attempted to leave without paying for the drugs, the dealer shot into his vehicle, killing the 2-year-old.

Garrick Clemente

In 1996, Garrick Clemente, a Black man, gave a neighbor four hundred dollars to paint a racial slur on his apartment door. Clemente's plan was to fake a hate crime. The motive for the hoax is unclear.

Sabrina Collins

In 1990, Sabrina Collins, a Black freshman at Emory University, claimed she was a victim of racial harassment. Collins told police that she had received a death threat and that someone had scrawled racial slurs on her dormitory walls. Several weeks later, Collins admitted she had written the death threat and scrawled the slurs. Her claims of racial harassment triggered protests by students and civil rights leaders on campus and in Atlanta.

Henry Crane

On New Year's Eve in 1995, Henry Crane notified police that he had been carjacked at gunpoint. He said the assailants were three Black men. After hearing a police broadcast about the incident, another police officer spotted the car and pulled it over. The woman driving the car told police that she and Crane had just had sex at a hotel. Crane had fabricated the hoax to avoid having his wife learn that he had been with another woman.

Tanya Dacri

In January 1989, Tanya Dacri, a White woman in Philadelphia, reported to the police that her 2-month-old son had been snatched from her in the parking lot of a shopping mall. According to her report, two Black men had kidnapped the infant. Police later found out that she and her husband had fabricated the story after murdering and dismembering the child and throwing his remains in a river.

Thomas Drogan and Louis Papaleo

In March 1993, two Yonkers, New York, police officers, Thomas Drogan and Louis Papaleo, got into a physical fight in the police station. The officers were fighting over who would file a report on a car fire that each had responded to earlier in the day. The fight left each officer with extensive cuts and bruises. One officer had to go to the hospital. In order to cover up their altercation, the pair invented a story that a Black man in a blue jacket and sneakers had beaten them. They said their attacker had evaded capture. The hoax was finally revealed by a fellow police officer who witnessed the fight in the police station. Officer Drogan was fired from the police force and Officer Papaleo was suspended for sixty days and put on probation for a year.

Dawn Frakes

In December 1995, Dawn Frakes, a Delaware state trooper, told police that she had been shot by a Black teenager. In fact, Frakes, who is White, had accidentally shot herself in the arm. Officer Frakes gave police a detailed description of her attacker, saying he went by the name "Willy." Frakes was suspended after it was determined that her story was a hoax.

Tina Gateley and William Karaffa

In 1993, Tina Gateley and her boyfriend, William Karaffa, both White, claimed that several Black youths had beaten up Gateley and taken her purse. Gateley was hospitalized for three days with broken ribs and other injuries. The pair told their story on local television and urged neighbors to call on police to make arrests in the case. Police investigators determined that the story was fabricated to cover up an incident of domestic violence. Karaffa had assaulted Gateley.

Matthew Gayle

In 1995, Matthew Gayle told police that his wife had been killed by a Black man wearing baggy pants and a red-and-white sweatshirt. According to Gayle, his wife was shot as the couple drove through an Orlando neighborhood. It was later determined that Gayle had paid a hit man ten thousand dollars to kill his wife. He concocted the hoax to collect on his wife's $150,000 insurance policy. Gayle was sentenced to life in prison.

Tonya Gibson, Tynnush Bush, Clayton Henley, William Gibson, and Gary Snyder

In August 1996, five White friends agreed on a racial hoax scheme. They decided to blame an accidental shooting on a fictional Black man. The quintet told police that a Black man had broken into their apartment and fired, hitting one of the five. Based on a description of the attacker, the police questioned and arrested John Harris, a Black man. Harris was taken to the scene of the shooting, and he was positively identified as the armed assailant. Police later informed the group that their friend, who had been hospitalized after the shooting, would survive and that Harris had an airtight alibi. At that point, the group admitted to making up the story.

Kendra Gillis

In November 1994, Kendra Gillis, a White female student at the State University of New York at Albany, reported that she had been attacked by a Black man wielding a knife. After police questioned her about inconsistencies in her story, she admitted that she had fabricated it. The real criminal was her father, who had physically abused her. No false report charges were filed against Gillis.

Joshua Green, Daniel Pratt, and Michael Crowley

In December 1994, three White men reported that they had been robbed of $3500 at the car wash where they worked. They told police that the assailant was a gun-wielding Black man. Less than a week later, the police discovered that the story was part of a plan the three men had devised to rob the car wash. All three men were arrested and charged with the theft. Green and Crowley were also charged with filing a false report.

Persey Harris, Ann Vigil, and Caryn Harris

In 1996, Persey Harris, a Black man, was sentenced to fifteen days in jail for filing a false police report. Harris and his cohorts told police that a restaurant owner had threatened them with a four-foot stick and shouted racial epithets at them. Harris later admitted that the fabricated incident was designed to be the basis of a civil lawsuit. Harris's partners were sentenced to community service.

Robert Harris

In January 1996, Robert Harris, a White man, claimed he and his fiancée had been shot and robbed on a quiet Baltimore street. Harris said the assailant was an armed Black man, wearing a camouflage jacket and black and white pants. Harris's fiancée died from her gunshot wounds. Within three days, Harris confessed that he had hired a hit man to rob the pair and kill his fiancée. Harris was motivated by the mistaken belief that he was the beneficiary of his fiancée's $250,000 insurance policy.

Jeffrey Hebert

In August 1995, Jeffrey Hebert told police that three Black men broke into his home, assaulted everyone there, then set the house on fire. Hebert, who is White, was the only survivor. He told police that following the attack the Black assailants ran into the woods nearby. Police became suspicious when they discovered contradictions in Hebert's story. Police had also observed that the wounds on Hebert's wrists, which he had said were the result of one of the assailants slashing him with a shovel, were consistent with a suicide attempt.

Brenda Hueneke

In 1995, Brenda Hueneke told police that a Black man had robbed her at knife point. She later admitted to making up the story and was charged with filing a false report.

Sonia James

In April 1996, Sonia James told police that her home had been vandalized and defaced with racial slurs. James, who is Black, claimed that furniture, clothing, and personal belongings had been destroyed by intruders. Community residents raised more than five thousand dollars for James and her infant son. She later told police that she had fabricated the scheme to defraud her insurance company.

Kathleen Johnston

In September 1994, Kathleen Johnston, a White female, reported that she had been assaulted and robbed. The Maryland woman said that she had been attacked by two Black males at the high school where she was a physical education instructor. After two months, she admitted that her wounds were self-inflicted, and she recanted her story. Johnston has since resigned from her teaching position.

Miriam Kashani

In 1990, Miriam Kashani, a student at George Washington University, reported that another White female student had been raped by two young Black men with "particularly bad body odor." The day following press reports about the crime, Kashani admitted she had made up the story. She said her goal was to "highlight the problems of safety for women."

Mark Lambirth

In 1995, Mark Lambirth, a White man, claimed that an American Indian man had forced him at gunpoint to drive from North Carolina to Colorado. Lambirth reported that in Colorado the car got stuck in the snow in a remote area. He told police that his kidnapper burned the car and made him walk up a mountain. After investigating the story, police concluded it was a hoax. Among other things, police observed a single set of foot tracks in the snow where Lambirth was allegedly taken.

Mark Lewis

In August 1993, Mark Lewis, a White, thirteen-year veteran of the Lake Worth, Florida, police department, filed a report stating that he had been hit on the head with a wrench. Lewis said his attacker was a Black man. After investigating the case, police officials concluded that the incident was a hoax. The hoax was staged to garner sympathy for a demotion Lewis had recently received and to support a claim that he experienced on-duty injuries.

Josephine Lupus

In November 1994, Josephine Lupus, a 21-year-old student at the State College at Old Westbury in New York, told police she had been robbed by a Black man. Lupus said the assault occurred one evening after she left class. She went on television and showed the cuts and marks she received from the attack. Lupus later admitted she had not been attacked by anyone.

Lucille Magrone

In 1990, White residents in Islip Terrace, New York, began receiving death threats. The letters, allegedly written by a Black man, threatened them with rape, robbery, and murder. One letter warned, "You people are all dead in 24 hours." White residents became fearful, some purchased dogs, some slept with bats at their bedside, and some believed that they saw intruders in their yard. Five months after the first menacing letter appeared, Lucille Magrone, a 48-year-old White woman, admitted to writing the letters. She said the incident was the result of stress she suffered from an assault, months earlier, by a Black man.

Ramon Martinez, Luis Mendez, and Joseph Degros

In January 1996, Ramon Martinez, an 18-year-old from Manchester, New Hampshire, told authorities that he had been shot in the foot. He said that a Black man shot him after a traffic dispute on a highway. Martinez's story was corroborated by Luis Mendez and Joseph Degros, who said they were with Martinez and witnessed the assault. Martinez later admitted he had accidentally shot himself.

Janet Maxwell

In 1993, Janet Maxwell, a 26-year-old White woman, claimed she had been kidnapped at gunpoint from a shopping mall by three Black men. Maxwell told police that she had been driven around in her car for ten hours, forced to take drugs, then raped. Police later determined that Maxwell made up the story so that her parents would not be angry at her for staying out all night.

Cecil McCool

In October 1995, Cecil McCool, a White man, accused two Black police officers of stranding his friend, Richard Will, another White male. McCool said that police had stranded the friend late at night in a high-crime Black neighborhood near Chicago, where the friend was later beaten and burned to death. In fact, McCool and his friend were driving through the neighborhood to purchase drugs, when police pulled them over for a traffic violation. The police took McCool into custody because he had an outstanding warrant. They directed Will to a pay phone three blocks away. Instead Will walked to a crackhouse where he was later killed.

Milton Metcalfe

In April 1993, Milton Metcalfe, a Black man from Cincinnati, reported that he and his girlfriend had been abducted and held at knife point. Metcalfe said that the crime occurred after he had offered a ride to two Black men. Metcalfe was charged with filing a false report after 911 records revealed that he was not at the location that was indicated in his police report. Metcalfe was convicted and spent one night in jail. His thirty-day jail sentence was suspended.

Richard Milam

In January 1994, Richard Milam told police that his wife had been murdered and that he had been stabbed. According to Milam, a masked Black man had attacked and robbed the pair outside of a restaurant. The police became suspicious of Milam's story when they discovered that his wife's death guaranteed he would receive a large insurance settlement. Nearly two years after the murder, police located a coworker of Milam's who said Milam had offered him money to kill his wife. Police took Milam into custody, whereupon he confessed to the murder.

Phillip Miller

In February 1994, Phillip Miller, a White convenience-store clerk, reported that he had been robbed. The Arkansas man said that two Black men had come into the store and robbed him at gunpoint of an unspecified amount of cash. A week later, Miller was charged with stealing the money and filing a false report.

Richard Nicolas

In July 1996, Richard Nicolas, a Black man, told police that while driving on a rural Maryland road with his 2-year-old daughter he was rammed from behind by car driven by a White man with long hair. The driver then pulled alongside Nicholas's car and fired a shot that killed his daughter. Nicolas has been charged and convicted of first degree murder. Months earlier he had taken out a fifteen-thousand-dollar insurance policy in her name, listing himself as the sole beneficiary.

Edward O'Brien

In July 1995, Edward O'Brien, a White teenager, reported that he had been robbed and knifed by two men. He said one of his attackers was Black and the other was Hispanic. A police investigation revealed that O'Brien had sustained the cuts while murdering his neighbor, whom he stabbed more than sixty times.

Brian Patterson

In March 1996, a White man told police that he had seen a Black man throw a White person over a bridge. Police searched the area and the river but did not locate a body. Patterson eventually told police that he had fabricated the story.

Dennis Pittman

In April 1996, Dennis Pittman, a White man, told police he had been carjacked. He said a Black assailant forced him at knife point to drive from Philadelphia to Atlantic City. Next, the assailant took off with his car. Shortly after the incident, Pittman admitted that he made up the story to avoid making any more car payments.

Maryrose Posner

In February 1994, Maryrose Posner, a White woman, alleged that she and her 2-year-old daughter had been approached at an ATM machine by a Black man with a gun. Posner told police that the armed attacker forced her to withdraw two hundred dollars from her account. Posner later admitted that she had made up the story to get attention from her busy husband.

Christopher Prince (Victim's name)

In 1994, a 12-year-old White girl from Virginia told police that a Black man had broken into her family's home and attempted to rape her. The girl identified her attacker as Christopher Prince, a 21-year-old Black man. Prince, who was arrested, charged, and convicted of burglary and attempted rape, was sentenced to a twelve-year prison term. He was released after fifteen months when the girl recanted her testimony. In 1995, Prince was pardoned by the governor, and in 1997 the Virginia Senate voted unanimously to award him $45,000 for wrongful imprisonment.

Reggie Rivera (Victim's name)

In 1993, four New York livery-van drivers and a mechanic, all of whom were Black, accused a White police officer, Reggie Rivera, of raping them. The two-year police investigation determined that the men, some of whom worked in the unlicensed van trade business, made false allegations. The allegations were part of a plot to get Officer Rivera fired because he had been cracking down on unlicensed van drivers.

Darlie Routier

In 1996, Darlie Routier, a White mother of three, told police that a White man, wearing dark clothes and a baseball cap, had broken into her home. She said the intruder stabbed two of her sons while they were sleeping. Routier had superficial stab wounds. In February 1997, Routier was convicted of capital murder for the death of the youngest child.

Judy Russell

In 1988, Judy Russell, a White federal prosecutor in New Jersey, reported that she had received death threats from two alleged terrorists facing extradition back to India. She later admitted she had written and mailed the letters to herself. This was done as part of a scheme to further incriminate the defendants at their extradition hearing. In 1989, Russell was acquitted of obstruction of justice charges, based on her insanity plea. The court recommended psychological counseling for Russell, since tests indicated she had multiple personality disorder.

Zhakeh Sarabakhsh

In October 1995, Zhakeh Sarabakhsh, an Iranian immigrant, claimed she had been bound, slashed, and left to die in a fire in her family's restaurant in Fargo, North Dakota. The police determined that Sarabakhsh had staged the hate crime herself. She had carved a swastika into her abdomen, tied herself up, and set fire to the restaurant.

Michael Shaw

In January 1995, Michael Shaw, a 21-year-old White man from Maple Shade, New Jersey, reported that a White toddler had been kidnapped by a Black man. According to Shaw, the girl's mouth had been bound with duct tape. The police quickly mounted an extensive air and land search for the child. One day later, Shaw admitted the story was false. Police believe he came up with the tale to get the afternoon off from work. Shaw was charged with making a false report to the police.

Susan Smith

In 1994, Susan Smith, a White women, told police that a young Black man carjacked her and drove off with her two young sons. Nine days after massive federal and state searches had been launched, Smith confessed to drowning her two boys in a South Carolina lake. Smith was depressed over a recent break-up with a boyfriend who did not want children.

Mounir Soliman

In November 1994, Mounir Soliman, a convenience store manager, claimed that two Black men robbed him of ten thousand dollars as he was carrying it to the bank. The description Soliman gave police was used to draw a composite sketch. Soliman ultimately confessed that he had taken the money.

Charles Stuart

In 1989, Charles Stuart told police that he and his wife had been shot by a Black jogger. Stuart and his pregnant wife, who lived in Boston, were on their way home after a birthing class. Stuart's wife and the unborn child died as a result of the gunshot wounds. Stuart identified a Black man from a police line-up as the criminal. The Boston case made national and international headlines. Police ransacked Mission Hill, a predominantly Black neighborhood, in search of the murderer. Stuart's brother, Matthew, informed police that Charles had concocted the hoax as a murderous scheme to collect his wife's insurance money. When Stuart learned the police were going to question him as a murder suspect, he committed suicide.

Lisa Tanczos

In September 1995, Lisa Tanczos told police she had been assaulted. Tanczos, a 30-year-old White woman, described her attacker as a muscular Black man in his late thirties who wielded a gun and a knife. The Allentown, Pennsylvania, woman claimed the assailant scratched her with the knife and used it to play a game of tick-tack-toe on her arm. Two months later, Tanczos said the same man attacked her at her home and again cut her with a knife. DNA evidence was used to show that Tanczos had fabricated the hoax (DNA was taken from the envelope of a card allegedly sent by the attacker to Tanczos's boss). In December 1996, Tanczos was sentenced to 350 hours of community service at a local Black church.

Paul Veach

In May 1995, Paul Veach, a 47-year-old White man from Des Moines, claimed that he had been robbed at gunpoint by a Black man with "light-colored hair in six-to-eight inch braids, a deformed pupil in one eye, acne scars on his cheeks, and one or two missing front teeth." Veach said he had been forced to drive around for six hours before being put out of his car. A police investigation revealed that Veach had made several ATM transactions at a local horse track. Veach subsequently admitted that he came up with the story to hide gambling loses, totaling $390.

Neva Veitch and David Craig

In 1989, Billy Joe Veitch of Georgia was brutally murdered. His wife, Neva, told police that she and her husband had been kidnapped by two Black men. According to Neva, the men killed her husband and tried to rape her. It was believed that the Veitches had been targeted by Blacks because they were KKK members. Neva Veitch detailed her attack at numerous Klan rallies. Two years later, David Craig, Veitch's lover (also a Klansman), confessed to police that he and Neva had killed her husband. The lovers had hoped to cash in on Billy Joe Veitch's insurance. Both were tried for murder. Craig, who was found guilty, committed suicide in prison.

Candice Wagner

In November of 1995, Candice Wagner, a 24-year-old White woman, reported that she had been kidnapped at gunpoint from a shopping mall parking lot. The Seattle woman described her attacker as a "short, slender Black man with a bad complexion" and claimed that he forced her to drive to an isolated area where he raped her. Wagner told police she escaped by kicking her attacker in the groin and driving to a friend's home. After police told her that parts of her story were inconsistent, Wagner admitted that her story was false.

Lisa Wight

In January 1996, Lisa Wight told police that a Black man attempted to rape her. Wight, a White woman employed as a courthouse deputy in New Jersey, claimed that she had been assaulted in a hallway of the federal courthouse where she worked. After intense questioning by the FBI, Wight admitted she made up the story. Wight was forced to resign her post.

Michele Yentes

In 1990, Michele Yentes claimed that she had been raped on the campus of Ohio State University. Yentes, who is White, told police that her assailant was Black. Police spent hours investigating her claim. Yentes later admitted that she had fabricated the rape. Yentes was charged with filing a false police report and fined fifteen thousand dollars.

Solomon Youshei

In 1995, Solomon Youshei, a jewelry-store owner, told police that he was robbed of five hundred thousand dollars in jewelry and twenty-seven hundred dollars cash. Youshei said the robbers were two well-dressed Black men wearing white gloves. Police determined that Youshei and his brother made up the story as part of an insurance scam.

Unnamed Racial Hoax Cases (Alphabetical by State)

Unnamed—Florida (1)

In 1994, a White 17-year-old high school student claimed that a young White male with long brown hair and wearing a "Metallica" T-shirt kidnapped her at gunpoint. She was abducted outside of a library at the University of South Florida and taken to a remote area where she was raped. Two days later, the young woman recanted her story. At the time of the alleged offense, the girl was at the house of her boyfriend, whom her parents had forbidden her to see.

Unnamed—Florida (2)

In July 1996, a White Florida woman claimed she had been raped and robbed by two Black men. According to her story, the men followed her into her home and slashed her with a steak knife. It was later determined that the story was a hoax.

Unnamed—Louisiana

A White woman in Baton Rouge told police that she had been sexually assaulted by a Black man. She said the man had a tattoo of a serpent on his arm. The alleged crime occurred in 1994. Police released a composite sketch of the "serpent man." As many as twenty-eight other women reported that they had seen or had been attacked by the pictured assailant. At the time the woman admitted to making up the story, police had targeted a suspect, whom they had planned to arrest.

Unnamed—Maine

In October 1994, a 7-year-old White girl told police she had been assaulted by a Black man. The attack occurred while she walked across a parking lot with two friends. Her friends corroborated her story. After initiating a statewide search for the assailant, the police discovered that the girls had made up the crime.

Unnamed—New Jersey

In March 1994, a young White woman reported that she and her 71-year-old mother-in-law had been attacked by a Black male intruder. The police investigation revealed that the woman had been in a fight with another woman and had come up with the story as a cover-up.

Unnamed—Virginia

In May 1995, a 39-year-old White man claimed that two Black men had cut him with his own knife and then taken his van at a traffic light in Fairfax

County. The man later admitted that he had parked the van and cut himself with his knife.

Unnamed—Wisconsin

In March 1996, a White woman in Madison, Wisconsin, told police that a Black man snatched her off of the sidewalk and raped her. She later admitted that the story was a fabrication. She was not charged with filing a false report.

Notes

NOTES TO CHAPTER 1

1. Numerous television shows offer mainstream portrayals of Blacks, including *Cosby* (downsized worker); *ER* (doctor); *Homicide* and *New York Undercover* (police officer); *Spin City* (mayoral staffer); *Pickett Fences* (prosecutor); *Dream On* (best friend and talk-show host); and *Dave's World* (plastic surgeon and best friend). For a detailed discussion of Black/White media portrayals, see Benjamin DeMott, *The Trouble with Friendship: Why Americans Can't Think Straight about Race* (1995).

2. See, e.g., "A Gallery of Twisted Images: The Black Man Distorted," *Emerge*, October 1995. Page 43 features pictures of Stepin' Fetchit, Amos 'n' Andy, Jimmie Walker (as J.J.), Mr. T, and Flip Wilson as "Geraldine."

3. Willie Horton is a Black man who while on a weekend furlough from prison raped and killed a White woman. In his 1992 presidential campaign, George Bush used television commercials featuring Horton to attack his opponent, Michael Dukakis. The voice-over in one commercial said, "Dukakis not only opposes the death penalty, he allowed first-degree murderers to have weekend passes from prison." Joe Feagin and Hernan Vera, *White Racism* 115 (1995).

4. Kevin Merida, "A Distorted Image of Minorities," *Washington Post*, October 8, 1995, A1. This article was the first in a three-part *Washington Post* series ("Reality Check: Attitudes and Anxieties about Race," October 8–10, 1995). For a more recent discussion of the impact of television news on racial stereotypes, see Howard Kurtz, "A Guilty Verdict on Crime, Race Bias," *Washington Post*, April 28, 1997, at C1.

5. Merida, "A Distorted Image."

6. Examples of White-Black buddy movies include *Nothing to Lose* (Tim Robbins and Martin Lawrence), *Gridlock'd* (Tim Roth and Tupac Shakur), *Pulp Fiction* (John Travolta and Samuel L. Jackson), *A Family Thing* (Robert Duvall and James Earl Jones), *Die Hard 3* (Bruce Willis and Samuel L. Jackson) *Lethal Weapon* (Mel Gibson and Danny Glover), and *Bulletproof* (Adam Sandler and Damon Wayans).

7. Spike Lee, *Do the Right Thing*, Universal Pictures (1989).

8. Marc Mauer and Tracy Huling, "Young Black Americans and the Criminal Justice System: Five Years Later," Sentencing Project (1995).

9. All Black male criminal justice majors at the University of Maryland (enrolled spring 1995) were invited to participate in the focus groups. Fifteen men (approximately 15 percent of the Black male majors) agreed to participate. The focus group sessions were held at the University of Maryland in July 1995. Two groups, one with seven participants, the other with eight, each met for one-and-one-half hours. Each participant received fifteen dollars. The author and colleague Ollie Johnson III, a Black male professor of political science and Afro-American studies, led the focus group discussions. Audiotapes of the focus groups were transcribed professionally. All names used for focus group participants are aliases.

10. See, e.g., Darrell Dawsey, *Living to Tell about It* (1996); Don Belton, ed., *Speak My Name* (1995); Daniel Wideman and Rohan Preston, eds., *Soulfires* (1996). See also John W. Fountain, "No Fare," *Washington Post,* May 4, 1997, at F1.

11. Trey Ellis, "How Does It Feel to Be a Problem?" in Don Belton, ed., *Speak My Name* 9 (1995). In the same book, see Robin D. G. Kelley, "Confessions of a Nice Negro, or Why I Shaved My Head," 13.

12. Lawrence Kasdan (1991), Twentieth Century Fox.

13. Twelve of the young men who participated in the focus groups agreed to take part in a follow-up interview. These interviews were conducted in November 1995.

14. Joshua Solomon, "Skin Deep," *Washington Post,* October 30, 1994, at C1.

15. Ibid.

16. The author interviewed Joshua Solomon in May 1995.

17. Chapter 7 includes a detailed discussion of the dynamics of White racism and Black crime.

NOTES TO CHAPTER 2

1. A. Leon Higginbotham, Jr., *In the Matter of Color* 28–29 (1978).

2. F. James Davis, *Who Is Black?* 5 (1991).

3. Michael Hindus, *Prison and Plantation* 145 (1980).

4. *State v. Maner* 2 Hill 355 (S.C. 1834) ("The criminal offense of assault and battery cannot at common law be committed on the person of a slave").

5. See Thomas Morris, *Southern Slavery and the Law, 1619–1860* 306 (1996).

6. A. Leon Higginbotham, Jr., and Anne Jacobs, "The 'Law Only as Enemy': The Legitimization of Racial Powerlessness through the Colonial and Ante-Bellum Criminal Laws of Virginia," 70 *North Carolina Law Review* 969, 1058 (1992).

7. See, e.g., Emily Field Van Tassel, "Freedom: Personal Liberty and Private Law: 'Only the Law Would Rule between Us,'" 70 *Chicago-Kent Law Review* 873 (1995).

8. Higginbotham, *In the Matter of Color* 23–24.

9. Higginbotham and Jacobs, "Law Only as Enemy" 1056.

10. Some states did make the rape of a slave girl under the age of 12 a criminal offense. See, e.g., Morris, *Southern Slavery,* 306 (discussing *State v. Jones,* involving

Mississippi statute that punished the rape or attempted rape of a mulatto or Black female by a mulatto or Black male).

11. See, generally, J. Clay Smith, "Justice and Jurisprudence and the Black Lawyer" 69 *Notre Dame Law Review* 1077, 1111 (1994).

12. See, e.g., ibid. at 1107 (citing Mississippi Code, penalty for helping slave obtain freedom); Higginbotham and Jacobs, "Law Only as Enemy," 1021 (discussing Virginia law).

13. See, e.g., Kenneth Stampp, *The Peculiar Institution* 214–215 (1956); Marvin Dulaney, *Black Police in America* 2 (1996).

14. Eric Foner, *Reconstruction: America's Unfinished Revolution, 1863–1877* 198 (1988).

15. Jason Gillmer, "*U.S. v. Clary*: Equal Protection and the Crack Statute" 45 *American University Law Review* 497, 538 (1995) (citing *An Act to Amend the Vagrant Laws of the State*).

16. Donald H. Zeigler, "A Reassessment of the *Younger* Doctrine in Light of the Legislative History of Reconstruction" 1983 *Duke Law Journal* 987, 993 (1983).

17. Douglas Colbert, "Challenging the Challenge: Thirteenth Amendment as a Prohibition against Racial Use of Peremptory Challenges," 76 *Cornell Law Review* 1, 41 (1990).

18. *U.S. v. Cruikshank* 25 F. Cas. 707 (1875), *aff'd* 92 U.S. 542 (1875). See also Colbert, "Challenging," at 60–61.

19. See, e.g., Trudier Harris, *Exorcising Blackness* 1–11 (1984); Gunnar Myrdal, *An American Dilemma* 562 (1944).

20. Myrdal, *An American Dilemma* 562.

21. W. E. B. DuBois, *Dusk of Dawn* 251 (1940).

22. See, e.g., Myrdal, *An American Dilemma* 561; Harris, *Exorcising Blackness* 7.

23. Myrdal, *An American Dilemma* 1347n. 25 (quoting Ray Stannard Baker).

24. Ibid. at 561; Harris, *Exorcising Blackness* 7.

25. U.S. Bureau of the Census, *Historical Statistics of the United States, Colonial Times to 1970, Bicentennial Edition, Part 2* 422 (1975).

26. Ida B. Wells-Barnett, *On Lynchings* 46–47 (1969).

27. U.S. Bureau of the Census, *Negro Population, 1790–1915* 436 (1969).

28. See, e.g., Lerone Bennett, *Before the Mayflower* 255–296 (1988); Derrick Bell, *Race, Racism, and American Law* 83–84 (1980).

NOTES TO CHAPTER 3

1. Michael Tonry, *Malign Neglect* 49 (1995).

2. Alfred Blumstein, "Racial Disproportionality of U.S. Prison Populations Revisited," 64 *University of Colorado Law Review* 743, 759 (1993).

3. John DiIulio, "My Black Crime Problem, and Ours," *City Journal* 14 (spring 1996) (emphasis in original).

4. William Wilbanks, *Myth of a Racist Criminal Justice System* 5–6 (1987).

5. See, e.g., Gary LaFree, "Official Reactions to Hispanic Defendants in the Southwest," 22 *Journal of Research in Crime and Delinquency* 213 (1985); Blumstein, "Racial Disproportionality" 1982; Patrick Langan, "Racism on Trial: New Evidence to Explain The Racial Composition of Prisons in the United States" 46 *Journal of Criminal Law and Criminology* 783 (1985).

6. Stephen Klein, Susan Martin, and Joan Petersilia, "Racial Equity in Sentencing," *RAND* (1988).

7. See, e.g., Robert Crutchfield, George Bridges, and Susan Pitchford, "Analytical and Aggregation Biases in Analyses of Imprisonment: Reconciling Discrepancies in Studies of Racial Disparity," 31 *Journal of Research in Crime and Delinquency* 166 (1994); Marjorie S. Zatz, "The Changing Forms of Racial/Ethnic Biases in Sentencing" 24 *Journal of Research in Crime and Delinquency* 69 (1987).

8. This raises the issue of racial classification. For example, the Uniform Crime Reports use five racial categories: White, Black, Asian, Native American, and Other. The UCR considers "Hispanic" an ethnicity and not a race. Because the arrest rates for Hispanics is included in other racial groups (a Hispanic person may be of any race) this may result in inflated figures for White and Black rates. The U.S. Census Bureau classifies Hispanics as a racial group. This makes analyses using both the UCR data and Census Bureau figures, necessary for discussing disproportionality, problematic.

9. Marvin Wolfgang and Bernard Cohen, *Crime and Race* 30–31 (1970).

10. See, e.g., DiIulio, "My Black Crime Problem" 14.

11. Blumstein, "Racial Disproportionality" 746.

12. See, e.g., U.S. Sentencing Commission, "Cocaine and Federal Sentencing Policy" 156, 161 (1995).

13. 116 S. Ct. 1480, no. 95-197 (1996).

14. See, e.g., Adina Schwartz, "'Just Take Away Their Guns': The Hidden Racism of *Terry v. Ohio*" 23 *Fordham Urban Law Journal* 317, 362 (1996); Ron Akers, *Criminological Theories: Introduction and Evaluation* 26–27 (1994).

15. Daniel Georges-Abeyie, "The Myth of a Racist Criminal Justice System?" in Brian MacLean and Dragan Milovanovic, eds., *Racism, Empiricism and Criminal Justice* 11 (1990). Georges-Abeyie's definition of informal stages includes racially derogatory courtroom language (e.g., a prosecutor referring to a Black defendant as an "animal"). For a detailed discussion of trial language, see Sheri L. Johnson, "Racial Imagery in Criminal Trials" 67 *Tulane Law Review* 1739 (1993); and Anthony V. Alfieri, "Defending Racial Violence," 95 *Columbia Law Review* 1301 (1995).

16. David Harris, "Driving While Black: Unequal Protection under the Law," *Chicago Tribune*, March 11, 1997, at 19; Tracey Maclin, "Some of Us All Too Familiar with 'DWB,'" *Houston Chronicle*, March 16, 1997.

17. Alvin Benn, "Black Leaders Set Up 'Harassment' Hotline," *Montgomery Advertiser*, March 6, 1996, at 2B.

18. Dennis Roddy, "Young Black Males Taught Lesson in Caution: Instruction on Dealing with Police Commonplace," *Pittsburgh Post-Gazette,* November 5, 1995, at A1.

19. Jerome McCristal Culp, Jr., "Notes from California: Rodney King and the Race Question," 70 *Denver University Law Review* 199, 200 (1993).

20. See, e.g., Michael Fletcher, "Driven to Extremes," *Washington Post,* March 29, 1996, at A1.

21. See, e.g., Robert Worden and Robin Shepard, "Demeanor, Crime and Police Behavior: A Reexamination of the Police Services Study Data," 34 *Criminology* 83 (1996).

22. See Yankelovich Partners, Inc., "African-American Study" 13 (1996). For a summary of this report, see Jervis Anderson, "Black and Blue," *New Yorker,* April 29/May 6, 1996, at 62.

23. See, e.g., David Moore and Lydia Saad, "No Immediate Signs That Simpson Trial Intensified Racial Animosity," *The Gallup Poll Monthly,* October 1995, at 3.

24. See, e.g., Nick Charles and Chrisena Coleman, "Criminally Suspect," *Emerge,* September 1995, at 24.

25. Gunnar Myrdal, *An American Dilemma* 542 (1944).

26. See, e.g., Fletcher, "Driven to Extremes"; Thomas Fields-Meyer, Maria Eftimiades, et al., "Under Suspicion," *People,* January 15, 1996, at 40; Ingrid Becker, "Black Actors Tell of Harassment by LAPD," April 12, 1991, UPI (LEXIS); Lolis Elie, "Luxury Car Misfortune," *Times-Picayune,* August 28, 1995, at B1 (Brian Taylor); and S. L. Price, "About Time: His Long Road to Becoming an NFL Coach: The Buccaneers' Tony Dungy Learned Hard Lessons about Race, Life, and Pro Football but Never Lost Hope," *Sports Illustrated,* June 1996, at 68 (Tony Dungy).

27. Arthur Colbert (college student pulled over by Philadelphia police and gun placed to his head); Joseph Gould (homeless man killed by White off-duty Chicago police officer); Malice Green (killed by Detroit police); Don Jackson (Long Beach, California, police officer who secretly videotaped a police assault against him. Jackson's head was slammed through a glass window); Rodney King (after high-speed chase, King was beaten by four Los Angeles police officers as other officers watched); Arthur McDuffie (Miami motorist beaten and killed by police officer. Acquittal of officer led to days of Miami riots); Desmond Robinson (undercover New York Transit officer who was shot in the back by a White officer who mistook him for a criminal); Brian Rooney (Wall Street businessman detained overnight with his 64-year-old mother after New York Transit police mistakenly believed he had entered the station without paying); and Ron Settles (college football star found dead in jail cell after being arrested for speeding. His family was awarded $760,000 in a wrongful death suit. The movie *The Glass Shield* was partly inspired by this incident). See, e.g., Pierre Thomas, "Police Brutality: An Issue Rekindled," *Washington Post,* December 6, 1995, at 1.

28. "Independent Commission on the Los Angeles Police Department, Report of the Independent Commission on the Los Angeles Police Department" 69 (1991).

See also "Developments in the Criminal Law—Race and the Criminal Process," 101 *Harvard Law Review* 1472 (1988).

29. Sandra Lee Browning, Francis Cullen, Liqun Cao, and Renee Kopache, "Race and Getting Hassled by the Police," 17 *Police Studies* 5–6 (1994).

30. See, e.g., *State v. Dean* 543 P.2d 425 (Ariz. 1975) (en banc); Erika Johnson, "'A Menace to Society': The Use of Criminal Profiles and Its Effects on Black Males" 38 *Howard Law Journal* 629 (1995); Emily J. Sack, "Police Approaches and Inquiries on the Streets of New York: The Aftermath of *People v. De Bour*" 66 *New York University Law Review* 512 (1991).

31. 517 U.S. 806 (1996).

32. See, e.g., Browning et al., "Race and Getting Hassled"; Robert Bogomolny, "Street Patrol: The Decision to Stop a Citizen," 12 *Criminal Law Bulletin* 544, 567–568 (1976) (study of police stops revealed that officers stopped Black males for "field interrogation" more frequently than would be expected based upon arrest rates); Al Reiss, "Police Brutality," in Richard Lundman, ed., *Police Behavior* 274, 278 (1980) (one in four Black men in Detroit report being stopped and questioned by police without good reason).

33. 42 U.S.C.S. sect. 14142 (1996).

34. *Traffic Stops Statistics Act of 1997*, 105th Congress, 1st sess., H.R. 118 (January 7, 1997).

35. Criminal Intelligence Report, State of Maryland, Maryland State Police, dated April 27, 1992 (*Wilkins v. Maryland State Police*, Civil Action No. MJG-93-468).

36. STIF officer John Appleby was forced to resign after an undercover operation revealed he was stealing drug money. See, e.g., "Ex-State Trooper Caught in Police Sting to Serve 18-month Sentence for Theft," *Baltimore Sun*, May 13, 1997, at 2B.

37. Three of these cases have been resolved. See, e.g., *Whitfield v. Bd. of County Commissioners of Eagle County*, 837 F. Supp. 338 (D. Colo. 1993) (out-of-court settlement for $800,000); *Washington v. Vogel*, 156 F.R.D. 676 (M.D. Fla. 1994) (dismissed for lack of standing). The Tinicum County case, brought by the Philadelphia American Civil Liberties Union, was settled for $250,000.

38. Tanya Jones, "Race Based Searches Prohibited," *Baltimore Sun*, January 15, 1995, at 1B.

39. Culp, "Notes from California" 206.

40. See Mark Curriden, "When Good Cops Go Bad," *American Bar Association Journal*, May 1996, at 61.

41. "City Liable in Teen's Death," *Washington Post*, March 22, 1996, at A18.

NOTES TO CHAPTER 4

1. Mark Terrill, "Text of the Simpson Letter," *Chicago Sun-Times*, June 18, 1994, at 7.

2. Humphrey Taylor, "Public Belief in O. J. Simpson's Guilt or Innocence Varies Greatly Not Just with Race but Also with Age, Education and Income," Harris Poll 1995, #21.

3. Christopher Caldwell, "Why the Simpson Case Endures," *Weekly Standard,* July 29, 1996, at 22 (author's emphasis).

4. Ibid.

5. William Raspberry, "Where's the Outrage from White America? Black Americans Put Their Faith in the System. They Were Let Down," *Washington Post,* May 1, 1992, at A27.

6. Meri Nana-Ama Danquah, "Why We Really Root for O. J.: The Superstar Suspect Embodies the Illusion of a Colorblind America," *Washington Post,* July 3, 1994, at C1.

7. See, e.g., Larry Dorman, "We'll Be Right Back after This Hip and Distorted Commercial Break," *New York Times,* September 1, 1996, at 13 (Tiger Woods indicates that he does not want to be limited to being a "Black" golfer).

8. Michael Eric Dyson, *Race Rules: Navigating the Color Line* 30 (1996).

9. Harry Edwards, "We Must Let O. J. Go: Separating Fact from Image," 86 *Sport* 80 (1995).

10. Regina Austin, "Deviance, Resistance, and Love," 1994 *Utah Law Review* 179, 180 (1994).

11. Robert Bork, a 1987 U.S. Supreme Court nominee, was heavily criticized for his anti-abortion court opinions. Liberal interest groups organized successfully to derail his candidacy. Many conservatives believe Bork was treated unfairly. Since then, "Borked" has been loosely used to describe any political nominee who is attacked because of his political views.

12. Clarence Thomas's full statement was:

> And from my standpoint as a black American, it is high tech lynching for uppity blacks who in way *[sic]* deign to think for themselves, to do for themselves, to have different ideas, and it is a message that unless you kowtow to an old order, that is what will happen to you. You will be lynched, destroyed, caricatured by a committee of the U.S. Senate rather than hung from a tree.

Reuters, *New York Times,* October 12, 1991, at 12.

13. Bill Carter, "In Interview, Simpson Appeals for Privacy," *New York Times,* January 26, 1996, at A16.

14. Paul Duggan and Hamil Harris, "Church Opens Arms to Simpson," *Washington Post,* August 29, 1996, at D1.

15. Avis Thomas-Lester, "O. J.? Oh, Brother!" *Washington Post,* September 1, 1996, at C5.

16. See, e.g., Leon Dash, "The Case against Clarence," *Washington Post,* June 9, 1996, at C2 (May 1996 debate in Prince George's County, Maryland, about whether Thomas should be allowed to address a predominantly Black junior high school assembly).

17. Yankelovich Partners, Inc., "African-American Study" 29–32 (1996) (prepared for the *New Yorker Magazine*).

18. W. E. B. DuBois, *The Souls of Black Folk,* in *Three Negro Classics* 215 (1965).

19. "Newsroom Diversity Continues Expansion, Though the Growth is Small, American Society of Newspaper Editors Report Shows," April 16, 1996 (press release) (Report states that there are a total of 55,000 newsroom journalists. Blacks account for 2,980 or 5 percent).

20. Richard A. White, *Association of American Law Schools Statistical Report on Law School Faculty and Candidates for Law Faculty Positions, 1995–1996,* Table 1B, at 3 (1996).

21. The NewsHour with Jim Lehrer, "Essay—American Mix," December 19, 1995, Transcript #5422.

22. See, e.g., Cynthia Kwei Yung Lee, "Beyond Black and White: Racializing Asian Americans in a Society Obsessed with O. J.," 6 *Hastings Women's Law Journal* 165 (1995).

23. Louis Aguilar, "Latinos, Asians Seek a Voice in Emerging National Discussion on Race," *Washington Post,* October 15, 1995, at A24.

NOTES TO CHAPTER 5

1. Richard Grant, "Mother of All Crimes," *Independent,* February 25, 1995, at 16.

2. Michael Grunwald, "For Boston, Harsh Reminder: Five Years Ago, Stuart's Racist Hoax Was Hatched—and Believed," *Boston Globe,* November 4, 1994, at 17.

3. Walter Watson, "Comedian Paul Mooney Uses Humor to Attack Racism," September 23, 1995, National Public Radio, Transcript #1979-7.

4. It is likely that the most common racial hoax is intraracial. These, however, do not attract the same degree of media attention as interracial hoaxes. Newspaper reports of crime hoaxes do not typically state the race of the parties involved. These are likely to be White-on-White hoaxes.

5. See generally, Dan Carter, *Scottsboro: A Tragedy of the American South* (1969). The Scottsboro injustices were addressed in *Powell v. Alabama,* 287 U.S. 45 (1932), which outlined the parameters of the Sixth Amendment right to a fair trial.

6. White-on-Black homicide is less prevalent than Black-on-White homicide. For 1995, White-on-Black murders made up 6 percent of all murders with Black victims, while Black-on-White murders made up 14 percent of all murders with White victims. U.S. Department of Justice, Uniform Crime Reports, "Crime in the United States, 1995," Table 2.8, at 17 (1996). The fact that Blacks are more likely to commit crime against Whites than Whites are to commit crime against Blacks may be due to the fact that there are more Whites to victimize.

7. Roni Rabin, "Hoax Fed on Prejudice: Frightened by Notes, Neighbors Suspected Black Family," *Newsday,* October 10, 1990, at 3.

8. Ibid.

9. See Simon Pristel, "Mastermind of Father-Son Jewel Heist Team Jailed," *Boston Herald*, September 20, 1996, at 6; Frank Devlin, "Alburtis Man Admits Gun Theft," *Morning Call*, February 28, 1996, at B3.

10. Douglas H. Palmer, Mayor of Trenton, New Jersey (press release, Thursday, January 12, 1995).

11. 505 U.S. 377 (1992).

12. 508 U.S. 476 (1993). In October 1989, Mitchell and some of his friends discussed a scene from the movie *Mississippi Burning*. In the scene, a White man beat a young Black boy who was praying. After this conversation, Mitchell and his friends decided to "move on some white people" and severely beat a White boy who was passing by. Ibid. at 2196.

13. Ibid. at 222.

14. Ibid.

15. Frederick Lawrence refers to the free-speech versus bias-crime debate as a "false paradox." He states, "[T]he apparent paradox of seeking to punish the perpetrators of racially motivated violence while being committed to protecting the bigot's right to express racism is a false paradox. Put simply, we are making this problem harder than it needs to be. We must focus on the basic distinction between bias crimes—such as racially motivated assaults or vandalism—and racist speech." Frederick Lawrence, "Resolving the Hate Crimes/Hate Speech Paradox: Punishing Bias Crimes and Protecting Racist Speech," 68 *Notre Dame Law Review* 673, 676 (1993).

16. This is an updated version of Justice Oliver Wendell Holmes's pronouncement that one does not have the right to "shout fire in a crowded theatre," *Schenck v. U.S.*, 249 U.S. 47, 51 (1919).

17. New Jersey A.B. 561 (1996) (proposed amendment to N.J.S. 2C: 28-4): "False Reports to Law Enforcement Authorities."

18. One case was found that may classify as a Black-on-Black hoax. In February 1996, Gerald Hill, a Black man, was charged in a twelve-hundred-count indictment. He was accused of abusing his four young children over a five-year period. Days following the indictment, three of the children stepped forward to recant their allegations, saying that a relative had forced them to make the statements. If the charges are false, this would be a Black-on-Black hoax. See "Bond in Abuse Case Stands: Judge Not Swayed by Kids' Recantation of Charges," *Chicago Tribune*, February 10, 1996, at 5.

19. Mari Matsuda, "Public Response to Racist Speech," in Mari Matsuda, Charles Lawrence, Richard Delgado, and Kimberlé Crenshaw, eds., *Words That Wound* 36 (1993).

20. Marc Fleischauer, "Review of Florida Legislation; Comment: Teeth for a Paper Tiger: A Proposal to Add Enforceability to Florida's Hate Crimes Act," 17 *Florida State University Law Review* 697, 706n. 34 (1990).

21. Lawrence, "Resolving the Hates Crimes/Hate Speech Paradox" 698.

22. See Fleischauer, "Review of Florida Legislation" 703.
23. N.J. AB 2553.
24. Charles Lawrence, "The Id, the Ego, and Equal Protection: Reckoning with Unconscious Racism," 39 *Stanford Law Review* 317, 322 (1987) (citations omitted).
25. William Raspberry, "Automatically Suspect," *Washington Post*, November 5, 1994, at A19. Following the Miriam Kashani rape hoax, the school president, in an address to the university community, wrote, "We must understand that our black students, faculty and staff and neighbors have been given offense and reason to feel concerned and anxious. They were special victims of the hoax." See also Jonetta Barras, "Blacks See Racism in Rape Hoax at GWU," *Washington Times*, December 12, 1990, at A21.

NOTES TO CHAPTER 6

1. The conference was retitled "Research on Genetics and Criminal Behavior: Scientific Issues, Social and Political Implications."
2. Ibid. at 2. The American Sociological Association committee assigned to investigate violations of the ethics code can choose from a range of actions: no sanction, suspension of membership, requested resignation, and termination of membership. Ibid. at 6.
3. Council on Ethical and Judicial Affairs, *Code of Medical Ethics* 13–14 (Chicago: American Medical Association, 1994).
4. The 1996–1997 Ethical Issues Committee of the American Society of Criminology is drafting a code of ethics.
5. Dinesh D'Souza, "Racism: It's a White (and Black) Thing," *Washington Post*, September 24, 1995, at C1. D'Souza discusses this conference in greater detail in *The End of Racism* 387–429 (1995).
6. For a discussion of the Pioneer Fund, see, e.g., Adam Miller, "Professors of Hate," in Russell Jacoby and Naomi Glauberman, eds., *The Bell Curve Debate* 162 (1995).
7. James Anderson, "On the Ethics of Research in a Socially Constructed Reality," *Journal of Broadcasting & Electronic Media* 353, 355 (summer 1992).
8. "Mainstream Science on Intelligence," *Wall Street Journal*, December 13, 1994, at A15. The fifty-two researchers who signed the statement include: Richard D. Arvey, Thomas J. Bouchard, Jr., John B. Carroll, Raymond B. Cattell, David B. Cohen, Rene V. Dawis, Douglas K. Detterman, Marvin Dunnette, Hans Eysenck, Jack Feldman, Edwin A. Fleishman, Grover C. Gilmore, Robert A. Gordon, Linda S. Gottfredson, Robert L. Greene, Richard J. Haier, Garrett Hardin, Robert Hogan, Joseph M. Horn, Lloyd G. Humphreys, John E. Hunter, Seymour W. Itzkoff, Douglas N. Jackson, James J. Jenkins, Arthur R. Jensen, Alan S. Kaufman, Nadeen L. Kaufman, Timothy Z. Keith, Nadine Lambert, John C. Loehlin, David Lubinski, David T. Lykken, Richard Lynn, Paul E. Meehl, R. Travis Osborne, Robert Perloff,

Robert Plomin, Cecil R. Reynolds, David C. Rowe, J. Phillipe Rushton, Vincent Sarich, Sandra Scarr, Frank L. Schmidt, Lyle F. Schoenfeldt, James C. Sharf, Herman Spitz, Julian C. Stanley, Del Thiessen, Lee A. Thompson, Robert M. Thorndike, Philip Anthony Vernon, and Lee Willerman.

9. "Reacting to *The Bell Curve*," *Education Week*, January 11, 1995, at 29–30.

10. American Psychological Association, "Intelligence: Knowns and Unknowns" (1995).

11. Ibid. at 39.

12. "Ideology and Censorship in Behavior Genetics," 35 *Mankind Quarterly* 327, 336 (1995).

13. The *Behavior Genetics Association* journal refused to publish Whitney's remarks. They were later published in *Mankind Quarterly*.

14. The Violence Initiative is the name given the federal grant that among other things was designed to identify and treat one hundred thousand inner-city children who have been labeled as genetically predisposed to commit crime. Peter Breggin, a Maryland psychiatrist, went on a one-man mission to show that the initiative, like the planned conference, was part of a larger plan by the federal government to promote genes and crime research. See, e.g., Peter Breggin, *The War against Children* (1994); Juan Williams, "Violence, Genes, and Prejudice," *Discover*, November 1994, at 93.

15. "Goodwin Apologizes for 'Inappropriate Remarks': Frederick Goodwin, Alcohol, Drug Abuse, and Mental Health Administration Director," 4 *Alcoholism and Drug Abuse Week* 3 (February 26, 1992). See also, Anne Davidson, "ADAMHA Chief Resigns amid Controversy over Remarks," 4 *Alcoholism and Drug Abuse Week* 1 (March 4, 1992); Daniel Goleman, *New York Times*, September 15, 1992, at C1.

16. See, e.g., Douglas Shuit, "Angry Blacks Say Conference Links Genetics, Crime," *Los Angeles Times*, October 14, 1993, at B1. (Community protests in response to the planning of a Los Angeles conference that would examine the relationship between drug abuse, mental disorders, and ethnic groups. Frederick Goodwin, who had been invited to speak at the conference, withdrew.)

17. During a panel discussion at the Maryland genes-and-crime symposium, Deborah Blum, a science reporter for the *Sacramento Bee*, stated that on more than one occasion she has encountered difficulty getting scientists to publicly criticize those scientists whose work they willingly contest in private (Sunday, September 24, 1995, audiotape on file with University of Maryland Audio Visual Media Archives).

18. Shannon P. Duffy, "In Abortion Flap, Judge Says SEPTA Not a Public Forum," *Legal Intelligencer*, August 20, 1996, at 5.

19. *Christ's Bride Ministries Inc. v. SEPTA*, 937 F. Supp. 425 (E.D. Penn. 1996).

20. An October 1996 review of twenty-three studies reported a link between abortion and breast cancer. See, e.g., David Brown, "Review of 23 Studies Links Abortion and Breast Cancer," *Washington Post*, October 12, 1996, at A3.

21. Claude M. Steele and Joshua Aronson, "Stereotype Threat and the Intellectual Test Performance of African Americans," 69 *Journal of Personality and Social Psychology* 797 (1995).

22. Adrian Raine stated, "I hope you can understand my emotions at feeling extremely hurt by such comments and suggestions that I would be racist. You've got to take my word for it" (panel titled "Evaluating the Research: Empirical and Conceptual Questions," Saturday, September 23, 1995, audiotape on file with University of Maryland Audio Visual Media Archives).

23. Alfred Lubrano, "The State of the Nation: Free Speech, Hate Speech? Kean College Hot under Blue-Collar," *Newsday,* January 30, 1994, at 7. Khalid Muhammad stated:

> The secret relationship between Blacks and Jews—the secret is they have lied to us. Now they tell us that they didn't play much of a role in the slave trade. . . . Jews were masters in high percentages, says U.S. Census. . . . According to the U.S. Census of 1830, a majority of southern Jews owned black slaves. How many? A majority. Ira Rosenwaike, a white Jew, a respected Jewish authority, who has published Jewish population studies, has revealed that as many as 75 percent of southern Jewish households held black men, women and children as slaves.

New Jersey Law Journal, January 24, 1994, at 16.

24. See, e.g., Ira Rosenwaike, *On the Edge of Greatness: A Portrait of American Jewry in the Early National Period* (1985). Rosenwaike reports that about one-half of all Jews in 1830 lived in the South, approximately 75 percent of those families owned slaves, and that, on average, Jewish slave owners were not large plantation owners.

25. Laurie Goodstein, "Black Studies Teacher Ignites Tense Debate: Remarks on Whites, Jews Create Furor in N.Y.," *New York Times,* August 18, 1991, at A3.

26. Frances Cress Welsing, *The Isis Papers: The Keys to the Colors* 4–5 (1991).

NOTES TO CHAPTER 7

1. Gary Kamiya, "Toni Morrison Tells the Publishers They Reinforce 'Racial Half-Truths,'" *San Francisco Examiner,* April 28, 1994.

2. Andrew Hacker, *Two Nations* 180 (1992).

3. The four journals are *Criminology, Justice Quarterly, Journal of Research in Crime and Delinquency,* and the *Journal of Criminal Law and Criminology.* The first two journals were selected because they are the official publications of the two largest professional organizations of criminologists, the American Society of Criminology and the Academy of Criminal Justice Sciences. The remaining two were chosen because of their wide readership and rank in the field of criminology. The search for articles on White crime and Black crime consisted of a review of titles and abstracts.

4. Edwin Sutherland, *White Collar Crime* 6 (1949).

5. Francis Cullen and Michael Benson, "White-Collar Crime: Holding a Mirror to the Core," 4 *Journal of Criminal Justice Education* 325, 334 (1993).

6. Ibid. at 332.

7. Andrew Hacker, "Caste, Crime, and Precocity," in Steve Fraser, ed., *The Bell Curve Wars* 97 (1995).

8. For a more detailed discussion of the role of the Black criminologist, see Katheryn K. Russell, "The Development of a Black Criminology and the Role of the Black Criminologist," 9 *Justice Quarterly* 667 (1992).

9. C. Wright Mills, *The Sociological Imagination* 178 (1959).

10. Robert Weissberg, "White Racism: The Seductive Lure of an Unproven Theory," *Weekly Standard*, March 24, 1997, at 19.

11. James Q. Wilson, "Crime, Race, and Values," *Society* 91 (November/December 1992).

12. Ibid.

13. Ibid. (emphasis added).

14. See, e.g., Wesley Skogan, "Crime and the Racial Fears of White Americans," *The Annals of the American Academy of Political and Social Sciences* (May 1995).

15. Ibid.

16. Jesse Jackson's complete statement was, "There is nothing more painful for me at this stage of my life than to walk down the street and hear footsteps and start to think about robbery and then look around and see its somebody white and feel relieved. How humiliating." John DiIulio, "My Black Crime Problem, and Ours," *City Journal* 14 (spring 1996).

17. See, e.g., ibid.; George Will, "A Measure of Morality," *Washington Post*, December 16, 1993, at A25; Susan Estrich, "Race in the Jury Room," *Washington Post*, September 11, 1996, at A23.

18. Andrew Hacker, "Malign Neglect: The Crackdown on African Americans," *The Nation*, July 10, 1995, at 45, 49.

19. See, e.g., Frankie Bailey, "Race, Law and 'Americans': A Historical Overview," in Michael Lynch and Britt Patterson, eds., *Race and Criminal Justice* 12 (1991).

20. See, e.g., Derrick Bell, *Race, Racism, and American Law* 29 (1992) (quoting speech given by Benjamin Franklin).

21. See Hacker, "Malign Neglect" 45. He recounts a hypothetical exercise he uses with his White students. He gives them the choice between having three hundred dollars in their wallets and having it taken by someone White or having one hundred dollars in their wallets and having it taken by someone Black. The majority of students select the first choice. "They would gladly pay the extra $200 to avoid a black assailant," 46.

22. Eric Clark, "A Tale of Two Nations: Racial Polarization in America," *Crisis* (July 1995).

23. Presumably referring to Blacks, in a discussion on the reaction to the verdict in the Simi Valley Rodney King trial, Wilson comments, "The racist bigotry now

being directed at the Ventura County jurors by people who did not sit through the trial or read the transcript is appalling." Wilson, "Crime, Race, and Values" 90–91.

24. Derrick Bell, *And We Are Not Saved* 245, 246 (1987).

NOTES TO CHAPTER 8

1. U.S. Sentencing Commission, *Cocaine and Federal Sentencing Policy* 122–123 (1995).

2. Ronald Smothers, "Wave of Prison Uprisings Provoke Debate on Crack," *New York Times*, October 24, 1995, at A18.

3. 846 F.Supp. 768 (E.D. Mo. 1994), *rev'd* 34 F.3d 709 (1994).

4. U.S. Sentencing Commission, *Cocaine* 163. For a detailed analysis of federal cocaine law, see William Spade, "Beyond the 100:1 Ratio: Towards a Rational Cocaine Sentencing Policy" 38 *Arizona Law Review* 1233 (1996).

5. 517 U.S. 806 (1996).

6. See, e.g., Associated Press, "Judge Is Forced to Lengthen Sentences for Crack," *New York Times*, November 27, 1995, at B5; Toni Locy, "Second Judge Rejects Guidelines for Sentencing in Crack Case: Pressure By D.E.A. Agent Cited as Term Is Reduced," *Washington Post*, July 21, 1994, at B1; Associated Press, "U.S. Judge, Citing Racism, Gives Black Defendant Lesser Sentence," *New York Times*, February 20, 1993, at 8.

7. Dorothy K. Hatsukami and Marian W. Fischman, "Crack Cocaine and Cocaine Hydrochloride: Are the Differences Myth or Reality?" 276 *Journal of the American Medical Association* 1580 (1996).

8. 481 U.S. 279 (1987).

9. See, generally, David Baldus, George Woodworth, and Charles Pulaski, *Equal Justice and the Death Penalty* (1990).

10. See, e.g., Marc Mauer, "Intended and Unintended Consequences: State Racial Disparities in Imprisonment," Sentencing Project (1997). (Fourteen percent of all Black men are either permanently or currently ineligible to vote.) For discussion of historical roots of disenfranchisement, see Randall Kennedy, *Race, Crime, and the Law* 87–88 (1997).

11. "Fraud Charges Filed," *Houston Chronicle*, April 11, 1996, at 23.

12. *Cato v. United States*, 70 F. 3d 1103 (9th Cir. 1995).

13. David Josar, *The Detroit News*, August 28, 1996, at D1.

14. Tim Golden, "Held in War, Latins Seek Reparations," *New York Times*, August 29, 1996, at A18.

15. Peggy Davis, "Law as Microaggression," 98 *Yale Law Journal* 1559, 1565 (1989) (quoting Chester M. Pierce et al., "An Experiment in Racism: TV Commercials," in Chester M. Pierce, ed., *Television and Education* 62, 66 [1978]).

16. "President Clinton's Weekly Radio Address," *Federal News Service*, March 29, 1997.

17. The *New York Times* and the *Washington Post* were the primary sources for the month-long search, conducted in February 1995.

18. At a November 11, 1994, faculty meeting, Rutgers president Francis Lawrence made the following statement, "The average SAT for African Americans is 750. . . . Do we set standards in the future so that we don't admit anybody with the national test? Or do we deal with a disadvantaged population that doesn't have that genetic hereditary background to have a higher average?" ("Rutgers Game Halted by Protesting Students," *Washington Post*, February 8, 1995, at A3).

19. "News Brief," *Washington Post*, February 11, 1995, at A2 (David Walden and Shawn Daniels of Missouri pleaded guilty to committing federal civil rights violations).

20. "Campus Protest against Slurs," *New York Times*, February 16, 1995, at A22.

21. "Confederate Flag Stays," *Washington Post*, February 19, 1995, at A12.

22. "News in Brief," *Washington Post*, February 17, 1995, at A2.

23. "School's Computer Game on Slavery Prompts Suit," *New York Times*, August 28, 1995, at A10.

24. Jacques Steinberg, "Racist Message Reveals Rift," *New York Times*, June 21, 1995, at B4.

25. See Ronald Smothers "Pilloried on a List That's Guilt by Name," *New York Times*, February 5, 1995, at A18. Union Point, Georgia, merchants, with the support of the mayor, imposed a ban against twenty-one Blacks. The ban prohibited the people on the list from entering the town's commercial business establishments. The list was devised as an anti-crime measure. Though some had been suspected of criminal activity in the past, none of the twenty-one had been convicted of any crime. In late February 1995, the ban was lifted. The U.S. District Judge who negotiated the settlement stated, "Their [store owners'] efforts to prevent crime were not motivated by any racial motivation" ("Georgia Shops Lift Ban on 21 Blacks," *Washington Post*, February 23, 1995, at A5). A civil action filed by several people named on the list was settled for $265,000, including attorneys' fees (Ronald Smothers, "Georgia Town Settles Lawsuit over List of 'Troublemakers,'" *New York Times*, February 20, 1996, at A12).

26. Karen Houppert, "More Than Words: Inside the Rutgers Student Movement," *Village Voice*, February 28, 1995, at 133.

27. Patricia Williams, "Spirit-Murdering the Messenger: The Discourse of Fingerpointing as the Law's Response to Racism," 42 *University of Miami Law Review* 127, 129 (1987).

28. Ibid.

29. See, e.g., Carol Castenada, "In Kentucky, Confederate Flag Is Fatal," *USA Today*, January 30, 1995, at 4A; Tony Horwitz, "A Death for Dixie," *New Yorker*, March 18, 1996, at 64.

30. Tom Gorman and Bettina Boxall, "Family Tells of Slain Gunman's Anger at Koon," *Los Angeles Times*, November 25, 1995, at A1.

31. Neil MacFarquhar, "Angry Calm at the Services for Teenager Slain by Police," *New York Times,* February 27, 1995, at B5 (author's emphasis).

32. "Rights Official Sees Danger from Police," *New York Times,* February 28, 1997, at A19 (author's emphasis).

33. Maya McNeilly et al., "Effects of Racist Provocation and Social Support on Cardiovascular Reactivity in African American Women," 2 *International Journal of Behavioral Medicine* 321 (1995).

34. Nancy Kreiger and Stephen Sidney, "Racial Discrimination and Blood Pressure: The CARDIA Study of Young Black and White Adults," 86 *American Journal of Public Health* 1370 (1996).

35. See, generally, Patricia Turner, *I Heard It Through the Grapevine: Rumor in African American Culture* (1993); Regina Austin, "Beyond Black Demons & White Devils: Anti-Black Conspiracy Theorizing and the Black Public Sphere," 22 *Florida State University Law Review* 1021 (1995).

36. Gary Webb, *San Jose Mercury News,* August 18–20, 1996.

37. See, e.g., Ambrose Lane, Sr., "Interview with Earl Ofari Hutchinson," WPFW radio talk show, September 16, 1996. (A caller raised a question about this conspiracy theory. Dr. Hutchinson disagreed that there was such a conspiracy.)

38. See, e.g., Pierre Thomas, "FBI Role in Impeachment Probed," *Washington Post,* February 26, 1997, at A10 (indicating that FBI may have withheld evidence in impeachment hearings of Black former judge Alcee Hastings).

39. Frank Rich, "The L.A. Shock Treatment," *New York Times,* October 4, 1995 (quoting Ben Stein).

40. Kennedy, *Race, Crime, and the Law* 4.

Selected Bibliography

Addis, Adeno. " 'Hell Man, They Did Invent Us': The Mass Media, Law, and African Americans." 41 *Buffalo Law Review* 523 (1993).

Alfieri, Anthony V. "Defending Racial Violence." 95 *Columbia Law Review* 1301 (1995).

Anderson, James A. "On the Ethics of Research in a Socially Constructed Reality." 36 *Journal of Broadcasting and Electronic Media* 353 (summer 1992).

Armour, Jody. "Race Ipsa Loquitur: Of Reasonable Racists, Intelligent Bayesians, and Involuntary Negrophobes." 46 *Stanford Law Review* 781 (1994).

Austin, Regina. "Beyond Black Demons & White Devils: Anti-Black Conspiracy Theorizing and the Black Public Sphere." 22 *Florida State University Law Review* 1021 (1995).

———. "'The Black Community,' Its Lawbreakers, and a Politics of Identification." 65 *Southern California Law Review* 1769 (1992).

Baldus, David, George Woodworth, and Charles Pulaski. *Equal Justice and the Death Penalty.* Northeastern University Press, 1990.

Barak, Gregg, ed. *Representing O. J.: Criminal Justice and Mass Culture.* Harrow and Heston, 1996.

Barnes, Robin. "Interracial Violence and Racialized Narratives: Discovering the Road Less Travelled." 96 *Columbia Law Review* 788 (1996).

Bastian, Lisa, and Bruce Taylor. "Young Black Male Victims." *Bureau of Justice Statistics* (December 1994).

Bell, Derrick. *Faces at the Bottom of the Well: The Permanence of Racism.* Basic Books, 1992.

———. *Race, Racism, and American Law.* Little, Brown, 1992.

———. *And We Are Not Saved: The Elusive Quest for Racial Justice.* Basic Books, 1987.

Belton, Don. *Speak My Name: Black Men on Masculinity and the American Dream.* Beacon, 1995.

Bennett, Lerone. *Before the Mayflower: A History of Black America.* Penguin, 1988.

Bernard, Thomas. "Angry Aggression among the 'Truly Disadvantaged.'" 28 *Criminology* 73 (1990).

Blumstein, Alfred. "Racial Disproportionality of U.S. Prison Populations Revisited." 64 *University of Colorado Law Review* 743 (1993).

Bogomolny, Robert. "Street Patrol: The Decision to Stop a Citizen." 12 *Criminal Law Bulletin* 544 (1976).

Breggin, Peter. *The War against Children.* St. Martin's Press, 1994.

Browning, Sandra Lee, Francis Cullen, Liqun Cao, Renee Kopache, and Thomas Stevenson. "Race and Getting Hassled by the Police." 17 *Police Studies* 1 (1994).

Brown-Scott, Wendy. "The Communitarian State: Lawlessness or Reform for African-Americans?" 107 *Harvard Law Review* 1209 (1994).

Butler, Paul. "Racially Based Jury Nullification: Black Power in the Criminal Justice System." 105 *Yale Law Journal* 677 (1995).

Carbado, Devon W. "The Construction of O. J. Simpson as a Racial Victim." 32 *Harvard Civil Rights–Civil Liberties Law Review* 49 (1997).

Carter, Dan. *Scottsboro: A Tragedy of the American South.* Louisiana State University Press, 1969.

Chiricos, Ted, Michael Hogan, and Marc Gertz. "Racial Composition of Neighborhood and Fear of Crime." 35 *Criminology* 107 (1997).

Colbert, Douglas. "Challenging the Challenge: Thirteenth Amendment as a Prohibition against the Racial Use of Peremptory Challenges." 76 *Cornell Law Review* 1 (1990).

Cole, David. "The Paradox of Race and Crime: A Comment on Randall Kennedy's 'Politics of Distinction.'" 83 *Georgetown Law Journal* 2547 (1995).

Cose, Ellis. *Rage of a Privileged Class.* HarperCollins, 1993.

Crenshaw, Kimberlé, Neil Gotanda, Gary Peller, and Kendall Thomas, eds. *Critical Race Theory.* The New Press, 1995.

Crutchfield, Robert, George Bridges, and Susan Pitchford. "Analytical and Aggregation Biases in Analyses of Imprisonment: Reconciling Discrepancies in Studies of Racial Disparity." 31 *Journal of Research in Crime and Delinquency* 166 (1994).

Cullen, Francis, and Michael Benson. "White-Collar Crime: Holding a Mirror to the Core." 4 *Journal of Criminal Justice Education* 325 (1993).

Cullen, Francis, Liqun Cao, James Frank, Robert Langworthy, Sandra Lee Browning, Reneé Kopache, and Thomas Stevenson. "'Stop or I'll Shoot': Racial Differences in Support for Police Use of Deadly Force." 39 *American Behavioral Scientist* 449 (1996).

Culp, Jerome McCristal, Jr. "Notes from California: Rodney King and the Race Question." 70 *Denver University Law Review* 199 (1993).

Daly, Kathleen. "Criminal Law and Justice System Practices as Racist, White, and Racialized." 51 *Washington and Lee Law Review* 431 (1994).

Davis, Angela J. "Race, Cops, and Traffic Stops." 51 *University of Miami Law Review* 425 (1997).

———. "Benign Neglect of Racism in the Criminal Justice System." 94 *Michigan Law Review* 1660 (1996).

Davis, F. James. *Who Is Black? One Nation's Definition.* Pennsylvania State University Press, 1991.

Davis, Peggy. "Law as Microaggression." 98 *Yale Law Journal* 1559 (1989).

Davis, Peter. "Rodney King and the Decriminalization of Police Brutality in America: Direct and Judicial Access to the Grand Jury as Remedies for Victims of Police Brutality When the Prosecutor Declines to Prosecute." 53 *Maryland Law Review* 271 (1994).

Dawsey, Darrell. *Living to Tell about It: Young Black Men in America Speak Their Piece.* Anchor Books, 1996.

Delgado, Richard. *The Rodrigo Chronicles: Conversations about America and Race.* New York University Press, 1995.

———. "Rodrigo's Eighth Chronicle: Black Crime, White Fears—On the Social Construction of Threat." 42 *Stanford Law Review* 503 (1994).

———. "Rodrigo's Ninth Chronicle: Race, Legal Instrumentalism, and the Rule of Law." 143 *University of Pennsylvania Law Review* 379 (1994).

DeMott, Benjamin. *The Trouble with Friendship: Why Americans Can't Think Straight about Race.* Atlantic Monthly Press, 1995.

DiIulio, John. "My Black Crime Problem, and Ours." 6 *City Journal* 14 (spring 1996).

D'Souza, Dinesh. *The End of Racism.* Free Press, 1995.

Du Bois, W. E. B. *The Philadelphia Negro.* Schocken Books, 1967.

———. *Three Negro Classics; The Souls of Black Folk.* 1965.

———. *Dusk of Dawn.* Discus, 1940.

Dulaney, Marvin. *Black Police in America.* Indiana University Press, 1996.

Dyson, Michael Eric. *Race Rules: Navigating the Color Line.* Addison Wesley, 1996.

Edwards, Harry. "We Must Let O. J. Go: Separating Fact from Image." 86 *Sport* 80 (1995).

Ellison, Ralph. *The Invisible Man.* Vintage, 1947.

Feagin, Joe, and Hernan Vera. *White Racism: The Basics.* Routledge, 1995.

Finkelman, Paul. "The Crime of Color." 67 *Tulane Law Review* 2063 (1993).

———, ed. *Race Law and American History 1700–1990: The African American Experience.* Vol. 4. Garland, 1992.

Fleishauer, Marc. "Review of Florida Legislation; Comment: Teeth for a Paper Tiger: A Proposal to Add Enforceability to Florida's Hate Crimes Act." 17 *Florida State University Law Review* 697 (1990).

Foner, Eric. *Reconstruction: America's Unfinished Revolution, 1863–1877.* Harper and Row, 1988.

Fountain, John W. "No Fare." *Washington Post,* May 4, 1997, F1.

Fraser, Steve, ed. *The Bell Curve Wars.* Basic Books, 1995.

Freeman, Alexa. "Unscheduled Departures: The Circumvention of Just Sentencing for Police Brutality." 47 *Hastings Law Journal* 677 (1996).

Gates, Henry Louis, Jr. "Thirteen Ways of Looking at a Black Man." *New Yorker,* October 23, 1995, 56.

Georges-Abeyie, Daniel, ed. *The Criminal Justice System and Blacks.* Clark Boardman, 1984.

Gibbs, Jewelle Taylor. *Race and Justice: Rodney King and O. J. in a Divided House.* Jossey-Bass, 1996.

Gillmer, Jason. "*U.S. v. Clary*: Equal Protection and the Crack Statute." 45 *American University Law Review* 497 (1995).

Hacker, Andrew. *Two Nations: Black and White, Separate, Hostile, Unequal.* Scribners, 1992.

Hagan, John, and Celesta Albonetti. "Race, Class, and the Perception of Criminal Injustice in America." 88 *American Journal of Sociology* 329 (1982).

Harris, Trudier. *Exorcising Blackness: Historical and Literary Lynching and Burning Rituals.* Indiana University Press, 1984.

Hawkins, Darnell F. "Explaining the Black Homicide Rate." 5 *Journal of Interpersonal Violence* 151 (1990).

———, ed. *Ethnicity, Race, and Crime.* State University of New York Press, 1995.

Herrnstein, Richard, and Charles Murray. *The Bell Curve: Intelligence and Class Structure in American Life.* The Free Press, 1994.

Higginbotham, A. Leon, Jr. *Shades of Freedom: Racial Politics and Presumption of the American Process.* Oxford, 1996.

———. *In the Matter of Color: Race and the American Legal Process.* Oxford, 1978.

Higginbotham, A. Leon, Jr., and Jacobs, Anne F. "The 'Law Only as an Enemy': The Legitimization of Racial Powerlessness through the Colonial and Ante-Bellum Criminal Laws of Virginia." 70 *North Carolina Law Review* 969 (1992).

Hindus, Michael. *Prison and Plantation: Crime, Justice, and Authority in Massachusetts and South Carolina, 1767–1878.* University of North Carolina Press, 1980.

Hoffman, Paul. "The Feds, Lies, and Videotape: The Need for an Effective Federal Role in Controlling Police Abuse in Urban America." 66 *Southern California Law Review* 1453 (1993).

Jacoby, Russell, and Naomi Glauberman, eds. *The Bell Curve Debate.* Times Books, 1995.

Jackson, Donald. "Police Embody Racism to My People." *New York Times,* January 23, 1989, A25.

Johnson, Erika. "A Menace to Society: The Use of Criminal Profiles and Its Effect on Black Males." 38 *Howard Law Journal* 629 (1995).

Johnson, Sheri L. "Racial Imagery in Criminal Trials." 67 *Tulane Law Review* 1739 (1993).

———. "Unconscious Racism and the Criminal Law." 73 *Cornell Law Review* 1016 (1988).

Kappeler, Victor, Mark Blumberg, and Gary Potter. *The Mythology of Crime and Criminal Justice.* Waveland Press, 1993.

Kennedy, Randall. *Race, Crime, and the Law.* Pantheon, 1997.

———. "The State, Criminal Law, and Racial Discrimination." 107 *Harvard Law Review* 1255 (1994).

Klein, Stephen, Susan Martin, and Joan Petersilia. "Racial Equity in Sentencing." *RAND* (1988).

Krieger, Nancy, and Stephen Sidney. "Racial Discrimination and Blood Pressure: The CARDIA Study of Young Black and White Adults." 86 *American Journal of Public Health* 1370 (1996).

LaFree, Gary. "Official Reactions to Hispanic Defendants in the Southwest." 22 *Journal of Research in Crime and Delinquency* 213 (1985).

LaFree, Gary, Kriss Drass, and Patrick O'Day. "Race and Crime in Postwar America: Determinants of African American and White Rates, 1957–1988." 30 *Criminology* 157 (1992).

Langan, Patrick. "Racism on Trial: New Evidence to Explain the Racial Composition of Prisons in the U.S." 76 *Journal of Criminal Law and Criminology* 666 (1985).

Lawrence, Charles, III. "The Id, the Ego, and Equal Protection: Reckoning with Unconscious Racism." 39 *Stanford Law Review* 317 (1987).

Lawrence, Frederick. "Resolving the Hate Crimes/Hate Speech Paradox: Punishing Bias Crimes and Protecting Racist Speech." 68 *Notre Dame Law Review* 673 (1993).

"Leading Cases." 101 *Harvard Law Review* 1472 (1988).

Lee, Cynthia Kwei Yung. "Beyond Black and White: Racializing Asian Americans in a Society Obsessed with O. J." 6 *Hastings Women's Law Journal* 165 (1995).

Lemelle, Anthony, Jr. *Black Male Deviance.* Praeger, 1995.

Lundman, Richard. "Demeanor and Arrest: Additional Research from Previously Unpublished Data." 33 *Journal of Research in Crime and Delinquency* 302 (1996).

Lynch, Michael, and Britt Patterson, eds. *Race and Criminal Justice.* Harrow and Heston, 1991.

MacLean, Brian, and Dragan Milovanovic, eds. *Racism, Empiricism, and Criminal Justice.* The Collective Press, 1990.

Maclin, Tracey. "Seeing the Constitution from the Backseat of a Police Squad Car." 70 *Boston University Law Review* 543 (1990).

Magee, Rhonda V. "The Master's Tools, From the Bottom Up: Responses to African-American Reparations in Mainstream and Outsider Remedies Discourse." 79 *Virginia Law Review* 863 (1993).

Mann, Coramae Richey. *Unequal Justice: A Question of Color.* Indiana University Press, 1993.

Matsuda, Mari, Richard Delgado, Charles Lawrence III, and Kimberlé Williams, eds. *Words That Wound: Critical Race Theory, Assaultive Speech, and the First Amendment.* Westview Press, 1993.

Mauer, Marc. "Intended and Unintended Consequences: State Racial Disparities in Imprisonment." *The Sentencing Project,* 1997.

Mauer, Marc, and Tracy Huling. "Young Black Americans and the Criminal Justice System: Five Years Later." *The Sentencing Project,* 1995.

Mayer, Jane, and Jill Abramson. *Strange Justice: The Selling of Clarence Thomas.* Houghton Mifflin, 1994.

McIntyre, Charshee. *Criminalizing a Race.* Kayode Publications, 1993.

McNeilly, Maya. "Effects of Racist Provocation and Social Support on Cardiovascular Reactivity in African American Women." 2 *International Journal of Behavioral Medicine* 321 (1995).

Miller, Jerome. *Search and Destroy: African-American Males in the Criminal Justice System.* Cambridge University Press, 1996.

Morris, Thomas. *Southern Slavery and the Law, 1619–1860.* University of North Carolina Press, 1996.

Morrison, Toni, ed. *Race-ing Justice, Engendering Power.* Pantheon, 1992.

Moynihan, Daniel P. *The Negro Family: The Case for National Action.* Government Printing Office, 1965.

Myers, Samuel L., and Margaret Simms, eds. *The Economics of Race and Crime.* Transaction Books, 1988.

Myrdal, Gunnar. *An American Dilemma: The Negro Problem and Modern Democracy.* Pantheon, 1944.

Patton, Alison L. "The Endless Cycle of Abuse: Why 42 U.S.C. 1983 Is Ineffective in Deterring Police Brutality." 44 *Hastings Law Journal* 753 (1993).

Poussaint, Alvin. "Black-on-Black Homicide: A Psychological Political Perspective." 8 *Victimology* 1 (1983).

Raper, Arthur. *The Tragedy of Lynching.* University of North Carolina Press, 1933.

Roberts, Dorothy E. "Deviance, Resistance, and Love." 179 *Utah Law Review* 180 (1994).

Russell, Katheryn K. "The Racial Hoax as Crime: The Law as Affirmation." 71 *Indiana Law Journal* 593 (1996).

———. "The Racial Inequality Hypothesis: A Critical Look at the Research and an Alternative Theoretical Analysis." 18 *Law and Human Behavior* 305 (1994).

———. "The Development of a Black Criminology and the Role of the Black Criminologist." 9 *Justice Quarterly* 667 (1992).

Sack, Emily J. "Police Approaches and Inquiries on the Streets of New York: The Aftermath of *People v. De Bour.*" 66 *New York University Law Review* 512 (1991).

Schafer, Judith K. "The Long Arm of the Law: Slave Criminals and the Supreme Court in Antebellum, Louisiana." 60 *Tulane Law Review* 1247 (1986).

Schwartz, Adina. "'Just Take away Their Guns': The Hidden Racism of *Terry v. Ohio.*" 23 *Fordham Urban Law Journal* 317 (1996).

Sheley, Joseph F. "Structural Influences on the Problem of Race, Crime, and Criminal Justice" 67 *Tulane Law Review* 2273 (1993).

Sherman, Lawrence. "Defiance, Deterrence, and Irrelevance: A Theory of the Criminal Sanction." 30 *Journal of Research in Crime and Delinquency* 445 (1993).

Skogan, Wesley. "Crime and the Racial Fears of White Americans." *The Annals of the American Academy of Political and Social Sciences* (May 1995).

Smith, J. Clay. "Justice and Jurisprudence and the Black Lawyer." 69 *Notre Dame Law Review* 1077 (1994).

Spade, William, Jr. "Beyond the 100:1 Ratio: Towards a Rational Cocaine Sentencing Policy." 38 *Arizona Law Review* 1233 (1996).

Stampp, Kenneth. *The Peculiar Institution.* Knopf, 1956.

———, ed. "Chattels Personal." In *American Law and the Constitutional Order: Historical Perspectives,* ed. Lawrence M. Friedman and Harry N. Scheiber. Harvard University Press, 1988.

Steele, Claude M., and Joshua Aronson. "Stereotype Threat and the Intellectual Test Performance of African Americans." 69 *Journal of Personality and Social Psychology* 797 (1995).

Steinberg, Stephen. *Turning Back: The Retreat from Racial Justice in American Thought and Policy.* Beacon, 1995.

Sulton, Ann, ed. *African American Perspectives on Crime Causation, Criminal Justice Administration, and Crime Prevention.* Sulton Books, 1994.

Sutherland, Edwin. *White Collar Crime.* Dryden Press, 1949.

Tassel, Emily F. "Only the Law Would Rule between Us." 70 *Chicago-Kent Law Review* 873 (1995).

Tillman, Robert. "The Size of the 'Criminal Population': The Prevalence and Incidence of Adult Arrest." 25 *Criminology* 561 (1987).

Tonry, Michael. *Malign Neglect: Race, Crime, and Punishment in America.* Oxford University Press, 1995.

Tucker, William. *The Science and Politics of Racial Research.* University of Illinois Press, 1994.

U.S. Bureau of the Census. *Historical Statistics of the United States, Colonial Times to 1970, Bicentennial Edition, Part 2.* Government Printing Office, 1975.

———. *Negro Population, 1790–1915.* Government Printing Office, 1969.

U.S. Department of Justice. *Uniform Crime Reports for the U.S., 1995.* Government Printing Office, 1996.

———. *Historical Corrections Statistics in the United States, 1850-1984.* Government Printing Office, 1986.

U.S. Sentencing Commission. *Cocaine and Federal Sentencing Policy.* Government Printing Office, 1995.

Verdun, Vincene. "If the Shoe Fits, Wear It: An Analysis of Reparations to African Americans." 67 *Temple Law Review* 597 (1993).

Wells-Barnett, Ida B. *On Lynchings: Southern Horrors, a Red Record, Mob Rule in New Orleans.* Arno Press, 1969.

Welsing, Frances Cress. *The Isis Papers: The Keys to the Colors.* Third World Press, 1991.

West, Cornel. *Race Matters.* Beacon Press, 1993.

Whitney, Glayde. "Ideology and Censorship in Behavior Genetics." 35 *The Mankind Quarterly* 327 (1995).

Wideman, Daniel, and Rohan Preston, eds. *Soulfires: Young Black Men on Love and Violence.* Penguin, 1996.

Wilbanks, William. *Myth of a Racist Criminal Justice System.* Brooks-Cole, 1987.

Williams, Patricia. "Spirit-Murdering the Messenger: The Discourse of Finger-pointing as the Law's Response to Racism." 42 *University of Miami Law Review* 127 (1987).

Wilson, James Q. "Crime, Race, and Values." *Society* 91 (November/December 1992).

Wilson, William J. *The Truly Disadvantaged: The Inner City, the Underclass, and Public Policy.* University of Chicago Press, 1987.

Wingate, C. Keith. "The O. J. Simpson Trial: Seeing the Elephant." 6 *Hastings Women's Law Journal* 121 (1995).

Wolfgang, Marvin, and Bernard Cohen. *Crime and Race: Conceptions and Misconceptions.* Institute of Human Relations Press, 1970.

Worden, Robert, and Robin Shepard. "Demeanor, Crime, and Police Behavior: A Reexamination of the Police Services Study Data." 34 *Criminology* 83 (1996).

Yankelovich Partners, Inc. *African-American Study.* Yankelovich Press, 1996.

Zatz, Marjorie S. "The Changing Forms of Racial/Ethnic Biases in Sentencing." 24 *Journal of Research in Crime and Delinquency* 69 (1987).

Index

About the Author

Katheryn K. Russell is an assistant professor of criminology and criminal justice at the University of Maryland, College Park. She has also taught at the American University School of Law, City University of New York (CUNY) Law School, Howard University, and Alabama State University. Professor Russell received her undergraduate degree from the University of California at Berkeley, her law degree from the University of California at Hastings, and her Ph.D. from the University of Maryland. Her 1994 article, "The Constitutionality of Jury Override in Alabama Death Penalty Cases," published in the *Alabama Law Review,* was cited by the U.S. Supreme Court in *Harris v. Alabama* (1995).

Russell was raised in Oakland, California, and currently resides in Maryland. Her email address is Krussel2@bss2.umd.edu.